# ETHICAL SHOPPING

# ETHICAL SHOPPING

*Where to Shop, What to Buy and What to Do to Make a Difference*

WILLIAM YOUNG
& RICHARD WELFORD

FUSION PRESS

First published in Great Britain by Fusion Press,
a division of Satin Publications Ltd.



Fusion Press
101 Southwark Street
London SE1 0JF
UK
e-mail: info@visionpaperbacks.co.uk
website: www.visionpaperbacks.co.uk

Publisher: Sheena Dewan
Cover design © 2002 Nickolai Globe
Printed and bound in the UK by Biddles Ltd.

ISBN: 1-904132-08-1

# Contents

# List of figures and tables

## Figures



## Tables

# Preface

> “ • Why are companies that make huge profits being accused of exploiting employees in developing countries?
> • Is child labour used?
> • How much are employees in developing countries paid compared to what I pay for the product?
> • What conditions are employees in developing countries working under?
> • Why do companies seem to have power over governments and world trade?
> • Which companies are treating their employees and/or suppliers in developing countries fairly?
> • What can the consumer do? ”

These questions are increasingly being asked by consumers concerned about the working conditions under which the products they buy are produced in developing countries. Consumers are becoming aware that products they buy may have been produced using child labour or in sweatshops, with workers suffering unsafe working conditions and employment conditions close to slavery. We often get the feeling that companies seem to have all the money and power while Western governments play politics with developing countries struggling with debt and poverty.

We know that in many parts of the world consumers eat so much that their health deteriorates, when at the same time millions of people in poor countries do not have enough to eat. We have seen children forced to work in factories to earn money for basic necessities. We also see many images of workers being forced to endure working conditions that would seem completely intolerable in the West. These conditions and these people exist so that products can be produced at low cost to fill the shelves of our shops. Many of the products we consume are, quite simply, being subsidised by the poor.

There is a real cause for concern therefore that some of the goods we consume in the rich world are made affordable by the suffering of the poor. In ethical terms the 'needs' and 'wants' of more affluent consumers are being met by corporations that are often accused of exploiting disadvantaged and oppressed workers.[1] Is there some way the consumer can influence this situation?

Any consumer with a conscience ought to be worried about some of the trends that we see as a result of free trade and globalisation. Not only are there some major environmental concerns about the transportation of so many goods around the world, but globalisation is also bringing about social change that is not always desirable for those in developing countries. This book can be used as an aid to consumers who want to use their purchasing power to make better, more ethical choices over purchases. It is a guide and handbook to becoming a more 'ethical shopper' and to pressurise retailers, producers and governments to change their practices to bring about an equitable world trading system.

Equitable trade aims to ensure, firstly, that employees and communities in developing countries benefit from similar working conditions enjoyed by workers in the developed world and, secondly, that consumers pay a fair price for the work done by people in those countries in comparison to the final price of the product. We should also expect transparency from companies, ie that they should tell us about their own and their suppliers' employment and working practices.

It is perhaps encouraging that we are witnessing increased concern about environmental and social issues and the plight of many of the poorest people in the world. Since we now live in a world where free trade is allowing many developing countries to expand, we have an obligation to ensure that that expansion is to the benefit of everyone in their communities – not just rich landowners and factory managers.

Such concerns have led to:

- the increase of Fairtrade products (53 per cent per annum growth since 1994);[2]
- more 'mainstream' companies developing codes of conduct on

employment and working conditions of employees;

- pressure on supply chains (in the US up to 85 per cent of large companies now have codes of conduct. In the UK many companies are starting to adopt them).[3]

This book aims to promote good practice in the field of trade and explains many of the concerns of consumers. We also examine methods used to tackle these issues by companies, charities and governments in the form of ethical trade, sound sourcing, fair trade and labels such as the Fairtrade Mark and RUGMARK. Perhaps, most importantly, we suggest ways in which consumers can act and begin to make a real difference in the world through their purchasing decisions. We help the consumer with the often difficult choice of what to buy by giving information on which high street retailers are addressing these issues for their own brand products.

This book arose out of academic research that the authors felt needed to be shared with a wider audience than academics. The aim of this book is to inform consumers of the issues and the action being taken by retailers (75 per cent of whom either do not have policies or have policies that are inadequate – see Chapter 22). We hope to encourage retailers and consumers to consider the consequences of their actions (or their failure to act). The responsibility is on consumers to buy products that are not produced under exploitative conditions and for retailers not to exploit workers in developing countries – it is as simple as that.

The writing of this book involved not only the authors but many people to whom we are most grateful: firstly, the University of Huddersfield for funding the initial academic research; Linda Orwin for helping with the initial research; Paul Holdsworth for helping with the last stages of the research; Sarah Young for editing the final scripts; Liz Puttick our literary agent and our publishers for making the project a reality; and our families, friends and colleagues for their encouragement.

As with a book of this type, there are the disclaimers. The views expressed in this book are solely of the authors and not the views held by the Universities of Huddersfield, Leeds or Hong Kong, Liz Puttick Literary Agent or the publishers. Any errors and omissions are the responsibility of the authors but information on the retailers' policies and activities are only as accurate as the information received from those retailers. Information in this book is as current as reasonably possible at publication.

William Young
March 2002

# 1 | The issues

Issues surrounding fair trade and equitable trade are complex. Often we can see a straightforward reason not to buy a particular product. More often, however, there will be decisions to make that are not so clear cut. Should one always boycott products made by children, which could lead to factories sacking young workers, leaving them to beg? Is it better to stimulate some employment in developing countries even if it is at very low wages? Should we buy cheap food that has been transported halfway around the world (nevertheless supporting the employment of poor people) or try to buy seasonal locally grown produce?

This first chapter introduces the issues surrounding ethical and fair trade and discusses some of the important terms used. We ask why ethical and fair trade has come to the forefront for companies and consumers in developed countries such as the UK.

*Information box*

- *Developed country* is a country with a developed economy such as the USA, Canada, Japan, Australia, New Zealand, the UK and other European countries.
- *Developing country* is a country still developing its economy and infrastructure such as African countries, Asian countries (except Japan), South American countries and East European countries.

Essentially the debate surrounding ethical and fair trade boils down to two main issues that the consumer should be concerned about: 1) helping the poor to move out of poverty through trade and not just aid; and 2) stopping companies exploiting cheap labour and bad working conditions in developing countries for profit.

## Poverty

It is difficult to escape images of poverty in the media and, of course, we know that a sizeable proportion of the world's people are living with inadequate food, clothing and shelter. Despite vast wealth creation in much of the world, the number of people living on less than a dollar a day is virtually unchanged from a decade ago at 1.2 billion. In some countries, nearly 50 per cent of the population remains mired in extreme poverty, not earning enough to buy even basic foodstuffs. Even in rich nations such as the United States, there are still many families who are homeless or cannot afford health care.[1] In the UK 34 per cent of children live in poverty (ie live in households with less than 50 per cent of the average UK income).[2] But poverty is not just about a lack of income. It is also about illiteracy, malnutrition among children, early death, poor health care and poor access to safe water. The United Nations Development Programme (UNDP), which is responsible for tackling poverty, addresses poverty as a denial of human rights. Good health, adequate nutrition, literacy and employment are not favours or acts of charity to be bestowed on the poor by governments and international agencies. They are human rights, as valid today as they were 50 years ago when the Universal Declaration of Human Rights was adopted.[3] The World Health Organisation (WHO) estimates that one-third of the children in developing countries are malnourished, while aid levels from most developed countries are actually falling. The United Kingdom is one of the lowest contributors per head of population (see Figure 1.1).[4]

By the late 1990s, the poorest fifth of the world's people living in the lowest-income countries had:[5]

- 1 per cent of world GDP;
- 1 per cent of world export markets;
- 1 per cent of foreign direct investment.

By contrast, the richest fifth in the richest countries controlled:

- 86 per cent of world GDP;
- 82 per cent of world export markets;
- 68 per cent of foreign direct investment.

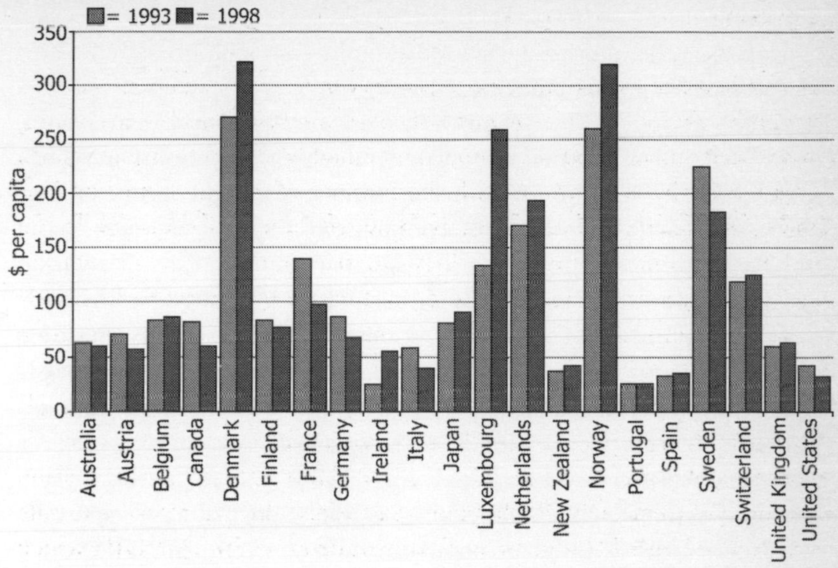


Figure 1.1 Aid levels from developed countries *(Graphics by MEEG, School of the Environment, University of Leeds)*

For the longer-term future, trade rather than just aid is seen as the hope for these countries – not least because most of them have little immediate prospect of industrialisation.[6]

> “Has globalisation lived up to the hope that developing countries would benefit from international trade?”

## Globalisation

Government deregulation, free markets, large multinational companies and exports have been seen by some as the best route to both economic and social development, with globalisation benefiting all. It is certainly true that economic growth in the world has benefited many people in developing countries, but the benefits from that growth are often unevenly spread. In many developing countries the poor remain in poverty despite growing exports partly because globalisation, driven by the competitive advantage that cheap labour provides, requires the maintenance of a low-wage economy in which to produce goods. In effect large companies make profits from producing goods in low-wage economies and selling them in high-wage economies.

During the 1990s, the complexities and problems associated with globalisation have become more apparent. Many people have not benefited, even where they have directly participated through employment in the global export markets, and social and economic problems in many developing countries have increased.[7] Developing countries are pressured to repay their debts and to increase their economic activity, often by encouraging the export of raw materials, to the detriment of the local population and environment. The prices of raw materials purchased in developing countries have increased at a slower rate than the price of finished products that are processed and sold in the developed countries.[8] Thus, the gap between what developing countries get for their outputs and the price that we pay for goods has increased.

> “Globalisation appears not to be benefiting the poor. It seems that the real winners are the large multinational companies based in rich countries – is this true?”

## Governments and multinational companies

One of the implications of free trade and globalisation is that we have seen an increase in the power of the multinational corporations, who with their huge capital resources have become nomadic. They are able to move from country to country seeking out new, more profitable opportunities. Moreover, they are often subsidised by governments keen to encourage capital flow into their countries. Whilst we are witnessing the globalisation of business, we see little evidence of the globalisation of government able to keep control of abuses of economic power.

Indeed, there has been a reduction in the role of government in the areas of both economic and social policy, with increased emphasis on the free market as the main mechanism for development. For the large companies that dominate world trade, barriers between nations have been broken down and it is often said that we are all now participants in a 'global village'. The problem is that that global village is not a democratic one. It is not even one where common values and norms exist. It is a village of increasing disparities between rich and poor – disparities welcomed by companies keen to maintain low wages in their production location.

The role of government in international development has diminished and it is perhaps not surprising that calls for change are to be found elsewhere. In many cases, the role of global governance is being taken up by a new informed civil society made up of coalitions of pressure groups, consumer organisations and non-governmental organisations (NGOs). We as consumers can be an important part of that new society as we make greater efforts to make choices in the products we purchase.

Pressure for greater corporate social responsibility is now growing, and ethical trade has evolved. Non-state and other actors have come to play an increasingly important role, as the relationship between market and society is mediated through differing means. Ethical trade has arisen in this context.[9] You will see in this book that many companies are making genuine efforts to deal with the ethical and moral dimensions of free trade. Others are paying lip service or ignoring the issues, adopting a 'head in the sand' mentality.

The gap between rich and poor amongst Southern populations continues to grow while a relatively small group of multinational corporations announce record profits.[10] Table 1.1 compares the richest countries to the richest companies. It is interesting to note that if General Electric and Wal-Mart (which owns Asda in the UK) were countries, they would be amongst the biggest 25 nations in the world![11] This means that large, powerful firms are increasingly dominating world trade and are able to use their huge influence with producers and suppliers to push down the price of their inputs.

The power and influence of large corporations result in an unfair system of trade. It is not in balance but dominated by rich multinational companies able to make or break producers in developing

Table 1.1 The richest countries (GDP) and companies (sales)

| Country/Corporation | GDP/Sales ($ million) | Country/Corporation | GDP/Sales ($ million) |
|---|---|---|---|
| 1 United States | 8,708,870.0 | 26 Exxon Mobil | 163,881.0 |
| 2 Japan | 4,395,083.0 | 27 Ford Motor | 162,558.0 |
| 3 Germany | 2,081,202.0 | 28 Daimler Chrysler | 159,985.7 |
| 4 France | 1,410,262.0 | 29 Poland | 154,146.0 |
| 5 United Kingdom | 1,373,612.0 | 30 Norway | 145,449.0 |
| 6 Italy | 1,149,958.0 | 31 Indonesia | 140,964.0 |
| 7 China | 1,149,814.0 | 32 South Africa | 131,127.0 |
| 8 Brazil | 760,345.0 | 33 Saudi Arabia | 128,892.0 |
| 9 Canada | 612,049.0 | 34 Finland | 126,130.0 |
| 10 Spain | 562,245.0 | 35 Greece | 123,934.0 |
| 11 Mexico | 474,951.0 | 36 Thailand | 123,887.0 |
| 12 India | 459,765.0 | 37 Mitsui | 118,555.2 |
| 13 Korea, Rep. | 406,940.0 | 38 Mitsubishi | 117,765.6 |
| 14 Australia | 389,691.0 | 39 Toyota Motor | 115,670.9 |
| 15 Netherlands | 384,766.0 | 40 General Electric | 111,630.0 |
| 16 Russian Federation | 375,345.0 | 41 Itochu | 109,068.9 |
| 17 Argentina | 281,942.0 | 42 Portugal | 107,716.0 |
| 18 Switzerland | 260,299.0 | 43 Royal Dutch/Shell | 105,366.0 |
| 19 Belgium | 245,706.0 | 44 Venezuela | 103,918.0 |
| 20 Sweden | 226,388.0 | 45 Iran, Islamic Rep. | 101,073.0 |
| 21 Austria | 208,949.0 | 46 Israel | 99,068.0 |
| 22 Turkey | 188,374.0 | 47 Sumitomo | 95,701.6 |
| 23 General Motors | 176,558.0 | 48 Nippon Tel & Tel | 93,591.7 |
| 24 Denmark | 174,363.0 | 49 Egypt, Arab Rep. | 92,413.0 |
| 25 Wal-Mart | 166,809.0 | 50 Marubeni | 91,807.4 |

countries. Many of the basic products we buy (sugar, chocolate, coffee, nuts, bananas and tobacco) are cheaper than they otherwise would be because of pressure to cut costs from the large trading companies. Many of the minerals that go into making the machines and vehicles upon which we rely in our daily lives are also part of this system and many people receive a bare pittance for their work and have a standard of living that is a bare twentieth of our own.[12]

> "Are there not international trade rules to protect the vulnerable and powerless?"

## The World Trade Organisation

The World Trade Organisation (WTO) claims to be the only global international organisation dealing with rules of trade between nations. At its heart are the WTO agreements, negotiated and signed by the majority of the world's trading nations and ratified in their parliaments. The goal is to help producers of goods and services, exporters and importers conduct their business.[13] On the other hand the WTO can be seen as constraining the freedom of most states to impose controls on trade, even for avowedly ethical (including environmental) reasons.

Freer trade is not necessarily fairer trade. The poorest 10 per cent of the world's population participate in less than one-half of 1 per cent of the world's trade. More trade liberalisation would not necessarily help. At the end of the last round of trade talks, it was predicted that Africa would lose out even further, suffering losses of between $300 million and $600 million per year if new agreements relating to trade liberalisation were implemented. Although trade rules are made by countries, it is companies that do the trading. It is the companies of the richest countries that have been able to make most of the gains from freer trade, often at the expense of smaller traders from developing countries. Instead of rushing into new talks on freeing trade, WTO members should address ways to make trade fairer for poor countries and poor people.[14]

> "Large companies and international politics cause problems associated with poverty – what does this have to do with me the consumer?"

## Cheap products

Consumers in developed countries demand cheap products such as food and clothes while production costs have increased. Hence, the only way companies can compete is either to move production to cheaper countries or, more commonly, to contract out the production to suppliers in developing countries. Developing countries tend to have lower production costs compared to developed countries for several reasons. Firstly, the standard of living is more expensive in developed countries. Labour is cheap in developing countries and stays cheap because there is little or no enforced employment legislation. Workers in developed countries are expensive to employ because companies have to:

- protect their health and safety at work;
- pay a minimum wage (which is a lot higher because of the expensive standard of living);
- keep working hours and the working week restricted;
- pay sickness, maternity and holiday leave; and
- pay taxes.

The basic rights of workers to receive fair wages, experience safe working conditions and receive welfare benefits are often taken for granted in the developed world. However, such 'privileges' are rarely implemented in developing countries, making it very cheap to produce products. Often developing countries as well as territories governed by Western countries attract business by having areas called free trade zones and export processing zones. These 'zones' are often free from the country's taxes and labour laws, including minimum wages, health and safety requirements, laws relating to the minimum working age and working hours. Employees in these zones work in poor conditions, sometimes in 'sweatshops' where suppliers make several brand products for different retailers in the same factory. Developing countries compete for business by offering lower and lower production costs, pushing down the working and human rights of employees.

Some raw materials such as coffee, cocoa and gold are sold through commodities markets. This causes problems for the growers, producers and miners who depend on the world market price for their livelihood. However, it is more often large multinational companies selling and buying commodities to maximise their profits that dominate the market. This situation is often not compatible with attempts to bring about fair and ethical trade practices.

> "How much are workers paid for producing the products we consume and use compared to other costs?"

## Profits and costs

The value of any product, in terms of its final price, is added to as it passes through various production stages and eventually reaches the consumer market. Free trade concentrates this value in the hands of rich corporate merchants, processors and retailers in the developed countries. Producers in the developing countries are commonly paid only a tiny part of the final price that consumers pay.[15]

Figures 1.2 to 1.5 illustrate end price audits of four products, namely bananas, jeans, coffee and chocolate.[16] These are products commonly sourced in developing countries and produced by workers earning very low wages. An end price audit takes the price the consumer pays for a product and breaks this back down into the shares that each part of the supply chain receives, ie who gets what. Typically, as can be seen in the cases of the four illustrated products, the producers in developing countries are paid 4 to 12 per cent for their work and the retailers in the developed world receive 25 to 60 per cent of the price of the product.

## Working conditions

There is a growing concern among consumers about the working conditions under which the poorest find themselves and about related human rights issues. We wonder whether the products we buy are made in factories where there are exploitative and dangerous working conditions. It is clear that the low wages paid to many workers in developing countries seem out of proportion to the prices that

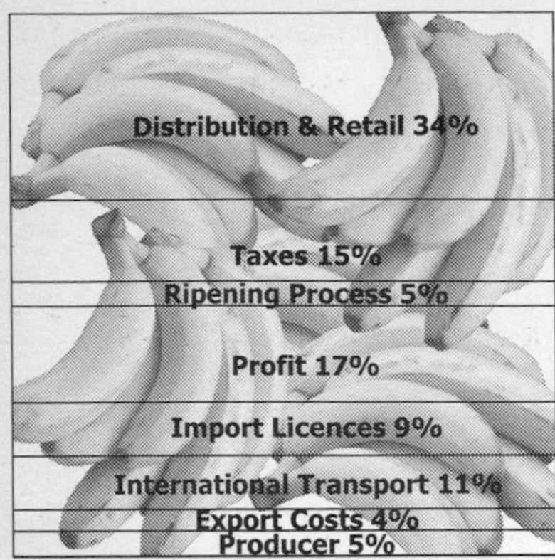


Figure 1.2 End price audit for bananas *(Graphics by MEEG, School of the Environment, University of Leeds)*

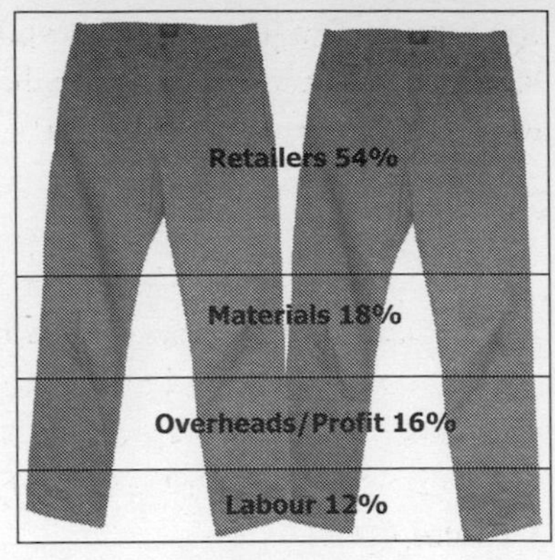


Figure 1.3 End price audit of a pair of jeans *(Graphics by MEEG, School of the Environment, University of Leeds)*

Figure 1.4 End price audit of coffee *(Graphics by MEEG, School of the Environment, University of Leeds)*

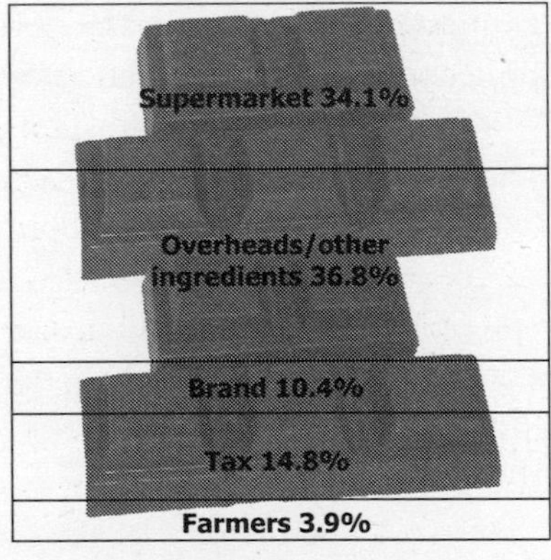


Figure 1.5 End price audit of a chocolate bar *(Graphics by MEEG, School of the Environment, University of Leeds)*

“How are workers treated when producing products for us?”

consumers pay in their local shops.[17] But other issues include forced labour, freedom of association, health and safety, child labour, working hours and discrimination (see the box below).[18]

*Information box*

- *Forced labour:* work carried out under the threat of penalty, eg bonded labour and forced labour in prison. Bonded labour is where a person is forced to work for no or minimal wage, to pay off a debt that the worker or his/her family owes to the employer.
- *Freedom of association:* ensures that workers are able to organise themselves into groups, usually trade unions, which negotiate pay and conditions collectively rather than on an individual basis. UNITE (Union of Needletrades, Industrial and Textile Employees) in the USA states that, in seeking higher profits, retailers and manufacturers look to contract out production in countries where workers are denied the right to organise their own unions. Even in countries that have the right to organise, companies often fight back against workers to prevent them from having a union. Companies often resort to tactics such as threatening or firing pro-union workers, even in the US. Workers must have the right to join independent unions of their own choosing. That is the only way that workers can bargain to increase their wages and improve their conditions.[19]
- *Health and safety:* standards of health and safety are low in many factories and work sites and in the agricultural sector in both developed and developing countries.
- *Child labour (in particular, the employment of children under 14 years old):* the charity Save the Children does not believe a ban on child labour is a good option. Most children who work do so to survive and, if they were banned from main-stream jobs, many would substitute illegal, dangerous work.[20] It is ironic that child labour in British mills was phased out 100 years ago only for products today to be produced by child labour in developing countries.

- *Wages and working hours:* low wages often do not support workers and their families and frequently government minimum wages are not enforced. Extra overtime is often compulsory, leaving workers with no choice but to work extremely long hours. UNITE argues that minimum wages are usually set so low that they keep workers in poverty. For example, in El Salvador, the minimum wage is 60 cents an hour. However, a recent study by Columbia University in the USA showed that workers must earn at least $1.73 an hour to pull themselves out of poverty. And in the Dominican Republic, the minimum wage only amounts to one-third of what the Dominican government estimates it takes to support a typical family. For workers to escape poverty, companies must agree to pay a living wage.[21] See Table 1.2 for examples of hourly rates for garment workers around the world.[22]
- *Discrimination:* because of ethnicity, religion, language, gender, sexuality, disability and age.

Key facts:

- 850 million people work less than they want or earn less than a living wage.[23]
- There are 250 million child labourers (one-quarter of all children aged between 4 and 14 years old in the world).[24]
- There are 20 million people who in effect are working as slaves.[25]
- A quarter of the world's 6 billion population lives in poverty on less than a dollar a day.[26]

Conditions that employees often face working in developing countries are:[27]

- 15-hour days;
- seven-day weeks;
- toilet break bans;
- shortened lunch breaks;
- cramped, stifling, dangerous shop floors;
- inadequate fire escape routes;
- beatings, lock-ins, withheld wages and summary sackings.

Table 1.2 Wages for garment workers around the world

| Country | Hourly rate |
|---|---|
| United Kingdom (legal minimum wage: £4.10) | £2.99–£4.61 |
| United States | £5.80 |
| Bangladesh | 4–14 pence |
| Burma | 3 pence |
| China (living wage: 60 pence an hour) | 16 pence |
| Colombia | 48–55 pence |
| Dominican Republic | 42 pence |
| El Salvador (living wage: 81 pence an hour) | 41 pence |
| Guatemala | 26–34 pence |
| Haiti (living wage: 40 pence an hour) | 21 pence |
| Honduras (living wage: 54 pence an hour) | 30 pence |
| India | 14–21 pence |
| Indonesia | 7 pence |
| Malaysia | 69 pence |
| Mexico | 34–37 pence |
| Nicaragua (living wage: 55 pence an hour) | 16 pence |
| Pakistan | 14–18 pence |
| Peru | 62 pence |
| Philippines | 40–52 pence |
| Romania | 17 pence |
| Sri Lanka | 28 pence |
| Thailand | 54 pence |

“I thought that there were international laws or standards protecting human and worker rights?”

## International standards

At the international level there are several standards covering human rights and labour standards. These include the following:

- Basic human rights standards are contained in the United Nations Universal Declaration of Human Rights (UDHR), which for example states, 'Everyone, without any discrimination, has the right to equal pay for equal work.'[28]
- The International Labour Organisation (ILO) has eight core labour conventions, which cover issues such as child labour, working hours, and health and safety.[29] See the box below for further information.
- The United Nations Convention on the Rights of the Child.

*Fundamental ILO conventions*

Eight ILO conventions have been identified by the ILO's governing body as being fundamental to the rights of human beings at work, irrespective of the levels of development of individual member states. These rights are a precondition for all the others in that they provide the necessary implements to strive freely for the improvement of individual and collective conditions of work.

Freedom of association

- Freedom of Association and Protection of the Right to Organise Convention, 1948 (No. 87)
- Right to Organise and Collective Bargaining Convention, 1949 (No. 98)

The abolition of forced labour

- Forced Labour Convention, 1930 (No. 29)
- Abolition of Forced Labour Convention, 1957 (No. 105)

Equality

- Discrimination (Employment and Occupation) Convention, 1958 (No. 111)
- Equal Remuneration Convention, 1951 (No. 100)

**The elimination of child labour**

- Minimum Age Convention, 1973 (No. 138)
- Worst Forms of Child Labour Convention, 1999 (No. 182)

**Ratification of the fundamental ILO conventions**

In May 1995, following the ILO's 75th anniversary and the discussions at the World Summit on Social Development, a campaign for the ratification of these conventions was launched by the Director-General of the ILO. Since then the ILO has registered over 70 ratifications and confirmations of previous obligations concerning the fundamental conventions. In addition, many countries are currently involved in formal ratification procedures or are in the process of examining or re-examining the appropriateness of ratifying the Organisation's fundamental conventions.

The ILO has 175 member states.

Web site: www.ilo.org

Unfortunately, national laws do not always correspond to these conventions, even when a country has signed them. For example, Britain did not incorporate a specific Human Rights Act into law until 2000, even though the UDHR was created in 1948. In the developing world, the ILO is working with many national governments to develop their labour laws and build capacity for improved enforcement.[30]

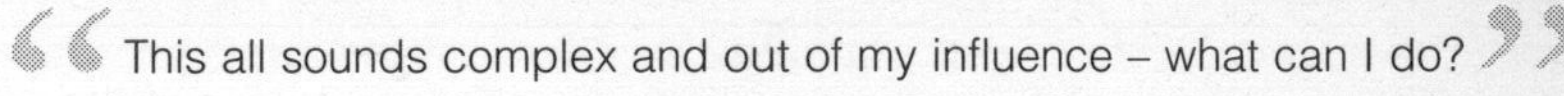


## Consumer power

The phrase 'responding to consumer demands' is often heard from companies. Indeed few companies would dispute that they must respond to the changing demands of their customers. But when it comes down to an issue such as ethical and fair trade, companies argue that there is little pressure from consumers.[31] Companies can change policies – as exemplified by the increase in organic food and the removal of genetically modified ingredients from products. In these cases companies felt they were under pressure to act because the consumer demanded it. Companies listened to consumers, albeit often indirectly through consumer groups such as the Consumers Association and pressure groups such as Friends of the Earth.

There is also a trend by companies to engage in stakeholder dialogue (communicating with all those directly affected by the company's activities), which includes talking to consumers. This emulates the environmental activities of companies in environmental reporting and transparency and creates an opportunity for consumers to express concerns over other issues such as ethical trade.

Much of the impetus behind recent developments in ethical trading can be attributed to the growth of a new set of expectations among consumers, including institutional consumers. There is a growing demand to seek assurances from companies that the products consumers buy have been produced in accordance with minimum labour standards. Survey evidence suggests that a majority of consumers are concerned about the human conditions under which goods are produced, although only a small, if growing, minority may be willing to pay a premium for ethical products. We also know that a negative ethical image associated with a brand or product can seriously affect sales. It is hard to imagine that a consumer would positively seek out products produced by forced or child labour or in grossly unsafe circumstances.[32]

What we have to recognise is that as consumers we do have a lot of power. Working together and alongside organisations promoting ethical trade we can make a real difference. By purchasing products produced according to sound ethical principles and avoiding products that are a result of exploitation in developing countries, we can begin to shape a fairer world. Businesses have shown that they are willing to listen to the concerns of consumers if they have a loud enough voice. We have an obligation to make our voices heard.

“So what should I do now?”

## Moving forward

There is clear evidence of a real need for change within the world trading system. Poverty and working conditions seem to be at odds with globalisation and company profits. Consumers and companies are becoming aware of the poor working conditions and inadequate wages of employees of suppliers in developing countries. So can we as individual consumers change the policies of companies? Of course we can! If companies are aware that consumers are not only buying ethical or fair trade products but are asking difficult questions this can only increase the spread of equitable trade policies. Later in this book there are tips on how we as consumers can use our power and increase the pressure on companies to act in more ethical ways.

# 2 | Ethical trade and fair trade

This chapter provides you with some information about fairer and more equitable trade. Firstly, it examines the similarities and differences between ethical and fair trade. Both offer a route for consumers to buy products produced under good working conditions as well as a route for producers in developing countries to trade under favourable trading conditions. Secondly, this chapter addresses the range of issues that the consumer needs to think about when purchasing goods.

## What is ethical trading or sound sourcing?

> *Ethical trading or sound sourcing is dedicated to improving the situation of employees in developing countries in the context of everyday consumer products. Ethical trading primarily directs its efforts at improving the conditions of employees by working with employers to ensure basic human and labour rights to develop and improve safe and decent working conditions, and general s tandards of living. Its objective is to achieve these aims for millions of waged workers, without this necessarily resulting in a retail price premium.*[1]

Companies in the UK operating ethical trading or more specifically sound sourcing policies often use 'codes of conduct' or 'codes of practice' to help producers, suppliers and the managers of their own operations to operate above 'accepted' minimum limits. These often include decent minimum wage levels, health and safety issues, employee rights and working practices. Companies have to implement these codes of conduct openly, and independently monitor and report on true progress for any positive effect to be achieved. So as long as we can rely on what companies tell us, consumers can buy from businesses operating ethical trade or sound sourcing schemes safe in the knowledge that the product has not been made through the exploitation of employees in developing countries.

At the moment ethical trade is a relatively new concept and is still being developed. Consequently there are only a few product 'lines' in retailer outlets that are conforming to an ethical code of conduct. Although such codes are being developed, most are only partially in operation. Many companies are aware of many of the issues but seem less than enthusiastic or confident about making any great changes until consumers buy sufficiently large numbers of products that have been sound-sourced. We as consumers can help to encourage companies to do more by making our purchases count and by asking questions about codes of conduct when we are considering making purchases of goods sourced in developing countries.

Companies can certainly get help with moving towards sound sourcing and the development of codes of conduct. One approach is for companies to join in the many industry initiatives that are beginning to spring up. Some companies have adopted the UK Ethical Trading Initiative (ETI) 'Base Code', which is voluntary (see the box on pages 21–22) but not certified, ie is a facilitator of the exchange of information. Going further, companies can choose to be certified (independently inspected for compliance) to the US Social Accountability 8000 (SA8000) standard (see the box on pages 22–23). The UN Global Compact (see the box on pages 23–24) is a voluntary charter that companies can sign up for, protecting the environment, labour rights and human rights.

There is also a range of industry-specific initiatives companies can get involved with. By way of an example, one initiative addresses the issue of illegal child labour in the carpet industry. The RUGMARK sign (see Figure 2.1) guarantees that carpet producers have an obligation to produce their carpets without employing illegal child labour. It enables the carpet buyer to contribute towards the removal of exploitative child labour.[2]

The range of products and potential products that can be ethically traded is only limited by the amount of materials and products produced in developing countries. The scope for increased ethical trade is therefore enormous. Most UK retailers could and should get involved in ethical trade.

Figure 2.1 The RUGMARK

## Global codes of conduct

Because of the failure to create an enforceable global code through international institutions like the United Nations, pressure on companies to be more socially and environmentally responsible has led to the adoption of voluntary company codes of conduct. Codes of conduct are statements that encompass the company's ethical practices and its responsibilities to uphold human rights, labour and environmental standards in all its operations and the operations of its suppliers. During the past six years, an increasing number of companies have formulated codes to be used as guidelines for relations with suppliers and to inform shareholders and the public what its standards are.[3]

The Principles for Global Corporate Responsibility: Benchmarks for Measuring Business Performance (Global Principles), written by the Interfaith Centre on Corporate Responsibility (ICCR), Ecumenical Council for Corporate Responsibility in Great Britain, and the Taskforce on the Churches and Corporate Responsibility in Canada, is a comprehensive tool to hold companies accountable to high standards that are measurable in relation to international human and labour rights conventions. Since the spring of 1999, a global network of religious and non-governmental organisations (NGOs) has been set up to utilise the Global Principles in 21 countries.[4]

The Global Principles is a useful accountability tool, as it gives socially responsible investors, grass-roots activists, NGOs and corporations a comprehensive set of principles, criteria and benchmarks to apply to their global operations. Codes can be effective tools if consumer, labour, religious and non-governmental organisations along with committed company officials work to make them strong, real and effective. Credible codes need to include:[5]

- processes to involve workers in formulating and revising the code;
- comprehensive international human rights, environmental and International Labour Organisation (ILO) standards including freedom of association, collective bargaining and the right to strike;
- standards that go beyond legal minimum compliance, especially to guarantee a sustainable living wage for workers for a regular work-week;
- standards that are implemented throughout the company;
- standards for a corporation's contact suppliers and vendors;
- clear monitoring processes that include internal monitoring and independent monitoring using NGOs that can provide independent verification of code compliance and enhance public credibility in the process;
- full access to the factories by monitors for unannounced and announced inspections;
- public transparency including periodic public reports on code compliance and how instances of non-compliance are addressed.

### *Ethical Trading Initiative (ETI)*

The Ethical Trading Initiative's role is to identify and promote good practice in the implementation of codes of labour practice, including the monitoring and independent verification of the observance of code provisions by companies.[6] It is an alliance of companies, NGOs and trade union organisations committed to working together to fulfil this role.

ETI member companies are committed to adopting codes based on internationally agreed standards, and moving to the demonstrable implementation of their codes. ETI is a learning organisation rather than a certification body. The ETI Base Code (which is voluntary and not certified by the ETI) contains the following provisions:

- no forced labour;
- freedom of association and the right to collective bargaining;
- safe and hygienic working conditions;
- no child labour to be used;
- living wages to be paid;
- no excessive working hours;
- no discrimination;
- regular employment to be provided; and
- no harsh or inhumane treatment.

These provisions reflect the relevant declarations and conventions of the United Nations and the ILO, including the core conventions of the ILO and its 1998 Geneva Declaration on Fundamental Principles and Rights at Work.

See retailer chapters to find which retailers are members.

Web site: www.ethicaltrade.org

*Social Accountability 8000 (SA8000) Standard*

The US-based NGO, Social Accountability International (SAI), has developed SA8000, a standard specifically covering ethical purchasing. It differs from company codes of conduct (including the ETI Base Code) in that it requires an accredited external auditing company to audit factories against a standard. Either purchasing companies such as retailers or their suppliers can use the standard.[7]

Based on the principles of international human rights norms as delineated in ILO conventions, the United Nations Convention on the Rights of the Child and the Universal Declaration of Human Rights, SA8000 has nine core areas:[8]

1. child labour;
2. forced labour;
3. health and safety;

4. compensation;
5. working hours;
6. discrimination;
7. discipline;
8. free association and collective bargaining;
9. management systems.

No UK company currently has this standard.

Web site: www.cepaa.org

*The UN Global Compact*

**The concept**[9]

The Global Compact is not a regulatory instrument or code of conduct, but a value-based platform designed to promote institutional learning. It utilises the power of transparency and dialogue to identify and disseminate good practices based on universal principles.

The Compact encompasses nine principles, drawn from the Universal Declaration of Human Rights, the ILO's Fundamental Principles on Rights at Work and the Rio Principles on Environment and Development. It asks companies to act on these principles in their own corporate domains. The Compact promotes good practices by corporations; it does not endorse companies.

**The nine principles**[10]

*Human rights*

The Secretary-General asked world business to:

- Principle 1: support and respect the protection of international human rights within their sphere of influence; and
- Principle 2: make sure their own corporations are not complicit in human rights abuses.

*Labour*

The Secretary-General asked world business to uphold:

- Principle 3: freedom of association and the effective recognition of the right to collective bargaining;
- Principle 4: the elimination of all forms of forced and compulsory labour;
- Principle 5: the effective abolition of child labour; and
- Principle 6: the elimination of discrimination in respect of employment and occupation.

*Environment*

The Secretary-General asked world business to:

- Principle 7: support a precautionary approach to environmental challenges;
- Principle 8: undertake initiatives to promote greater environmental responsibility; and
- Principle 9: encourage the development and diffusion of environmentally friendly technologies.

Web site: www.unglobalcompact.org

## Fair trade

Fair trade was introduced to ensure a better deal for farmers, growers and small-scale producers who in the past have often found that, because of their remoteness or size of operation, they were unable to obtain a fair price for their products.[11] Fair trade targets these disadvantaged communities and organisations, working with them to enable them to be involved in international trade. Building up the skills and capacity of producer groups is central, enabling them to trade more effectively with fair trade organisations and, for some, to begin to export to mainstream buyers in developed economies.[12]

Even more importantly, fair trade companies often provide prepayment so that crops can be purchased without getting into insupportable debt, as well as paying a guaranteed minimum price above the market-place norm. They also include an additional 'social premium' so that farmers and growers can invest in their businesses without going into debt, and support local social welfare programmes such as education and health initiatives. The local community decides democratically how to invest their extra income, making participation and joint responsibility of key importance. Providing access to information about global markets is an important feature of fair trade. Fair trade is a practical way of helping producers establish themselves into the world supply chain. It is not a charity, but a sensible commercial practice that emphasises human values.[13]

Fair trade is organised primarily in two ways. The first is through national labels such as the Fairtrade Mark in the UK.

*The Fairtrade Mark*

The Fairtrade Foundation awards an independent consumer guarantee – the Fairtrade Mark (see Figure 2.2) – to individual products which meet Fairtrade criteria regarding terms of trade and conditions of production.[14]

The main points of meeting the Fairtrade Mark criteria are:[15]

- Production conditions:
  - Small-scale farmers can participate in a democratic organisation.
  - Plantation/factory workers can participate in trade union activities and have decent wages, housing, and health and safety standards.
  - No child or forced labour.
  - Programmes for environmental sustainability.
- Fairtrade terms of trading:
  - A price that covers the cost of production.
  - A social 'premium' to be used by the producers to improve their living and working conditions.
  - Advance payment to avoid small producer organisations falling into debt.
  - Contracts that allow long-term planning and sustainable production practices.

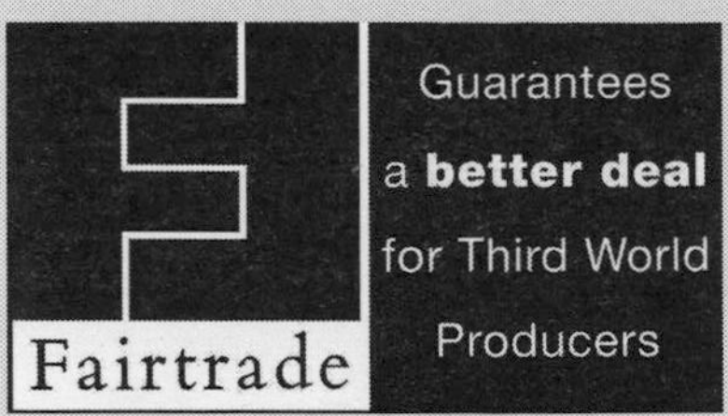


Figure 2.2 The UK Fairtrade Mark

Some Fairtrade Mark companies and their products include:

- Cafédirect (instant and ground coffee, and tea);
- Clipper Teas (tea bags and loose-leaf teas);
- Co-op (bananas, and milk chocolate with Divine);
- Divine (milk chocolate bar – The Day Chocolate Co);
- Equal Exchange (teas, coffees, honey, sugar, cocoa);
- Green & Black's (chocolate and cocoa);
- Hampstead (speciality teas);
- Oxfam (chocolate and cocoa);
- Ridgways (tea bags and loose tea);
- Traidcraft (chocolate, cookies, snack bars).

There are over 1,000 fair-trade-labelled products in 17 countries with sales of £120 million in Europe. In the UK, sales of Fairtrade Mark products have increased by about 53 per cent per year over the last five years.

The other route to fair trade is by organisations creating their own initiatives and working with others. Organisations such as Oxfam, Traidcraft and The Body Shop International have developed a reputation for selling fair trade products using their own criteria. These organisations might have some products with the Fairtrade Mark but in general apply fair trade principles to some or most of their products and practices as well as participating in development, political and charity activities.[16] These organisations have expanded the fair trade principles into handicrafts, clothes and beauty products as well as food products.

## Supply chain management

Corporate procurement and outsourcing of manufacturing is a huge and financially risky activity that involves complex relationships with suppliers and should include ethical and fair trading issues. Hence, the 'ethicalness' of a retailer is inextricably linked to the 'ethicalness' of those who supply it with goods and services, and the working conditions in its suppliers' suppliers and so forth.[17] Retailers can push ethical trade practices along the supply chain to suppliers but different product lines have different challenges. Some supply chains are simple, such as horticulture (eg vegetables). Here there are only grower, exporter, importer and retailer in the supply chain and so it is relatively easy to manage and implement good working conditions.[18] Other products such as cocoa have complex supply chains, ie grower, collector, local trader, international trader, commodities market, processor, merchandiser and retailer. Clearly, here it is more difficult for retailers to verify working conditions of employees in the supply chain.[19] So the complexity of implementing an ethical trading code of conduct into different product supply chains depends on:[20]

- length of supply chain;
- diversity of suppliers;
- diversity of retailing;
- business and legal implications;
- stability in the supply chain;
- trust in the supply chain.

In order to optimise the well-being of workers, socially responsible supply chains should include emphasis on good governance, good working practices, health, safety, security, compensation and investment in the future.[21] In the case of some products such as cocoa, the simplest method for retailers is to cut through the complex supply chain and source directly from the growers to ensure good working conditions and the payment of fair prices (as required by fair trade principles). Some retailers have numerous own-brand products where control should be much easier. This applies particularly to supermarkets. For example, Asda has over 30,000 different own-brand products with their own supply chain. Implementing ethical trade or fair trade principles should be standard practice for new supply chains. For existing product lines, ethical and fair trade practices should be phased in over time so that suppliers can improve working practices.

## Problems with ethical and fair trade

Consumers should be aware that there are difficulties in implementing and ensuring ethical and fair trade:

- Some developing countries have argued that developed countries are using ethical and fair trade as an excuse to impose trade barriers to stop the loss of jobs to lower-waged economies.[22] They argue that ethical standards will force up the costs of production and will result in a loss of competitive advantage.
- Using companies with profit motives as the vehicle for improving labour standards contains inherent limitations, and is not a substitute for a broader development strategy.
- As codes of conduct are adopted voluntarily by individual companies, their coverage is only partial in the context of total employment. They are limited to those suppliers servicing the relevant companies in developing countries. Suppliers who do not wish to (or cannot) meet the conditions laid down in the code are free to shift to other markets.
- Some of the stakeholders involved in ethical and fair trade, especially groups representing the interests of marginalised workers, have no commercial power, which undermines their ability to participate on equitable terms with companies.
- Ethical and fair trade can be seen as the imposition of Western values on other cultures. As a result, the voices and interests of those groups in developing countries could well be overlooked or misrepresented, undermining the usefulness of codes. A major challenge will be how to represent the needs and interests of weaker groups in the process, and ensure this is not merely a top-down paper exercise.
- Retailers have been accused of not operating by the very codes of conduct they impose on suppliers.
- Codes of conduct are a top-down solution that are heavily

biased in the retailers' favour. Often they are not flexible enough for suppliers or local conditions.

These problems are, of course, complex. What is important though is that we act in a way that seems most ethical for us, bearing in mind some of the tensions and contradictions implied above. Business will also have to think about many of these issues. But the way for them to overcome contradictions is simply to be clear and transparent about their values. Increasingly companies are producing 'values statements' and we should push them to think more about ethical and fair trade issues.

In conclusion, ethical and fair trade can be complementary to, but cannot be a substitute for, other forms of regulation or labour standards implemented through government regulation or international organisations. They are also only part of a broader range of standards covering issues such as the environment.[23] For companies, regulation provides a level playing field within which employers operate, and helps to ensure a more stable labour market environment. Good employment standards can also complement the attainment of higher levels of productivity in a company, increasing employee commitment and quality of work.

From the consumer point of view, changing labour standards cannot be ignored. Governments and companies only start changing if there are pressures on them from a variety of sources. The consumer can help apply this pressure through purchasing fair trade products from retailers who have implemented a code of conduct. Consumers can also become informed and active through pressure groups that force governments and companies to take note of the poor and exploitative working conditions in developing countries.

# 3 | What should we expect from business?

## Sustainable development

The continuing ability of the environment to supply raw materials and assimilate waste while maintaining biodiversity and a quality of life is being increasingly undermined. If growth and development are to take on new responsible paths we have to find a way that will not further degrade the environment in which we live and not create many of the social tensions that we now observe. In its simplest form, sustainable development is defined in the Brundtland Report as development that meets the needs of the present generation without compromising the ability of future generations to meet their own needs.[1] Such a simple statement has profound implications. It implies that, as a minimum, all human activity must refrain from causing any degree of permanent damage through its consumption of environmental resources. Business has a big role to play in this. But it also implies that business has an obligation to ensure that it is responsible on a range of social issues too.

Tackling sustainable development from the perspective of the firm is not an easy task. To talk of a sustainable company is perhaps meaningless because, however big or small the organisation, it cannot be seen in isolation from the society in which it operates. However, it may be possible to talk of a business acting in a way that is consistent with sustainable development. We should expect to see businesses adopting policies that can help to achieve a more sustainable society. Business must examine a range of issues (many of which are contradictory) inherent in sustainable development. These include issues of ethics, debates around globalisation and free trade, the thorny issue of consumption and marketing as well as aspects of local economic development and responsibilities to local communities.

There can be little doubt that social and environmental concern has in general increased over the last 30 years. In the 1990s that real concern became so great that legislators, regulators, policy makers and some intergovernmental organisations have given environmental considerations their proper place amongst all the other competing objectives of a modern pluralist society. Different stakeholders and non-governmental organisations (NGOs) have championed various objectives that they see as necessary parts of sustainable development. Businesses have responded in different ways. Many have been resistant to change, others have been accommodating and now some are being increasingly proactive. A small minority have even become champions themselves, showing what can be achieved by searching for social and environmental excellence. These are the companies given five-star ratings in this book.

The concept of sustainable development is a radical one, requiring every organisation and every person to think in time dimensions longer than a generation and placing an emphasis on both rights and responsibilities. There are a number of reforms that businesses can and should adopt to minimise their negative impacts on the environment and social development. There is even a need to consider just how we do business and think about the ways that the capitalist system often forces businesses to maintain a competitive advantage. If this means exploiting more and more natural resources and labour working in developing countries, then it is hardly consistent with sustainable development.

As a starting point, business needs to recognise that the issues surrounding human life and economic activity are an interdependent part of wider social and ecological processes that sustain life on earth. They must operate within sustainable processes or they will, in turn, bring about the demise of present societies. That requires fundamental reforms of the structures and processes that have caused the problem in the first place. That means finding new ways of doing business, of including workers in change processes, of organising trade so as to protect the developing world and indigenous populations, and of sustaining all other life forms on the planet.

We cannot rely on established governmental structures, technology and science to bring about real change. A technological breakthrough allowing the whole world to consume more and everybody to have higher living standards might happen one day. But we cannot rely on that. There is a need for business to engage in a more radical rethink of many of the issues that face society and, as part of that, we need to think carefully about enterprise culture.

What nobody can provide, however, is a formula for the precise way in which businesses must operate into the future. When Karl Marx was once asked to describe what a communist society would look like, he replied that he could not write recipes for the cookshops of the future. We can, however, point to the inadequacies of many current strategies and point to the direction along which organisations must tread. We can provide a series of suggestions and demands for business and hope sincerely that there will be sufficient societal pressure to encourage the business community further to take steps forward.

## The challenge of sustainable development and consequences for business strategy

Social and environmental concerns are not particularly new; they have been a matter of public concern for over a quarter of a century. As scientific and technical knowledge relating to the cause and effect of environmental damage has become more complete, the pressure to change the ways in which industry behaves has increased. Individuals are also changing their patterns of behaviour, and industry is having to respond to the seemingly endless demands of the new, environmentally aware consumer. Indeed, such are the wide-ranging pressures being put on business from a range of diverse stakeholders that business will increasingly have to account for its actions if it is going to survive in the market-place. With increased information availability, more sophisticated targeting of companies by pressure groups and a greater wish to see companies as good corporate citizens, the very strategy of a business has to be sensitive to increasing social and environmental demands.

In its early stages, the environmental debate in industry was largely one of words rather than action. More recently, businesses have recognised the need to improve their environmental performance but we have seen only a few businesses begin to change in a way that can bring about a lasting reversal of trends towards environmental destruction. This is compounded by the process of globalisation and the emphasis on free trade that blurs the frontiers of a single business's activities. While it is difficult for industry to reject the general need for environmental protection, its response has too often been piecemeal, adopting bolt-on strategies aimed at fine-tuning its environmental performance within the constraints imposed by a traditional capitalist society. To date there have been a lot of publications aimed at telling businesses how they can achieve a measure of environmental improvement (and now many that talk of the need for social accountability), but there has been rather less debate about the very way in which business operates that will lead to real progress. There is a need to develop practical solutions to meet the challenge of sustainable development. And at the heart of the issue there is a need to tackle trade, making it more consistent with sustainable development and protecting developing countries and their citizens.

Traditionally the view of the corporate world has been based on the idea that the investments and innovations of industry drive economic growth and satisfy the demands of the consumer. However, in doing so, be it because of the resources that it consumes, the processes that it applies or the products that it manufactures, business activity has become a major contributor to environmental destruction. Many commentators have argued that we need to find new technologies and to develop more efficient methods of production. But the very basis of that argument needs to be examined carefully. Growth can no longer be a sole objective that stands alone and pays no heed to its environmental consequences now and into the future. Growth is only justifiable if it is associated with development.

For a long time now free market economists have told us that, if harnessed correctly, the market mechanism can be utilised to develop the solutions that are so vital if the environment is to be protected. But to date the free market has failed to bring about equitable distribution of income, it has failed to protect the developing world and it has done little to protect the planet. The free market approach was heralded as the way to create wealth in developing countries, and free trade is supposed to be the vehicle for this. Yet free trade has brought with it a greater emphasis on cost reduction, and in developing countries competitive advantage is often maintained by keeping wages as low as possible. This is hardly consistent with development.

Business strategy therefore has to embrace the concept of sustainable development. This is going to be a difficult task, because at times that concept may not be entirely consistent with other strategies such as growth, profit maximisation, creating shareholder value and investment. Conflict will not always occur, of course: the many stories of companies reducing their costs through the adoption of traditional environmental management principles are now so overwhelming that one is left wondering why not every company is doing it. But where conflict does occur, businesses have choices to make. Those will be difficult choices and businesses will have to think carefully about the consequences of their decisions. The bottom line, however, is that ultimately it will be the senior managers who will have to make those choices. There will be little that many of us can do about it. But what we can expect is that businesses become increasingly transparent and accountable in their strategic decision making and that they are then able to explain to stakeholders why they took one path rather than another. Then we as consumers can make a choice as to whether we want to buy their products.

Ultimately, the most we can expect of businesses is that they make their values clear. Based on an assessment of these values and a similar assessment of their actions, we as consumers and citizens can decide whether we want to do business with them. In this book we have tried to use the information provided by companies to help you make better choices as a consumer. With the common usage of the Internet, information about companies is increasingly available and we have seen campaigners against organisations such as McDonalds and Shell use this medium to rather good effect. In the so-called McLibel case and in the case of Shell's embarrassment over both the sinking of the Brent Spar and its activities in Nigeria, the image of the company (and one can only assume its long-term profitability) was compromised. In both cases it was the arrogance of the company's business strategy that ultimately led to their problems.

## Sustainable development and implications for industry

One major obstacle preventing sustainability from being achieved is the overall level and type of consumption experienced in the Western world. Consumers who are relatively wealthy seem reluctant to reduce their own levels of consumption significantly. While increasingly governments are adopting economic instruments such as taxes, subsidies and product labelling schemes to reduce and channel consumption towards more environmentally friendly alternatives, there is also a need for education amongst consumers. In addition, though, industry has a role to play in educating its customers and suppliers and all businesses must be encouraged to increase their own internal environmental efficiency further by reassessing the very ways in which they do business and measuring and assessing their environmental performance.

The fact that lies behind the concept of sustainable development is that there is a trade-off between continuous economic growth and the sustainability of the environment. Over time, through greater and greater exploitation, growth causes pollution and atmospheric damage, disrupts traditional ways of living (particularly in the developing world), destroys ecosystems and feeds more and more power into oligopolistic industrial structures. The concept of sustainable development stresses the interdependence between economic growth and environmental quality, but it also goes further in demonstrating that the future is uncertain unless we can deal with issues of equity and inequality throughout the whole world. It is possible to make development and environmental protection compatible and to begin to deal with the problems caused by a lack of consideration of equity issues, by following sustainable strategies and by not developing the particular areas of economic activity that are most damaging to the environment and its inhabitants.

Economic development and environmental protection can be made compatible, but this requires quite radical changes in economic practices throughout the world including a reassessment of globalisation and free trade. Mass consumption is not possible indefinitely and, if society today acts as if all non-renewable resources are plentiful, eventually there will be nothing left for the future. But more importantly than that, mass consumption may cause such irreparable damage that humans may not even be able to live on the planet in the future.

There is often a fruitless search for a universal and single definition of sustainable development. Development is a process and not easily defined but what is more important is that we begin moving towards a development path that is environmentally and socially responsible. At least in part, this means treating economics, social issues and environmental issues not as three separate and individual concepts that have to be managed, but as important parts of a bigger whole. Often good business (in traditional terms) is environmentally friendly and socially responsible, but perhaps more often there are conflicts that will have to be resolved.

It seems clear therefore that industry must seek to provide the services demanded by consumers with the minimum social and environmental impact at all stages. This is a far-reaching challenge as it involves a reformulation not only of sourcing and production processes but of products and trading mechanisms. While many consumers may be unwilling to reduce the overall levels of consumption to which they have become accustomed, they have proved willing to select the goods that produce a reduced environmental impact. In this book we try to help the consumer think about a range of social issues as well, by considering fair trade and equitable trade. Companies need to focus their strategies and marketing campaigns on supplying goods with a sustainable differential advantage. In so doing the producer has to accept responsibility for the environmental and social impacts of the materials and processes used at the production stage and for the final product and its disposal. In many ways, therefore, industry has to take on a whole range of new responsibilities towards the economy.

We must not forget, however, that a key part of the sustainable development concept (which is often conveniently ignored by industry) relates to equity issues. The massive inequality in wealth and standards of living displayed across the world makes sustainable development harder to achieve. Those living in the developing world often aspire to the standards of living of the developed world and we know that from an environmental stance such aspirations are presently not achievable. But what right do people in the developed world have to deny other human beings development in the same unsustainable way in which they themselves have developed? We can see that social and environmental improvement is inextricably linked to wider issues of global concern that do need to be addressed. Equity has also to be tackled at the level of the firm, however. New forms of industrial organisation should seek to empower workers and increase their decision-making powers, to increase democracy in the workplace and to share profits with the workforce, alongside improving environmental performance. This demands a more holistic and ethical approach to doing business that values workers as an integral and valuable part of the organisation rather than a resource to be hired and fired as external market conditions change.

## The corporate response to sustainable development

Environmental legislation in most industrialised economies is increasingly plugging the gaps that allow environmental degradation to happen. Firms (and their directors) attempting to hide their illegal pollution are now subject to severe penalties. However, businesses should recognise that it is not only ethical to be environmentally friendly but, with the growth of consumer awareness in the environmental area, it will also be 'good business' in a more traditional sense. Now that attention is also switching to the social concerns highlighted by the concept of sustainable development, industry is beginning to feel pressure from a number of its stakeholders to demonstrate that it is a good corporate citizen.

Firms clearly have a role to play in the development of substitutes for non-renewable resources and innovations that reduce waste and use energy more efficiently. They also play a part in processing those materials in a way that brings about environmental improvements. But they clearly also have a role in shaping societies and helping to provide a good social infrastructure. Many companies are politically powerful, some might say even more powerful than many of the governments around the world. Such power can be harnessed for good and sometimes it is. However, large transnational corporations are often cited as creating large degrees of social unrest and conflicts in countries where they operate. This is particularly true with regard to the operations of large firms outside their Western 'homes'.

Accusations of human rights abuses, corruption and cosy relationships with military dictators do not fit easily with the type of social responsibility demanded by the concept of sustainable development.

Within the pluralist society in which we live a whole range of pressures is beginning to create the preconditions that are necessary to encourage businesses to respond to the environmental challenge. Industry is beginning to develop new technologies and techniques that may help to move the global economy towards sustainability. Whilst accepting that the answer will not lie in technology alone, this process must continue. The rapid growth of public environmental awareness in recent years has also placed new pressures on industry. These pressures can take many forms as individuals collectively exercise their environmental conscience as customers, employees, investors, voters, neighbours and responsible citizens. But it is perhaps the NGO movement and its ability to expose industry actions that is most interesting. In general, the growth of a 'civil society' means that industry may not have the power in the future that it has now. Often referred to as the 'second superpower', civil society (aided by the type of information availability we have already discussed) has the potential to mitigate the excesses of business. This has to be seen as a good thing, and businesses are going to have to be prepared to tackle this new force. To do so is simple: it requires companies to be more transparent, more accountable and more honest.

A strategy for responding to the demands of sustainable development must begin with real commitment on the part of the whole organisation. This may mean a change in corporate culture, and management has an important role to play. In leading that commitment and laying out the organisation's corporate objectives with respect to social and environmental issues, management has to be the catalyst for change. Indeed it needs to rethink its whole rationale and reassess the very structures in its own organisation that act as impediments to change. Further, change has to be ongoing, and management must be ever mindful of the full range of (often competing) objectives to which it is subject. Management has to find compromise between these objectives if they conflict, and design corporate strategies that are operational, consistent and achievable. Change will have to be addressed in a systemic way, dealing with the company as a whole rather than in a compartmentalised way. There is also a need to look towards the 'larger picture' rather than being driven by product-specific considerations.

Moreover, corporate structures should not be rigid, and the identification and development of corporate strengths should be seen as more important than the continuation of 'business as usual'. When it comes to the integration of social and environmental considerations, co-operative strategies need also to be considered. All too often competition has been the dominant ideology in business, but increasingly co-operative strategies between businesses and involving the public and regulatory agencies can bring about benefits. Single-minded competitive strategies run the risk of isolating businesses from new developments, expertise and public opinion that are invaluable to the socially and environmentally aware company.

## Sustainable development in an international context

One of the characteristics of post-war Europe has been growing integration associated with the European Union. But that trend, more recently, has been mirrored in other parts of the world. International trade is dominated by the global triad of Europe, North America and Japan, and all OECD countries have found their economies becoming more interdependent and inter-related through the growth of trade, technology transfer and global communications networks. Through the mass media it has often been models of Western consumer culture that have been relayed across the planet and into the developing world. Yet global inequality persists between the higher-income and lower-income countries and there are considerable differences within the lower-income countries themselves.

In many ways, no country can see itself as independent. The global spread of industrial activity along with the expansion of information systems means that no country can insulate itself from the external economic climate. Neither can countries insulate themselves from the growing pollution and social disruption caused by industrialisation and consumerism. Perhaps most intrusive, however, are the activities of the transnational corporations (TNCs), which bring with them their own corporate cultures and dominate international trade and production. They are therefore responsible for significant levels of transnational environmental damage.

The rapid evolution of an international economic system has not been matched by international political integration or international laws to regulate that system. The consequence is that many businesses operate above the law and above national boundaries and are able to set their own international economic agenda. Moreover, by creating a situation where many developing world countries are dependent on their patronage, employment and technology, they often wield considerable political power as well. This is hardly a scenario that can be reconciled with sustainable development.

Many firms today do business worldwide and source their raw materials from a range of countries. Although this presents great opportunities, it also poses some problems, some ethical dilemmas and many opportunities for abuse. Unethical practices have a critical effect on the image of companies at home and abroad. Union Carbide's acceptance of lower operating standards in its developing world operations led to the Bhopal accident on 3 December 1984 when a gas (methyl isocyanate) leaked from their plant; approximately 3,800 people died, 40 had permanent total disability and 2,680 experienced permanent partial disability. The lesson to be learnt is that standards and controls must be even more rigidly applied in countries where workers and managers may be less competent than they are in more economically and educationally advanced countries. A major ethical question also revolves around the sourcing of raw materials from parts of the world where indigenous populations are adversely affected. The drive for low-cost inputs leads to the exploitation of such people and the abuse of their land, and attacks their fundamental right to lead their lives as they would wish.

Trade is therefore a source of increased opportunities for many people in developing countries. However, it is also a threat if it involves exploitation of natural resources and people. Business is the major driver of increased trade and therefore as a minimum we should expect companies to ensure that what trade is done is consistent with the highest principles of ethics and of sustainable development.

## Conclusions

Business has a big role to play in moving the world towards a more sustainable path. The way forward seems to be to combine a more ethical business approach with an increase in the awareness of consumers. This approach stresses the need for new social contracts between those who produce, source and trade goods and those who buy them. Sustainable development demands both a local and a global approach (based on local action and organisation); it demands a reconsideration of equity and a new stress on equality. There are serious limits to the capacity of national sovereignty to deal with the threats to the environment. There may be a need for new national and supranational forums and a recognition of interdependence at the global level (although real action should be at the local or regional level). Further, such institutions need also to be more creative and leave aside accepted wisdom and theories maintained by the status quo. We need to develop further the notions of individual responsibility and collective strategy at the political level and drive this down to the business level.

But businesses must take their roles seriously as well. They can be facilitators for sustainable development through the adoption of high principles and the adoption of policies associated with the highest environmental and social standards. They can also be educators and campaigners and integrate the various strands of sustainable development into their decision-making processes. If we are going to move towards a more sustainable world we should accept no less.

# 4 | Conflicts between sustainable development and free trade

## Introduction

There can now be little doubt that the environmental damage caused to the planet over the last few decades has got to a point where it is causing untold damage to humans and to other species. Much of that damage is irreversible, and the massive use of non-renewable resources has taken little account of the needs of future generations. The situation is getting worse, impacting on human health, biodiversity and the social infrastructure of many societies. There is now clear evidence of climate change, and we are losing the areas of wilderness left on the planet at an alarming rate. Governments have demonstrated little real effort directed at reversing these trends, preferring to leave the task to the voluntary efforts of businesses, pressure groups, other non-governmental organisations and individuals. Perhaps more than anywhere, the environmental crisis is most acute in the developing world where it is directly impacting upon the lives and health of local populations. Moreover, environmental crises are directly linked to many of the social problems that we now observe.

Business has to accept a very large share of the responsibility for the crisis. Businesses are central to a system of production and consumption that is destroying life on Earth, and if we continue with this path not one area of wilderness, indigenous culture, endangered species or uncontaminated water supply will survive the global market economy. The often uncritical acceptance of trends towards globalisation, free trade and the emphasis on the need for (naive measures of) economic growth make the situation worse. If trends towards uncontrolled free trade mean that production shifts to low-wage economies where labour is continually under pressure to produce more at lower costs, then this is hardly consistent with any type of development. In parallel, if growth in the developed world simply results in underdevelopment in the developing world, then this simply widens the inequities that are inconsistent with a move towards sustainable development.

Given the current international economic order, what is likely is that the future environmental crises, which are inevitable, will occur not in those countries at the root of the industrialisation process, but in developing countries that are currently growing at the fastest rates, where business activity is expanding rapidly and where institutional structures are least able to deal with the consequences of accelerating production and consumption.

## The international economic order

In line with the move towards the globalised, free market economy, governments have created an international environment of deregulation, because free markets unrestrained by governments are supposed to result in higher economic growth as measured by gross national output. The primary responsibility of industrial policy seems to be to provide an infrastructure that will help corporations expand their commercial activities. In this respect, governments seek to enforce the rule of law with respect to property rights and contracts – without which the capitalist system comes to a halt. Privatisation has been espoused over the last 15 years and we have seen valuable national assets shifted from the control of governments to the private sector in the name of efficiency. Thus the very role of governments has been to transfer more and more power into the corporate private sector.

Around the world, governments and intergovernmental agencies have shifted towards the more conservative view of economics and industry. The left talks of the stakeholder society and no longer of vested interests and the living standards of the working classes. It now embraces social democratic principles and democratic capitalism. But, in general, mainstream political parties have not embraced green ideas and have shown only a limited commitment to sustainable development. They have consistently lacked any real leadership on social and environmental issues and their policies have been devoid of any radical green ideas or vision.

More fundamentally, however, we must now recognise that politicians and governments no longer have sole control over the management of nations. They may still be able to wage war with their massive stocks of destructive arms, but the management of the economic process has to be done in co-operation with business. Of the hundred biggest economic institutions in the world today, about half are countries and half are companies. Only recently have businesses become the major agents in determining how societies and cultures are defined, but they are now expert at it. Indeed, it is business that has created the consumer culture, the fast food culture and insatiable materialism. It is business that often seems to set out its vision of the world's monoculture with its global products, global messages and mass markets. It is even business that supports and sponsors the politicians and political parties that will give it what it wants.

Moreover, large corporations have a significant advantage over governments. They are able to cross national boundaries much more easily. The transnational corporations with their massive stocks of private capital are much more influential on the global stage than any government or even intergovernmental agency can be. The capital that they use to broker agreements replacing vital natural resources with industrial plant is essentially nomadic. This means that a large corporation is able to change the direction of development of the many countries dependent on its patronage to suit whatever short-term objective seems paramount at any point in time. What development there is in the developing world, for example, is often directed, dependent development – the aspirations of indigenous populations and local environmental concerns are rarely given any real priority. The institutions of government and the intergovernmental agencies that are supposed to protect the greater interest are failing to do so.

There is, therefore, what we might call a 'governance gap'. Whilst we have seen the growth and globalisation of business we have not seen an equivalent globalisation of government. There has been no globalisation of democracy and virtually no successful initiatives to introduce international regulations governing the behaviour of companies. There is no requirement for companies to be accountable to a global audience, only financially accountable in those countries where they decide to declare their profits. This represents a fundamental problem where the power of corporate elites far exceeds the power of any democratically elected institution. In many ways corporations really do now rule the world.

Business so often begins with the premise that free trade is here, it is a reality and there is nothing you can do to stop the trend. End of story. In taking that line it cleverly sidesteps any debate over the inherent contradictions between globalisation, free trade and sustainable development. Whilst ignoring that debate, it seems content to see the full effects of globalisation resulting in a global shift of business out of high-wage economies and towards low-wage economies. And business itself, constrained as it is by its dependence on growth and globalisation, might result in being a major barrier to sustainable development. Here we can outline three sets of contradictions: between business and the international economic order; between the international economic order (including trends towards globalisation and free trade) and sustainable development; and between business and sustainable development. Although business might be responsible to a large degree for some of the abuses created by free trade, we will see that it is also constrained by the system that it often espouses. Let us deal with these contradictions.

## *Business and the international economic order*

Businesses are actually constrained by the pressure that globalisation exerts upon them. The need to make profits in a highly competitive international market-place means that costs have to be continually driven down. There is little room in corporate budgets for anything that is not perceived as strictly necessary or for anything that does not have a short payback period in a traditional business sense. Such intense competition drives out the scope for creativity, reflection and responsibility. It does not allow for any organisational slack. For many Northern companies, simply surviving and maintaining employment in such a hostile environment is difficult.

As if to make the situation worse, competitors in low-wage

economies with access to Northern markets are able to undercut domestic firms and have free access to their markets. Low wages become a major source of competitive advantage and therefore high wages (as paid to workers in the North) become a source of inefficiency. Job cuts are made or the company itself relocates to a low-wage economy. Human beings become little more than factors of production, and when the globalised system makes them inefficient they are simply substituted out of production.

The emphasis on cost reduction as a source of competitiveness often therefore turns out to be destructive. Moreover, even when companies switch to producing in low-wage economies that is not the end of the potential for cost reduction. The exploitation of the natural environment follows with firms clearing forests, mining in unsustainable ways and convincing governments to let them have access to more and more resources in order to aid development. Social and environmental responsibility comes pretty low down on any such business agenda. And when breaches of any such responsibility are easy to hide (as they commonly are in the developing world) then it does not even focus at all.

## *The international economic order and sustainable development*

The international economic order is fixated on growth: the quantitative increase in nation output per year. The bottom line here is that growth and development are different things. In some cases a degree of growth has benefited development. However, the type of growth we are now witnessing, brought about by the international economic order, is often not consistent with development. Since development is about a qualitative improvement in the lives of human beings it is difficult to see how low-wage economies, the destruction of natural resources and the undemocratic political power of corporations are consistent with such development. In addition, economic growth in one part of the world actually requires a degree of underdevelopment in other parts of the world in order to provide the cheap labour and resources to fuel competitiveness. Thus the international economic order becomes divisive and stimulates as much underdevelopment as it creates growth.

Further, what development there is, is often not sustainable either economically or environmentally. It is too often based on treating the environment as a free good and tends to result in high levels of pollution. It relies on easy access to resources. But such factors cannot last for ever and there is an inevitability about economic collapse following environmental collapse. The future could as easily be about resource wars as some harmonious free enterprise global economy.

The whole process of globalisation means that trade in goods and services, capital and labour is free to move around the world as necessary. This greatly reduces the ability of individual firms to put in place policy instruments and other measures consistent with sustainable development. The introduction of environmental regulation or taxation could lead to a degree of (perceived) uncompetitiveness and result in less favoured treatment by powerful transnationals. Thus, there is a power vacuum, and national communities are weakened and are simply not able to respond to sustainable development. Indeed, the international economic order, with the support of multilateral financial agencies and the World Bank, takes developing-world countries in completely the wrong direction.

## *Business and sustainable development*

Clearly the constraints discussed above mean that business actually has a very hard task if it wants to internalise policies and strategies that are consistent with the move towards more sustainable development. But the nature of company behaviour often makes the situation even worse. Since firms seek to maximise profits (even though much of these profits are consumed inside the firm rather than distributed to shareholders), then there will always be an incentive for firms to externalise costs. In the developed world there are many social and environmental costs imposed on companies: minimum wages, national insurance contributions, welfare programmes, health and safety measures, pollution control, liability for accidents and so on. Many of these social costs can be externalised simply by a shift of location. Indeed, what globalisation creates is a process of lowering standards, which some companies are happy to go along with. They actually create a situation where policies that could move us towards sustainable development, but that would result in costs being imposed on business, are not possible.

Instead, business espouses the voluntary approach, where we are supposed to sit back and trust companies to move to a situation more consistent with sustainable development. Most people do not actually trust big business any more. There is little evidence that much of business is interested in sustainable development, but unfortunately rather a lot of evidence of businesses being involved in human rights violations, illegal payments to governments, corruption and negligence over pollution controls. But they are now so powerful people think that there is little that anyone can do about it.

Business is yet to realise that if the international economic order continues and that if the demands of sustainable development are ignored, then they are bringing about their own demise. There is an environmental crisis in the world, but perhaps it is not yet of the magnitude that will force business (and governments) to face up to its real responsibilities. The problem is that when business eventually gets around to acknowledging its true role, it may be too late.

## Conclusions

It would be wrong to suggest that all companies are bad. Indeed, this book will show that many large companies are adopting environmental management strategies and thinking about their social responsibilities in terms of trade. But we must also recognise that failure to deal with inequities often brought about by free trade cannot be attributed to business alone. Businesses often struggle with a free market economic order that is sometimes inconsistent with sustainable development, and that forces them continually to drive costs down in order to survive. In such a system, it is little wonder that businesses often view environmental protection and social responsibility as relatively low priorities. Nevertheless, in a world where businesses are increasingly powerful and in a world where they are actually able to create more effective change than many governments, we should still expect them to take a lead.

Thus we are left with the question relating to what companies ought to try to achieve. We must recognise that we live in an increasingly globalised economy where companies will only survive if they can maintain a degree of competitive advantage. But rather than see this as a barrier to social and environmental improvement and to sustainable development, we ought to regard it as an opportunity. In this respect, companies can build upon the competitive advantage that already exists, stressing real differentiation strategies associated with environmental protection and social responsibility. Through a greater degree of accountability and transparency, and effective communications, they can create a new norm that requires every business to perform in a way more consistent with sustainable development.

It will be seen in the chapters to follow that some companies (awarded five stars) are beginning to pursue policies consistent with sustainable development: producing less products of higher quality, reducing environmental and social impacts and putting a new emphasis on equitable and fair trade. It is important that business continues to develop accounting and reporting techniques as a way of tracking and providing information on achievements in these areas, and this, in turn, will help consumers make better choices. This is going to be very challenging for businesses, but we see signs that they are responding to this challenge. With the growth of information available about firms (provided by both themselves and their detractors) through media such as the Internet and books like this, it is going to be much easier for us all to make more informed choices about the products we buy. Business policies consistent with sustainable development are nevertheless still required to accelerate the move towards a situation more consistent with an equitable world.

# 5 | Communicating the difference

## Tell the truth and nothing but the truth

No company can be a sustainable company unless it is a successful company. That means that it has to achieve its traditional business objectives as well as try its best to act in a way that is consistent with sustainable development, adopting fair trade and equitable trade principles. For many people there may appear to be a number of conflicts here. It is often assumed that being socially and environmentally sensitive will cost money. However, there are many case studies of companies where this is not the case. But even where operationalising sustainable development in the business organisation does add to costs, then this is still consistent with good business, just so long as the benefits of differentiating the company and its products in that way exceed the costs. Therefore, what is very important in a company that wants to move in the direction of sustainable development is the ability to differentiate its products and its overall corporate image. The most effective way of doing this is through open and honest communications with stakeholders and particularly through efforts to educate and influence customer choice.

There is therefore a role for the company in persuading its consumers to act in ways that are consistent with sustainable development, whilst at the same time making sure that its own profile is both environmentally and socially responsible. In the past, however, marketing and particularly the concept of 'green marketing' may have impeded the creation of a sustainable society. The fact of the matter is that many companies did not tell the whole truth, some deliberately misled and misinformed their customers and others were downright dishonest. What we should now expect of businesses is that they tell us the truth and the whole truth. And if they get found out telling lies then we should be prepared to switch away from those companies and even mount boycotts of their products.

Traditionally, the concept of 'green marketing' often seems to be more associated with hype and overzealous claims about a product's environmental impact than anything positive associated with giving consumers full information about it. It has had a history associated with false claims and misleading statements about environmental 'credentials' and has led to a situation where many consumers simply do not believe some of the claims associated with greener products. In many ways this has caused problems for those companies that are genuinely trying to differentiate their products based on some sort of environmental and social responsibility profile. It means that companies now not only must convince consumers of the validity of their product claims but must also become associated with having a sound corporate image. Thus business should make an effort to promote sustainable development, particularly in the areas of education and campaigning.

Because the concept of sustainable development requires us to take a holistic view of business, marketing is seen as akin to 'total management', embracing a wide array of disciplines from the inception and creation of new products, cost management and the pricing of goods, through sourcing, procurement and logistics management to promotion, sales and after-service – the front line between the firm and its customers. But it also embraces the overall profile of the company, its reputation, corporate image, sponsorship, education programmes and campaigning activities. Indeed, if used ethically and effectively, it is argued here, the traditional marketing tool can make a significant contribution to moving us down the path towards sustainable development. Because businesses are so powerful and because retailers, in particular, have such close contact with individuals, there is a significant contribution for the business world to make in this sort of process.

Marketing is dependent on the structures, processes and systems within which the firm operates. This includes the competitive, economic, political, social and cultural spheres to which the marketing strategy has to be matched. There is nothing inherently evil in the marketing function but it ought to be ethical, honest and compatible with sustainable development. In part it represents a culture change process that emphasises co-operation rather than competition, eliminates sales hype and provides honest information to the consumer. Its selling techniques are non-stereotypical, non-exploitative and open to public scrutiny. Marketing should stress education and point to the need for both social and environmental responsibility on the part of both producers and consumers.

The context in which business operates has been changed because of a growing public familiarity with environmental issues. This is likely to continue and the consumer is going to be more and more sophisticated in his or her choices and in what he or she believes from the corporate message. The next decade will also see people embracing a range of social issues and the marketing function of business will have to respond to this as well. It is likely that people will become less trusting of companies, and indeed catastrophes such as the Exxon Valdez oil spill, the Chernobyl nuclear incident and the chemical spillage in Bhopal, India only highlight to consumers that much of the world's ecological destruction has been caused directly by the drive towards more and more output without regard to ecological protection and safety.

This situation means that the way a firm communicates with the outside world through its products, services and other activities is going to have to be more open and honest. Moreover, companies will have to recognise that consumers will switch away from the companies' products if they believe that the companies are not acting in a reasonable way. We know that many people do change their buying choices because of negative impressions of particular companies. Companies therefore need to think much harder about the ways they are portraying themselves and build ethical and ecological considerations into their communications strategies.

The marketing function can therefore be seen as a very wide one. It must encompass all the operations and activities of the firm, emphasise the social and environmental life cycle impact of a product (from getting the raw materials through to throwing away) and look carefully at an organisation's corporate image. It must be involved in setting ecological criteria for product design, it must carefully consider the packaging and promotion of products and it should be open and honest about the achievements of the firm from an ecological perspective and be able to demonstrate commitment to do even more. More than anything, it needs to give the consumer honest and accurate information about products, their source and modes of manufacture so that better-informed decisions can be made.

Advertising policies should adapt to changing conditions by displaying a more ethical approach to business and an increased distaste for stereotypical or offensive images. Advertising should be specific and all claims will have to be capable of proof to overcome the chronic public scepticism resulting from traditional approaches to marketing and dishonest claims. The role of advertising needs to be extended to be compatible with the education and campaigning role of business advocated in this chapter.

## Marketing and sustainable development

It has been argued that marketing ought to represent a discrete shift in emphasis away from traditional sales approaches, putting stress on certain aspects of a product, towards an ethical approach that takes a holistic view of the social and environmental aspects of the product from cradle to grave and considers the context in which it is produced. Marketing is about the provision of information about the product, its sourcing and the conditions under which it was manufactured. It therefore represents product stewardship at its best and ought to demonstrate sound sourcing and adherence to principles of equitable and fair trade.

The stakeholder concept emphasises the need to satisfy a whole range of often disparate demands. The role of sustainable marketing is to track these demands and to try to satisfy them where appropriate. For example, there will be demands from customers for socially and environmentally friendly products at reasonable prices with high-quality attributes, demands from shareholders for profitability and dividends, and demands from employees for fair wages and job security. Where conflict between competing aims exists, it has been the stakeholders with most power (usually measured in crude financial terms) who win the battle. However, if our ultimate aim is sustainable development, all other demands must be considered as secondary to this and profit-centred strategies must be replaced by more holistic and integrated approaches. A starting point must be to make stakeholders aware of one another's demands in an open and honest way. This approach has been alien to many organisations in the past but it must be part of an organisation's corporate culture if the company is honestly to claim that it is seeking to improve the whole of its social and environmental performance.

The most important lesson to be learnt from the stakeholder concept is that co-operation is as important as competition. Relations of trust have to be developed with stakeholders and this is best built up by honesty and openness. Companies that are serious about improving their social and environmental performance should have nothing to hide and therefore the disclosure of as much information as possible, without giving away competitive advantages, is central to a sustainable strategy. Therefore both product-specific information and company profiling and reporting are crucial if the consumer is to make a decision relating to both the purchase of a product and from whom it is bought. A preference for buying products from companies that can exhibit a positive social and environmental image is likely to be a characteristic of consumer preferences in the future.

Although social and environmental considerations are increasingly important to the consumer, such attributes alone will be insufficient to sell a product. Not only must the product recognise traditional market requirements (ie it must be fit for the purpose for which it was intended, have the desired quality and delivery attributes and be price-competitive), it must also consider its profile and the profile of its producer with regard to wider ecological issues such as worker rights, the treatment of women and minority groups, animal testing and any impact on the developing world and indigenous populations. In other words the company must be capable of responding to a whole range of issues consistent with sustainable development. Failure to meet these basic requirements will ultimately result in failure of the product.

Marketing cannot be looked at in isolation however. The effects of launching a new product or reorienting an existing one to have superior social and environmental attributes will have ramifications for procurement, finance, human resources, production processes and delivery. The fundamental key to a green marketing strategy is to approach the problem in a systemic way, undertaken through research and planning. Consideration of longer timescales for activities will also be important.

Sustainable marketing requires the company to reconsider even some of the basic assumptions about doing business. For example, it may not be consistent with sustainable development for a company to continue to try to persuade the consumer simply to buy more and more. An education process teaching the consumer to buy less may actually be more appropriate. Whilst this might, at first, be seen as bad business, the experience of companies such as Dow Chemicals, which has educated farmers to purchase fewer fertilisers, has shown that rather than losing customers, one can actually gain the trust of more customers such that business is retained and overall sales actually increase at the expense of other less enlightened companies.

Central to any sustainable marketing strategy will be the identification of new issues, market trends and the state of scientific knowledge and technology. Market research and accurate information will be needed to build successful campaigns. Marketing requires information to be effective and we should expect accurate information on the social and environmental impact of both a company and its products. A continuous flow of information and data is needed on both processes and products and central to this will be life cycle analysis, social and environmental audits and dialogue with stakeholders. These need to be ongoing activities producing information relating to the overall performance and social and environmental conduct of the whole organisation. However, information is often collected in a rather haphazard sort of way and this leads to a narrow and piecemeal focus. There is therefore a need for some sort of information system where information is collected and collated in a planned and productive way and from which reports are produced and published and product information is derived. The aim of such a system must be to enable managers to make more effective decisions, to act as a database for answering queries from stakeholders and to aid in education and campaigning initiatives.

## Communications

Communications are a key element in any marketing process. Accurate information about products and wider social and environmental aspects of processes should be communicated to all stakeholders and particularly customers. In particular, at the centre of the communications process should be a product stewardship approach where advice and help about the use and disposal of the product should be given to all those who will come into contact with it after it has left the factory gates. There is, of course, no magic method or style of promotion and information provision. Essentially, explaining the attributes of an environmentally friendlier, socially responsible or fair trade product should be approached in just the same way as any other communication message. The central message should always be visible, understood, relevant and honest. The company should be prepared to prove what has been said and be open to further questions about its overall social and environmental profile.

Companies that are promoting an environmentally friendly image will have to be very precise about what they say and truly practise what they preach. Drawing attention to the environmental aspects of a business will increasingly draw attention from a more sceptical public and better-informed media. If there is something about a product or organisation worth communicating then the key question must be to whom do you communicate? Undoubtedly the first group to concentrate on is the consumers of the product.

However, the sustainable development message may be rather more difficult to communicate than many surveys of consumer attitudes might suggest. While theoretically willing to buy alternative products, we know that most consumers are not, in practice, happy about giving up the brands they know and the price, quality and performance standards they have come to expect, especially for alternative, more uncertain purchases that might actually be at a higher price. One of the problems is that past marketing campaigns with respect to greener products have made situations worse by being deceitful. Many consumers have become confused, cynical and disillusioned with greener products. Companies cannot therefore jump to conclusions about consumers' understanding of, and likelihood to respond to, communications about fair trade and equitable trade products. Moreover, trying also to explain a product's socially responsible profile can result in even bigger dilemmas. There is therefore a need to look very closely at markets and consumer behaviour before effective communications can be developed. In the main, the onus will be on companies to educate consumers, simplify social and environmental issues (without decreasing their importance) and then offer product solutions. Marketers should also think about the profile of the company as a whole and consider campaigning strategies consistent with this profile.

The consumer will also be affected indirectly through the behaviour of competitors and through the media, politicians and a range of pressure groups. There are therefore many other key targets for any communications. Increasingly, business-to-business communication is becoming more and more important for manufacturers and suppliers. If a company (and particularly a retailer) is developing its social and environmental stance, it is going to be more demanding of the social and environmental practices of its suppliers.

The first consideration concerning communication is often not what to say about the company or product but whether there is anything to say at all. There are two concerns here. Firstly, communicating a less-than-thorough or dubious social or environmental initiative runs the risk of alienating consumers and opinion formers if there are gaps in the message, inaccuracies in the claims or secrets in the organisation. In overstating claims, negative regulatory or pressure groups and media responses could endanger the product, service or corporate integrity. Bad publicity could negate everything the company was trying to achieve and would certainly act against any positive corporate image that the company was trying to foster. Secondly, there is an issue concerning whether a certain message is appropriate to consumers at all. The impact of the message will depend on how aware, committed and educated the consumers of a product are and on the particular market characteristics in which the product is sold. In the first instance a company needs to establish whether social and environmental considerations are or could be significant in their markets, and whether appropriate messages could confer a competitive advantage.

There are a number of communications techniques that can be used to get the message across. However, in order to be effective it is important that, whichever methods are chosen, they are used within an integrated and co-ordinated strategy of moving towards a situation consistent with sustainable development. Even now, consumers are still swamped with the clichéd, generic imagery of greening in environmental messages: rainbows, trees, plants, green fields, dolphins and smiley planets. At the other end of the scale far too many messages have assumed detailed consumer knowledge across a range of other issues. There is a need to explain each issue where appropriate and then stress the reason why the consumer should prefer one particular product to its competitor products. When it comes to profiling the social responsibility of products the problems are even more apparent since social issues are less well defined and may be more difficult to communicate. Nevertheless the creative skills of marketers can produce a difference and are capable of differentiating products based on elements of sustainable development. It requires hard work and some experimentation but is nevertheless vital if businesses are to help to promote the importance of sustainable development.

In terms of communicating effectively, companies should not over-assume people's knowledge or altruism when it comes to any social or environmental issues. Neither should they under-assume how much consumers like their current brands and labels. The majority of consumers will not be impressed with complicated explanations of why one product is more socially responsible or environmentally friendly than another. Those communicating the difference need to find simple and honest messages about why one product should be preferred. Perhaps most importantly, however, the company needs to create a positive profile of itself and all its activities in order to gain the trust of consumers and help to add credibility to any specific product claims made.

Communications through the medium of advertising are likely to form part of any marketing strategy. However, it has already been suggested that clichéd imagery and stereotypical role models are hardly consistent with a move towards strategies consistent with sustainable development. Sexist, racist and homophobic categorisations of people are more likely to cause offence to educated consumers than convince them to buy a particular product or service. Moreover, the tokenism paid to minority groups that is apparent in many commercials is equally offensive and will be interpreted as a cynical attempt to appear ethical.

## Education and campaigning

Perhaps more than any other institution in the world, companies have the ability to educate many people about the important concept of sustainable development. Through education programmes with their workers, suppliers and customers they can have an impact on many more people than traditional educators can reach. Large corporations may well have literally millions of people buying their products every year and that access to people gives business both a significant role and a responsibility to push messages associated with moving down the path of sustainable development.

In the future businesses will also be campaigners (we have seen some evidence of this already). They will realise that there is a very thin dividing line between marketing, education and campaigning. They will see that they and their products become more attractive when they take a particular line on a popular public issue (eg GM food, animal testing, human rights, fair trade, etc). Therefore, business has a huge role that it can productively play in educating its staff and its customers, engaging in debate surrounding development and campaigning on a range of important issues.

## Conclusions

Communications and marketing will be central to any business organisation committed to social and environmental improvement. However, it must be recognised that ethical and sustainable approaches must be central to the communications function. Moreover, communication is more than simply about selling products; it is also about educating the consumer about better use of a product in environmental terms and it is about being part of a wider campaign to move business towards sustainable development. It therefore represents a discrete shift away from the more unethical and spurious green marketing strategies so common to date. Key elements of the marketing strategy include the need to recognise and chart changing consumer trends, to have clear strategies aimed at differentiating the company's marketing mix and to have integrated and effective information systems. It is not enough to promote products alone. Any organisation needs to examine its overall impact on and commitment to the environment. The green company will also be a campaigning company and be committed to spreading an ethical communication message about sustainable development.

Companies that are keen to identify their more environmentally friendly products within their marketing strategy will also be aided by third-party eco-labelling schemes, based on seals of approval, which will be able to confer a recognised accreditation for a particular product. As a minimum the assessment approach should be based on a full life cycle assessment of a product category and suitable minimum criteria laid down for the award of a label. However, the schemes that are in existence will have to take on wider ecological criteria including fundamental human and animal rights if they are to retain their credibility and really act as an effective tool to take us towards sustainable development. Increasingly consumers' attention will be based on corporate performance as well as individual product profiles and therefore any strategy will have to focus on the widest possible aspects of environmental impacts. Companies that take the environment seriously need therefore to adopt a proactive communications strategy that is much more holistic than the narrower marketing so often employed by more traditional firms.

# 6 | What can you do? The route to the ethical shopper

Previous chapters have detailed the problems of globalisation, demands for cheap products in developed countries and the unregulated labour market in developing countries. The consumer should think about ceasing to support shops that actively exploit workers in developing countries. We all need to decide whether we are really happy to eat, wear and use products that have been produced through the often greedy practices of large multinational corporations. Products might make our lives easier, happier or more fashionable but is this justified if it is at the expense of another human being's human rights?

We need to ask ourselves: can the consumer do anything about global problems such as poverty? Can the consumer stop multinational companies exploiting workers in developing countries in order to ever-increase profits? The answer is that we can! As consumers and customers we have enormous power. We can use this power to promote ethical and fair trade. Rather than shopping with just style, price and convenience in mind, another criterion is crucial. We need to be mindful of issues associated with ethical and fair trade. Ask yourself if the shop you are about to enter is using sweatshops and child labour to keep its prices down and make profits.

This chapter will take you through methods for avoiding shops that exploit human rights and for putting pressure on retailers for positive and real change to the way products are produced in developing countries. In summary we must think about the following checklist:

- Be informed:
  - Find information on retailers and product manufacturers.

- Ask questions:
  – Find the right person to ask about a company's ethical trading policy.
- What to ask:
  – Know the crucial questions to ask your retailers about their practices.
- Buying strategies (become an ethical shopper):
  – Develop buying strategies to optimise ethical and fair trade.
- Campaign for a fairer world
  – Pressurise retailers to adopt ethical trade practices and sell other ethical and fair trade products.
  – Join and be active in pressure groups such as Oxfam, Christian Aid, the New Economics Foundation, CAFOD, Traidcraft and the World Development Movement.

## Be informed

Ethical and fair trade are relatively new, fast-moving areas with more and more products being produced under ethical and fair trade conditions. The practical implementation of ethical and fair trade practices is evolving with experience. Consequently the whole concept of ethical and fair trade is still being debated. It is important to keep informed about this debate and to be aware of retailers and brand manufacturers who are addressing ethical and fair trade issues and, more importantly, those who are not!

In essence, the main areas to remain informed about are:

- the issues covered in Chapter 1, ie globalisation, poverty, sweatshops, child labour, bonded labour, working conditions, government action, the World Trade Organisation, the activities of the International Labour Organisation and the United Nations as well as pressure group activities;
- the progress of ethical and fair trade issues through organisations such as the Ethical Trading Initiative (ETI) and the Fairtrade Foundation;
- the progress (or lack of it) of retailers in positively tackling

> the issue of the production of their products as well as the ingredients/materials for those products. The baseline is usually the implementation of a code of conduct for suppliers certified by independent inspectors. Current best practice is exemplified by products certified with the Fairtrade Mark for making real progress in not only working conditions but also trading agreements and community development.

How do we stay informed about ethical and fair trade? There is a wealth of information about the issues surrounding globalisation and working conditions, some information about ethical and fair trade schemes but little information on retailers' and brand manufacturers' activities. The reasons for this are mixed. The big issues such as globalisation and child labour are on the agendas of government and international organisations (such as the UN and WTO) and are easy subjects to discuss at a general level. When it comes actually to implementing policies and actions, it becomes hard, and governments are constrained by political issues at a national scale between countries and by international agreements, for example made through the WTO. In other words, pressure placed on developing countries by the government of a developed country would cause political problems because companies in the developed country want their products made cheaply in developing countries and often exploit the natural resources that are exhausted in their own country, eg wood, oil, metals, food crops, cheap labour and so on.

Then we come to companies' involvement in respect of the use of cheap labour, poor labour standards and discriminatory practices. Most companies are reluctant to disclose information about the working conditions of their suppliers' employees because companies state that the factories producing their products belong to their suppliers. Further, companies' products are made at a fraction of the price in developing countries compared to European and North American countries and companies do not want to impose standards that would change this low-cost advantage.

Ethical and fair trade schemes are still a small part of the market compared with conventional unfairly traded goods. Schemes to promote improved supply conditions and trading practices are often managed by pressure groups and development organisations that are understaffed and working on scarce resources. Compared with the public relations budgets of the big supermarkets, for example, their financial resources are very limited. It is very difficult for them to compete with multinational companies that spend millions of pounds trying to persuade the consumer to buy their products through advertising, image promotion and branding. Companies are not keen to highlight ethical and fair trade because the consumer can then, rightly, ask why the company's other products are not produced under these schemes. A brand such as Gap or Nike can be seriously damaged if bad working practices are exposed.

There are several ways to stay informed about these issues:

- Newspapers. The press covers stories of unfair trading practices, although more often than not newspapers highlight sensationalist stories such as the exploitation of children.
- Television news and documentaries. Recently the BBC and Channel 4 have produced such programmes.
- Specialist magazines such as *Ethical Consumer, Pure, New Consumer* and *New Internationalist.*
- Newsletters and Web sites of ethical and fair trade organisations such as the Ethical Trading Initiative and the Fairtrade Foundation.
- Membership and Web sites of development and pressure organisations such as Oxfam, the World Development Movement, Save the Children, Slavery International, Actionaid, Traidcraft, Amnesty International and others.
- Web sites of national and other government agencies such as the UK Department for International Development (DFID), the United Nations Global Compact, the International Labour Organisation and the European Parliament.
- Companies. Most companies (especially retailers) have Web sites and those that have codes of conduct usually place them on their Web sites. It is useful to keep an eye on companies that do not currently have codes of conduct. In addition, some companies, especially those with high-profile campaigns against them such as Nike and Gap, have extensive information on their activities with regard to ethical trade.
- The Internet. There is increasing information on the Internet from the organisations listed above, companies including

retailers and various other information and campaign Web sites (see Chapter 23 for further information).

## Ask questions

It is evident that most of the organisations actively involved in ethical and fair trade are development organisations and pressure groups. Commonly, companies only start to address issues of working conditions and human rights because of adverse media attention created by these groups. Companies do not want their brands to have the stigma of sweatshops or child labour, which could lead to a drop in sales. They have tended in the main to be reactive – but the important point is that they do react. If enough pressure is put on them, they have a track record of change.

Retailers and brand manufacturers are keen not to lose customers through boycotts such as the long-standing and continuing boycott of Nestlé products. In addition, retailers are keen to develop new product ranges where they perceive a demand (as with organic and non-genetically modified foodstuffs). To put pressure on retailers you should think about the shops you regularly go to and consult the relevant chapter in this handbook to find out if they are addressing ethical and fair trade. Then, when you have the opportunity, ask them what progress they are making generally on ethical trade and in particular in stocking fair trade products such as Fairtrade Mark products. The best way to ask is either through your local retailer (through shop assistants or the shop manager) where you shop or through the company's customer services (if available).

## What to ask

The more people who ask the right questions, the more shops and other companies will respond to a new tide of public pressure. We might ask for example whether clothes we are considering buying were made under decent conditions. The care tag tells you how to treat the garment, but not how the worker who made it was treated. Here are some questions to ask the shop manager:

- Sweatshops thrive when they are hidden. Does your company know where the product was made and how the workers who made it were treated?
- Do you have a list of all the factories around the world that make your products? Does it include the wages and working conditions in each factory? Can I see it?
- Does your company guarantee that the workers who made this garment were paid a living wage, enough to support their families?
- Does your company have a code of conduct that protects human rights and monitors child labour and unsafe conditions in all the factories that make the products you sell? Can I see it? How do you enforce these rules?

## Buying strategies (becoming an ethical shopper)

Staying informed and thinking about what you are buying are the key ways to becoming a more ethical shopper.

The first step is to question your overall buying process:

- What do I buy?
- Why am I buying this product? Do I really need it?
- Where do I buy my products?
- Am I sure that this product has not been produced under oppressive working conditions?
- Do I agree with the practices of the company I am buying from?

The general idea behind questioning your overall buying behaviour is that by doing so your buying philosophy will be easier to implement than by questioning each product every time. In other words, if you decide to change where you buy products, for example to locally produced products from local shops or from fair trade organisations such as Oxfam and Traidcraft, it may be easier than questioning the source of every product you buy from the tens of thousands of products available at your supermarket.

The process of changing from the products you normally buy to ones that are not produced under oppressive regimes can be difficult. Firstly, this area is changing fast and the number of retailers and brand manufacturers addressing working conditions is increasing. On the other hand, some companies that have stated that they are committed to improving working conditions have been exposed as doing just the opposite! Secondly, to move from being a 'mainstream' shopper to an 'ethical' shopper may take time. Finding alternative ethically produced products or deciding that in fact you do not need that shampoo (despite the advert claiming that it will change your life) may be hard. The answer may be to remind yourself that you really do have the power to change the lives of people producing cheap products.

There is also the issue of boycotting specific companies for bad practice. This can be done either in line with boycott calls from pressure groups or your own boycotts. Many pressure groups ask supporters and the public to boycott certain companies because of infringements of human or employee rights or environmental impacts. There are many pressure groups based on a boycott of a specific company. These boycotts aim to put pressure on a company either to change its practices or to close. Own boycotts can involve avoiding a certain product or company or a product group because of ethical issues that you believe in.

## Campaign for a fairer world

A way to move companies towards addressing the conditions under which their employees work is to campaign actively against them. One way to get involved in campaigning is to join a pressure group that has similar views to yours. You can be active in that pressure group's activities such as demonstrations, informing the public and media and organising boycotts.

# 7 | Carpet retailers

## Working conditions in the carpet industry

Concerns in terms of ethical and fair trade in the carpet industry involve mostly knotted wool rugs and carpets, 86 per cent of which are imported from developing countries such as Iran, Pakistan, India and Turkey. It is hard to believe today, but young children with small flexible hands still toil under terrible conditions, making hand-knotted carpets that are sold in the US and Europe for huge prices. Contrary to popular belief, these children are employed illegally and rarely receive adequate wages for their labour. Instead, they are exploited, receiving only a fraction of the money adults would receive for the same work. Carpet manufacturers continue to employ children for this very reason; they are the main source of cheap labour. Children are unable to form unions, they are easily intimidated, often abused and beaten and they cannot demand decent wages.[1]

Demand for child labour in this industry is so high that children are often sold by desperately poor parents to the owners of illegal carpet factories. The children are then forced to work long hours, day and night, unable to attend school, and often suffer from malnourishment. This perpetuates a cycle of poverty since most of these children never get the education and training needed to obtain the skills they would require to get a better-paid job. Throughout their adult lives, they live on a subsistence basis and remain desperate enough to send their own children off to work, repeating the cycle.[2]

Children who have been bought often have to work 12 to 14 hours a day without payment. Mistakes and minor faults are punished severely – a common punishment involves the child being hung upside down. There is rarely medical care to treat the common injuries caused by using sharp knives to turn the carpet knots.

## Initiatives

As outlined in Chapter 2, RUGMARK (see Figure 7.1) is a consumer label that offers the best assurance that illegal child labour has not been used. At the moment in the UK only B&Q, the Co-op and Odegard (a carpet gallery) are committed to only buying carpets that are RUGMARK certified; other companies and independent stores stock some RUGMARK-labelled carpets. RUGMARK does more than just certify products however. It runs rehabilitation centres for children 'rescued' from illegal carpet factories where they can learn reading and writing skills. They also participate in awareness-raising discussions on health, social issues and the law.

Figure 7.1 The RUGMARK

RUGMARK attempts to inspect 10 per cent of carpet factories a month. The system is paid for by exporters who contribute 0.25 per cent of the carpet's export value. Meanwhile importers of RUGMARK carpets agree to contribute 1 per cent of the export value to a development fund. When you purchase a RUGMARK carpet, you can also take pride in knowing that:

- A portion of the price you pay goes to provide schooling and other welfare support to former child workers, their families and communities.
- You are helping to bring attention to the disturbing problem of child labour in the carpet industry.
- You are letting carpet retailers know that you will not purchase carpets made by children.
- The loom on which your carpet was made is registered with RUGMARK.
- RUGMARK inspectors have open access to the factory or loom where your carpet was produced.[3]

To be certified by RUGMARK, carpet manufacturers sign a legally binding contract to:

- produce carpets without illegal child labour;
- register all looms with the RUGMARK Foundation;
- allow access to looms for unannounced inspections.

Inspectors are trained and supervised by RUGMARK. Carpet factories are monitored regularly. Each labelled carpet is individually numbered so that the carpet's origin can be traced back to the loom on which it was produced. This protects against counterfeit labels. Non-profit child welfare organisations, not affiliated with RUGMARK, also have access to RUGMARK-certified factories to ensure that no children are employed.[4]

RUGMARK state that:[5]

- RUGMARK inspectors rescue on average one child carpet weaver per week.
- More than 2 million carpets carrying the RUGMARK label have been sold in Europe and North America since 1995.
- RUGMARK carpets are sold in approximately 300 stores throughout the US.
- Nearly 1 million children are 'employed' in the hand-knotted carpet industry worldwide.
- The US constitutes the largest market for hand-knotted carpets, importing $422,549,000 worth of rugs in 1998.
- 80 per cent of US consumers would avoid businesses identified with unfair labour practices.
- India:
  – Since 1995, 1,334 children have been liberated from carpet looms by RUGMARK India.
  – Four RUGMARK schools currently provide education to 1,172 former child weavers.
  – 230 Indian exporters, representing approximately 15 per cent of all registered carpet looms, are licensed under RUGMARK.
  Pakistan:
  – RUGMARK Pakistan issued its first labels in 1999. Two-thirds of the 20,154 registered looms have already been inspected and approved for certification.

– RUGMARK Pakistan operates three schools and is affiliated with an additional eight, providing education to 744 children from carpet-producing communities.
– Approximately 75 per cent of Pakistan's carpet weavers are female children under the age of 14.
Nepal:
– Since 1996, 407 carpet children have been rescued for RUGMARK rehabilitation.
– 188 children attended RUGMARK schools in 2000.
– Manufacturers representing 65 per cent of Nepal's carpet exports are certified by RUGMARK.
– The estimated number of Nepali child weavers is 1,800.

RUGMARK's rehabilitation and education efforts are integral to its overall efforts to end child labour. Since 1995, RUGMARK schools in India, Nepal and Pakistan have offered educational opportunities to more than 2,000 former child weavers and children from weaving communities. In India and Nepal, roughly one-third of the students are girls and two-thirds are boys. In Pakistan, these proportions are reversed, reflecting the ratio of working girls and boys found by RUGMARK inspectors in each country.

RUGMARK places a priority on encouraging community-based rehabilitation. This means that every effort is made to reunite the children with their families, so that they do not become alienated from their communities, and they are not 'pampered' in RUGMARK programmes. So far, 150 children in Nepal have been reunited with their families and in India, more than 300.

Four levels of support are given to children who return to live with their families, depending upon need:

- support for school fees;
- support for books;
- support for uniforms;
- support for other materials.

Since RUGMARK support is provided until a child reaches the age of 18 or grade 10, whichever comes first, the children are encouraged to attend vocational training by the age of 14. This way they will be able to support themselves when the programme assistance ends. Interest and aptitude of the child, as well as market value of the skill, are considered during enrolment. The educational programmes are designed so that children first go through an intensive non-formal training for literacy and numeracy, preparing them for formal education. From there, the vocational training prepares children for joining the workforce.

In Nepal, the non-formal programmes are designed by the government and are meant to take two years to complete. Many children finish the programme within eight months, showing that when they are not working and are given proper nutrition they are able to excel as students. Formal educational programmes include English language training, Hindi, maths and science. An emphasis is also put on physical fitness and extra-curricular pursuits, such as music. As of February 2000, RUGMARK India has offered adult literacy programmes to carpet weavers and a self-help programme that enables mothers of child weavers to learn to generate income.[6]

RUGMARK Foundation USA provides three examples of children who have been rescued by RUGMARK inspectors:[7]

- Laxmi Shrestha is a 10-year-old RUGMARK student. Rescued from a Nepali carpet factory by RUGMARK inspectors at the age of six, Laxmi lives at a RUGMARK rehabilitation centre and attends fourth grade at a nearby private school. She is one of the most studious and disciplined children in her programme. Laxmi's family of six moved to Kathmandu after a landslide wiped out their property in a nearby village. Her alcoholic father refused to take responsibility for Laxmi, her mother and three sisters, so Laxmi's mother began weaving carpets to support the family. She brought Laxmi and her older sister Mina to the carpet factory, so that they, too, could work. The sisters were found three and a half years ago by RUGMARK inspectors and now attend school with RUGMARK's support. Laxmi plans to continue her studies through high school. RUGMARK pays for her tuition, books, uniforms, food and lodging. While she lives separately from her mother, they see each other regularly. Before, Laxmi had no hope of gaining an education. Now she intends to complete a full course of study and live a better life.
- In 2000, the youngest child ever to be found weaving as a bonded labourer was found by RUGMARK inspectors in India

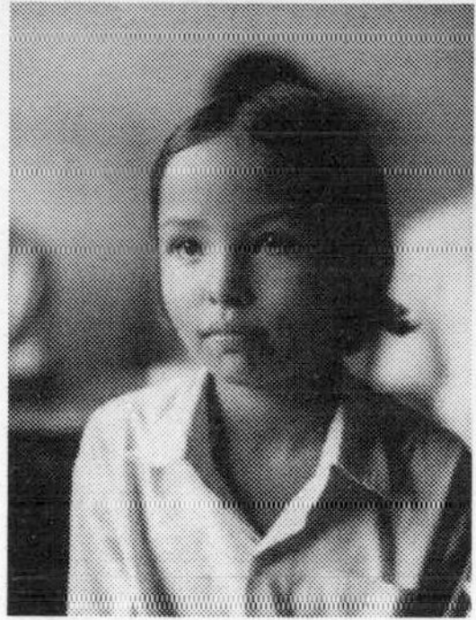

Figure 7.2 Laxmi Shrestha *(Mr Robin Romano, RUGMARK)*

Figure 7.3 Raju *(Mr Robin Romano, RUGMARK)*

Figure 7.4 Razia Sultana *(Mr Robin Romano, RUGMARK)*

and was enrolled in the Balashrya Centre for Bonded Labourers. At the age of seven, Raju was sold into bondage by his parents who were very poor and could not afford to take care of him. The sum his parents received from the loom owner for Raju's ongoing labour was the equivalent of about $50. After weaving carpets day in and day out for the better part of a year, Raju was rescued by RUGMARK inspectors. While signs of malnourishment are still present on Raju's face, his most prominent features are his sparkling smile and eyes. He enjoys learning Hindi, English, maths, music and science at the RUGMARK Balashrya Centre, and stands out among his peers as the most energetic. Before, Raju could not have dreamt of a life outside a carpet loom shed. Now he dreams of a different future: to be a policeman when he grows up, so that he can prevent other loom owners from forcing children to work.

- In the predominately male-dominated, Muslim culture of Pakistan, village girls rarely have the opportunity to gain a proper education. Most girls stay at home, weaving carpets side by side with their mothers. In fact, 75 per cent of carpet weavers in Pakistan are girls. Razia Sultana, a 13-year-old student at RUGMARK Pakistan's new school in Faisalbad, has the chance to live a different life. Razia studies, along with 20 other girls and four boys, because RUGMARK funds their education to keep them off carpet looms. Razia studies Urdu, maths and English. A shy, but intelligent girl, Razia does not know what her future holds. But now she has choices: something she did not have before RUGMARK.

## The British carpet industry

The carpet industry in Britain is large with just over £1.4 billion of sales in 2000 (see Table 7.1).[8] Carpets are subdivided by production process:

- Woven carpets are the traditional means of manufacture. Traditionally made of wool, more recently with artificial fibres, the vast majority use a mix of the two. This represents the quality end of the market. Axminster and Wilton are two well-known types of carpet. The former is more versatile, with the use of any number of colours being possible. Wilton is the top-quality product, though usually limited to a maximum of five colours since all fibres run throughout the carpet, thus providing a thick and luxurious pile.
- Tufted carpets are a relatively modern development – a US invention from the 1940s that gained ground in the UK less than 40 years ago. These carpets are manufactured by punching the fibre into a jute or synthetic backing and keeping it in place by an adhesive. They originally used only nylon, but polypropylene is now the more common fibre. As with woven carpets, a mix of wool and artificial fibres is common.
- Fibre-bonded carpets, including needleloom, are made by meshing together a blend of fibres to form a web, which is treated by heat or resin impregnation.
- Carpet tiles may be fibre-bonded, fusion-bonded or tufted.
- Other carpets include sisal, coir and seagrass.

There are also other types of floor coverings made from a wide variety of synthetic products (particularly vinyl), ceramics, cork, linoleum, stone and wood. Their purpose is to produce a smooth, easy-to-clean and durable floor covering. These are not covered in this book.

Table 7.1 UK retail sales of flooring (2000)

| Type of Carpet | % |
| --- | --- |
| Tufted carpet | 73 |
| Axminster carpet | 4 |
| Wilton carpet | 5 |
| Other carpets | 2 |
| Vinyl flooring | 8 |
| Wood flooring | 1 |
| Laminated flooring | 6 |
| Other smooth flooring | 1 |

The main retailers of carpets in the UK are:

- independent specialists (45 per cent of market);
- carpet specialist chains (30 per cent of market);
- furniture and specialist chains (11 per cent of market);
- department stores (8 per cent of market);
- DIY sheds (2 per cent of market); and
- others including mail order, factory shops and market stalls (4 per cent of market).

## Carpet retailers' rankings

We surveyed the biggest carpet retailers. Only three companies operating through seven branded outlets dominate the carpet retailing industry. It is unclear to what extent the carpets sold through these outlets are manufactured in developing countries because of the lack of information supplied by these retailers.

Table 7.2 Five-star rating system of retailers

| Symbol | Explanation |
| --- | --- |
| 5 stars | 1. Company has a published comprehensive code of conduct.<br>2. Company has independent inspectors of factories for compliance with code of conduct.<br>3. Company has a comprehensive public reporting system detailing |

| | |
|---|---|
| | number of factories/suppliers in developing countries and results of inspections. |
| | 4. Company has own fair trade scheme for all or some products. |
| | 5. Company has demonstrated that it is moving beyond implementing basic human and working rights in factories/suppliers and acting on sustainable development values. |
| 4 stars | 1. Company has a published comprehensive code of conduct. |
| | 2. Company has independent inspectors of factories for compliance with code of conduct. |
| | 3. Company has a comprehensive public reporting system detailing number of factories/suppliers in developing countries and results of inspections. |
| | 4. Company has own fair trade scheme for all or some products. |
| 3 stars | 1. Company has a published comprehensive code of conduct. |
| | 2. Company has independent inspectors of factories for compliance with code of conduct. |
| | 3. Company has a comprehensive public reporting system detailing number of factories/suppliers in developing countries and results of inspections. |
| 2 stars | 1. Company has a published comprehensive code of conduct. |
| | 2. Company has independent inspectors of factories for compliance with code of conduct. |
| 1 star | 1. Company has a published (available to the public via Web site or shops or on products) comprehensive code of conduct. |
| ½ star | Company has a code of conduct or is developing a code of conduct. |
| # | Company without own-brand products. |
| > | Company has no operations in developing countries. |
| X | Company has no code of conduct. |
| Δ | Company wants information to remain confidential. |

Table 7.3 Five-star ratings for carpet retailers

| Symbol | Carpet Retailers |
|---|---|
| 5 stars | None |
| 4 stars | None |
| 3 stars | None |

| | |
|---|---|
| 2 stars | None |
| 1 star | None |
| ½ star | None |
| # | None |
| > | None |
| X | Allied Carpets |
| | Carpetland |
| | Carpetworld |
| | General George |
| Δ | Carpet Depot |
| | Carpetright |
| | Harris Carpets |

## Detailed survey results

The survey results are presented in the tables below:

- Retailers that wanted their information to be confidential (Table 7.4).
- Retailers that have no code of conduct (Table 7.5).

Table 7.4 Carpet retailers that wanted their information to be confidential

| Carpet Retailers | Parent Company |
|---|---|
| Carpet Depot | Carpetright Plc |
| Carpetright | Carpetright Plc |
| Harris Carpets | Carpetright Plc |

Table 7.5 Carpet retailers with no code of conduct

| Carpet Retailers | Parent Company |
|---|---|
| Allied Carpets | Allied Carpets Group Plc |
| Carpetland | Allied Carpets Group Plc |
| Carpetworld | Carpetworld Ltd |
| General George | Allied Carpets Group Plc |

# 8 | Clothes retailers

## Introduction

More than half of the £25 billion[1] worth of clothes sold in Britain every year is imported. With about 40 large retail chains, 150 medium-sized retail chains and 30,000 independent clothes stores, the clothes retailer is the dominant high street feature. Marks & Spencer, Arcadia Group, Next, Littlewoods, Bhs and Mothercare have the biggest retail sales in the UK with about 45 per cent of the total market between them.[2]

## Working conditions

The clothes market was one of the first to utilise low-cost production facilities available in developing countries, exploiting poor working conditions and minimal employee wages. 'Sweatshops' is the common term used by campaigners to explain the conditions commonly found in clothes manufacturers in developing countries. Some famous brand names have been 'exposed' as having clothes produced under poor working conditions or exploiting child labour.

The rag trade is an industry on the move. Traditional manufacturing facilities in Europe have often closed down because of the fierce cost competition in Asia. However, in Asian countries where wages have been rising, manufacturing has shifted again to even lower wage economies, for example in Central America. Here, women commonly make less than £2 a day working in excess of 10 hours. Seated at rows of sewing machines, each woman stitches the same part of a piece of clothing over and over again. She then passes the garment to her neighbour to sew another part and it is passed along the assembly line. Employees are not permitted to talk to one another and there is little ventilation for the factory, which is made hotter by steaming industrial irons used to press clothing. Overtime is common at no extra pay. Visiting such factories, one can see products bearing the common high street brands.

## Initiatives

The clothes sector has seen the greatest development of codes of conduct and organisations pressurising companies to implement them, especially in the United States. Some of the major initiatives for the clothes sector are mentioned here.

For 30 years the Interfaith Centre on Corporate Responsibility (ICCR) in the USA has been a leader of the corporate social responsibility movement. ICCR's membership is an association of 275 Protestant, Roman Catholic and Jewish institutional investors, including national denominations, religious communities, pension funds, endowments, hospital corporations, economic development funds and publishing companies. ICCR and its members press companies to be socially and environmentally responsible. Each year ICCR-member religious institutional investors sponsor over 100 shareholder resolutions on major social and environmental issues. The combined portfolio value of ICCR's member organisations is estimated to be $110 billion.[3]

ICCR 'affirms a global approach to corporate responsibility. ICCR encourages and challenges corporations to use their resources positively to develop communities, to respect worker rights and to enhance the human rights of people. As the globalisation of the economy develops rapidly, so have the problems of people, particularly women and children, who labour in sweatshops for low wages producing products for the global market-place. All people everywhere have a basic human right to a sustainable living wage and equal employment opportunity. All communities everywhere have a basic right to expect corporations to contribute to the sustainable economic development of their society.[4]

'ICCR members file resolutions and participate in dialogues with US companies, particularly in the apparel, footwear and automotive industries. The agenda is to hold companies accountable for the labour practices of their vendors and suppliers in order to:

- enforce high labour, human rights and environmental standards for their suppliers;
- affirm the right of workers to organise and bargain collectively;
- pay a sustainable living wage for a regular work-week;
- be publicly transparent; and
- participate in independent monitoring programmes with local religious, human rights and other non-governmental organisations.

ICCR is focusing its efforts on a number of major companies including Alcoa, Delphi, Disney, Gap, Hasbro, Kohl's, Nike, Sara Lee, Sears, Wal-Mart and Warnaco.'[5]

The European Clean Clothes Campaign (or the 'CCC' as it is popularly called) aims to improve working conditions in the garment and sportswear industry. The CCC started in the Netherlands in 1990. At that time, shops in the Netherlands were not taking any responsibility for the working conditions under which the clothes they sold were made. Now there are Clean Clothes Campaigns in 10 Western European countries and it is more difficult to find retailers in these countries who deny this responsibility. Campaigners are regularly in touch with organisations in a variety of countries, including those where garments are produced, and in this way work together as a network to draw attention to labour rights issues in the garment industry.

Since the main demand of the Clean Clothes Campaign is that retailers live up to their responsibility to ensure that garments are produced in decent conditions, it is important to be clear about how we define good working conditions. Guiding principles for the improvement of working conditions can be found in the basic conventions issued by the International Labour Organisation (ILO), a United Nations body, plus the international principles regarding fundamental rights in the workplace. These principles are: freedom of association, the right to collective bargaining, no discrimination of any kind, no forced or slave labour, a minimum employment age of 15, safety and health measures, a working week of 48 hours maximum and voluntary overtime of 12 hours maximum, a right to a living wage and establishment of the employment relationship (a contract). Early on, the need for a common code to campaign around was raised. As a result, at the European level the CCC developed a code, called the 'Code of Labour Practices for the Apparel Industry Including Sportswear', in which the principles listed above are elaborately described.

In their campaigning, the CCC demands that retailers adopt the standards outlined in the Code of Labour Practices, implement those standards and create a system to continuously monitor that those standards are being upheld. They also ask that companies agree to a system of independent verification. The CCC believes that retailers should ensure that the clothes they sell are made under good labour conditions. Retailers and the major garment companies do more than just sell clothes to consumers – they are also the buyers of these clothes in Asia or Eastern Europe, and therefore they can and should use their power to improve labour conditions.[8]

The Fair Labour Association (FLA) in the USA is a non-profit organisation established to protect the rights of workers in the United States and around the world. The FLA Charter Agreement created a first of a kind industry wide code of conduct and monitoring system. The agreement lays the foundation for the creation of an independent monitoring system that holds companies publicly accountable for their labour practices, as well as those of their principal contractors and suppliers around the world. The FLA accredits the independent monitors, certifies that companies are in compliance with the code of conduct, and serves as a source of information for the public. The companies participating in the FLA are Adidas-Salomon, GEAR For Sports, Levi Strauss & Co, Liz Claiborne, Nike, Patagonia, Reebok, Eddie Bauer, Phillips-Van Heusen and Polo Ralph Lauren. They have agreed to open up their factories to inspections by independent external monitors. The founding non-government organisation members of the FLA include the International Labour Rights Fund, the Lawyers Committee for Human Rights, the National Consumers League, the National Council of Churches and the Robert F. Kennedy Memorial Centre for Human Rights. To date, 159 colleges and universities have affiliated with the FLA to ensure that companies producing goods under their licences are operating in accordance with the principles espoused by the FLA.[7]

USAS (United Students Against Sweatshops) in the USA is an international student movement of campuses and individual students fighting for sweatshop-free labour conditions and workers' rights. USAS believes that university standards should be brought in line with those of its students, who demand that their school's logo is emblazoned on clothing made in decent working conditions. They have fought for these beliefs by demanding that universities adopt ethically and legally strong codes of conduct, full public disclosure of company information and truly independent verification systems to prevent sweatshop conditions. Ultimately, USAS is using the power of student numbers to affect the larger industry that thrives on sweatshops.[8] There has been little activity in UK universities, mainly because clothes with university logos are not linked to branded clothes companies such as Nike as is the case in the USA. It is however disappointing that student unions in the UK are not putting their campaigns against the ill effects of globalisation into action by checking the suppliers of the products they sell such as clothing items with university logos.

Labour Behind the Label (LBL) is a UK network of organisations supporting garment workers' efforts to defend their rights and improve their wages and conditions. Activities include awareness raising, campaigns and solidarity actions. LBL includes overseas aid organisations, eg Oxfam and CAFOD, as well as all major UK textile unions and homeworking organisations. Also included are alternative trading organisations like Traidcraft and small solidarity groups such as Central America Women's Network and Women Working Worldwide. LBL works to draw attention to the plight of workers both in the UK and around the world. It works to facilitate international solidarity between workers and the exchange of information, and calls on companies to:

- abide by the internationally agreed core conventions of the UN's International Labour Organisation;
- commit themselves to a living wage and to the independent verification of labour standards;
- take responsibility for improving working conditions globally.[9]

## Clothes retailers' rankings

The tables below show the results of a survey of the 66 largest clothes retailers in the UK in relation to ethical trade and sound sourcing policies (commonly called 'codes of conduct'). None of these retailers are involved in fair trade products but some organisations, such as Traidcraft, sell fair trade products in a few product lines (see Chapter 17). Many clothes retailers either sell their own branded products, such as Marks & Spencer, or sell individually branded clothes, or a mixture of both, such as Moss Bros. The survey only covers retailers' own branded products. The retailers were contacted though their customer service centres and asked if their products were produced in developing countries and if these operations are covered by codes of conduct.

Table 8.1 Five-star rating system of retailers

| Symbol | Explanation |
|---|---|
| 5 stars | 1. Company has a published comprehensive code of conduct.<br>2. Company has independent inspectors of factories for compliance with code of conduct.<br>3. Company has a comprehensive public reporting system detailing number of factories/suppliers in developing countries and results of inspections.<br>4. Company has own fair trade scheme for all or some products.<br>5. Company has demonstrated that it is moving beyond implementing basic human and working rights in factories/suppliers and acting on sustainable development values. |
| 4 stars | 1. Company has a published comprehensive code of conduct.<br>2. Company has independent inspectors of factories for compliance with code of conduct.<br>3. Company has a comprehensive public reporting system detailing number of factories/suppliers in developing countries and results of inspections.<br>4. Company has own fair trade scheme for all or some products. |
| 3 stars | 1. Company has a published comprehensive code of conduct.<br>2. Company has independent inspectors of factories for compliance with code of conduct. |

| | |
|---|---|
| | 3. Company has a comprehensive public reporting system detailing number of factories/suppliers in developing countries and results of inspections. |
| 2 stars | 1. Company has a published comprehensive code of conduct.<br>2. Company has independent inspectors of factories for compliance with code of conduct. |
| 1 star | 1. Company has a published (available to the public via Web site or shops or on products) comprehensive code of conduct. |
| ½ star | Company has a code of conduct or is developing a code of conduct. |
| # | Company without own-brand products. |
| > | Company has no operations in developing countries. |
| X | Company has no code of conduct. |

**Table 8.2 Five-star ratings for clothes retailers**

| Symbol | Clothes Retailers |
|---|---|
| 5 stars | None |
| 4 stars | None |
| 3 stars | C&A |
| 2 stars | Burton |
| | Dorothy Perkins |
| | Evans |
| | Hawkshead |
| | Littlewoods |
| | Miss Selfridge |
| | Primark |
| | Principles |
| | Principles Menswear |
| | Racing Green |
| | Timberland |
| | Top Man |
| | Top Shop |
| | Wade Smith |
| | Wallis |
| | Warehouse |
| 1 star | Gap |

| | |
|---|---|
| | Marks & Spencer |
| | Monsoon |
| | New Look |
| | Original Levi Stores |
| | Outfit |
| ½ star | Adams |
| | Benetton |
| | Blazer |
| | Diesel |
| | Edinburgh Woollen Mill |
| | Etam |
| | French Connection |
| | Hugo Boss |
| | Jaeger |
| | Laura Ashley |
| | Mackays |
| | Matalan |
| | Moss Bros |
| | Mothercare |
| | Next |
| | Oasis |
| | Peacock's |
| | River Island |
| | Ted Baker |
| | The Suit Company |
| | Thrifty |
| | Viyella |
| # | None |
| > | Giorgio Armani |
| | Thomas Pink |
| X | Alexon |
| | Austin Reed |
| | Bay Trading |
| | Bhs |
| | Bon Marché |
| | Dash |
| | DKNY |
| | Eastex |

Emporio Armani
Esprit
Freemans
Gucci
Hobbs
Jigsaw
Mark One
Polo Ralph Lauren
Tie Rack
Yves Saint Laurent

---

Example codes of conduct from clothes retailers are set out in the Appendix.

## Detailed survey results

The survey results are presented in the tables below:

- Retailers that do not have suppliers in developing countries (Table 8.3).
- Those retailers that do have suppliers in developing countries and have a code of conduct (Table 8.4). This table summarises the content of their codes of conduct, including policies in relation to freedom to join employee associations, child labour, forced labour and violence against employees. In addition, the table covers whether or not the code of conduct is mandatory for all the retailer's suppliers, if compliance by suppliers to the code of conduct is checked by independent (to the retailer and the suppliers) inspectors and finally whether the retailer is a member of the Ethical Trading Initiative (see Chapter 2).
- Retailers that are developing a code of conduct (Table 8.5).
- Retailers with no code of conduct (Table 8.6).

Table 8.3 Clothes retailers with no operations in developing countries

| Clothes Retailers | Parent Company |
|---|---|
| Giorgio Armani | Armani Group |
| Thomas Pink | Thomas Pink Ltd |

Table 8.4 Clothes retailers with a code of conduct

| Clothes Retailers | Parent Company | Forced labour | Collective bargaining | Freedom of association | Health and safety | Child labour | Wages | Working hours | Equality | Job security | Harsh/inhumane treatment | Mandatory? | Independently inspected? | Member of ETI? |
|---|---|---|---|---|---|---|---|---|---|---|---|---|---|---|
| | | Contents of Code of Conduct | | | | | | | | | | | | |
| Benetton | Benetton (UK) Ltd | * | | | | | | | | | | | | |
| Burton | Arcadia Group Plc | X | | X | X | X | X | X | X | | X | X | X | |
| C&A | C & A/Brenninkmeyer | X | | X | X | X | X | | X | | X | X | X | X |
| Diesel | Diesel Group UK | | | X | | X | X | X | X | | | X | | |
| Dorothy Perkins | Arcadia Group Plc | X | | X | X | X | X | X | X | | X | X | X | |
| Edinburgh Woollen Mill | Grampian Holdings Plc | + | | | | | | | | | | X | | |
| Etam | Etam Plc | X | | | X | X | X | X | X | | X | | | |
| Evans | Arcadia Group Plc | X | | X | X | X | X | X | X | | X | X | X | |
| French Connection | French Connection Group Plc | * | | | | | | | | | | | | |
| Gap | Gap Inc | X | X | X | X | X | X | X | X | | X | X | | |
| Hawkshead | Arcadia Group Plc | X | | X | X | X | X | X | X | | X | X | X | |
| Jaeger | Coats Viyella Plc | X | | X | | X | | | X | | | X | | |
| Laura Ashley | Laura Ashley Holdings Plc | * | | | | | | | | | | | | |
| Littlewoods | The Littlewoods Organisation Plc | X | X | X | X | X | X | X | X | X | X | X | | X |
| Mackays | Mackays Stores (Holdings) Plc | X | | X | X | X | X | X | X | | X | X | | |

| | | | | | | | | | | | | | | |
|---|---|---|---|---|---|---|---|---|---|---|---|---|---|---|
| Marks & Spencer | Marks & Spencer Plc | | X | X | X | X | X | X | | | | X | | X |
| Matalan | Matalan Plc | X | | | X | X | X | X | X | X | X | X | | |
| Miss Selfridge | Arcadia Group Plc | X | | X | X | X | X | X | X | | X | X | X | |
| Monsoon | Monsoon Plc | X | X | X | X | X | X | X | X | X | X | | | X |
| Mothercare | Mothercare Plc | X | X | X | X | X | X | X | X | X | X | | | X |
| New Look | New Look Group Ltd | X | X | X | X | X | X | X | X | | X | X | | |
| Next | Next Plc | X | X | X | X | X | X | X | X | X | X | | | |
| Oasis | Oasis Stores Ltd | X | X | X | X | X | X | X | X | | X | X | | |
| Original Levi Stores | Clanstock Ltd | X | | X | X | X | X | X | X | | X | X | pilot | X |
| Outfit | Arcadia Group Plc | X | | X | X | X | X | X | X | | X | X | X | |
| Peacock's | Peacock's Stores Ltd | X | | X | X | X | X | X | X | | X | X | | |
| Primark | Associated British Foods Plc | X | X | X | X | | X | | X | | X | X | X | |
| Principles | Arcadia Group Plc | X | | X | X | X | X | X | X | | X | X | X | |
| Principles Menswear | Arcadia Group Plc | X | | X | X | X | X | X | X | | X | X | X | |
| Racing Green | Arcadia Group Plc | X | | X | X | X | X | X | X | | X | X | X | |
| River Island | Lewis Trust Group Ltd | | | | X | X | X | X | X | | | X | | |
| Ted Baker | Ted Baker Plc | X | | | X | X | X | X | X | X | X | X | | |
| Thrifty | Coats Viyella Plc | X | | X | | X | | | X | | | X | | |
| Timberland | Timberland (UK) Ltd | X | X | X | X | X | X | X | X | | X | X | X | |
| Top Man | Arcadia Group Plc | X | | X | X | X | X | X | X | | X | X | X | |
| Top Shop | Arcadia Group Plc | X | | X | X | X | X | X | X | | X | X | X | |
| Viyella | Coats Viyella Plc | X | | X | | X | | | X | | | X | | |
| Wade Smith | Arcadia Group Plc | X | | X | X | X | X | X | X | | X | X | X | |
| Wallis | Arcadia Group Plc | X | | X | X | X | X | X | X | | X | X | X | |
| Warehouse | Arcadia Group Plc | X | | X | X | X | X | X | X | | X | X | X | |

+ Information confidential at request of retailer

* Code of conduct unavailable

**Table 8.5 Clothes retailers developing a code of conduct**

| Clothes Retailers | Parent Company |
|---|---|
| Adams | Adams Childrenswear Ltd |
| Blazer | Moss Bros Group Plc |
| Hugo Boss | Moss Bros Group Plc |
| Moss Bros | Moss Bros Group Plc |
| The Suit Company | Moss Bros Group Plc |

**Table 8.6 Clothes retailers with no code of conduct**

| Clothing Retailers | Parent Company |
|---|---|
| Alexon | Alexon Group Plc |
| Austin Reed | Austin Reed Group Plc |
| Bay Trading | Alexon Group Plc |
| Bhs | Measuremarket |
| Bon Marché | Bon Marché Holdings Ltd |
| Dash | Alexon Group Plc |
| DKNY | Donna Karan International Inc |
| Eastex | Alexon Group Plc |
| Emporio Armani | Armani Group |
| Esprit | Esprit (UK) Ltd |
| Freemans | Freemans Plc |
| Gucci | Gucci Group NV |
| Hobbs# | Peace & Quiet Ltd |
| Jigsaw | Jigsaw |
| Mark One | Northworld Ltd |
| Polo Ralph Lauren | Ralph Lauren Ltd |
| Tie Rack | Tie Rack Plc |
| Yves Saint Laurent | Gucci Group NV |

# try to be socially responsible but too small to have independent inspectors

# 9 | Department stores

## Introduction

Department stores vary greatly and sell a range of products covered in other chapters such as clothes, household goods and footwear. The issues surrounding these products are detailed in the relevant chapter. Traditionally department stores have not sold their own branded products but this is now changing along with the increasing number of branded franchises in department stores. These franchises are often individual fashion labels selling their products, usually clothes, direct to the consumer. This chapter only surveys department stores producing own-brand products. If department stores do not sell own-brand products, then their franchises are ignored. Department stores should however engage in pushing ethical trade principles up the supply chain by requiring franchises trading in their stores to implement ethical trade principles into the production of their products.

Table 9.1 illustrates that the only department store that has a code of conduct – Debenhams – is one of the largest, with 22 per cent of the market.[1] It is surprising that only one has a code of conduct, especially in view of the size of department stores such as John Lewis and House of Fraser.

Table 9.1 Major department stores' share of market by sales performance in 2000

| Department Store | % of Market |
|---|---|
| John Lewis | 30.0 |
| Debenhams | 22.1 |
| House of Fraser | 12.9 |
| Allders | 8.1 |
| Harrods | 6.8 |
| Selfridges | 5.7 |

| | |
|---|---|
| Fenwick | 4.0 |
| Harvey Nichols | 2.1 |
| T J Hughes | 2.0 |
| Bentalls | 1.9 |
| Beatties | 1.7 |
| Beales | 1.1 |
| Liberty | 0.9 |
| Jenners | 0.7 |

## Department stores' rankings

Table 9.2 Five-star rating system of retailers

| Symbol | Explanation |
|---|---|
| 5 stars | 1. Company has a published comprehensive code of conduct.<br>2. Company has independent inspectors of factories for compliance with code of conduct.<br>3. Company has a comprehensive public reporting system detailing number of factories/suppliers in developing countries and results of inspections.<br>4. Company has own fair trade scheme for all or some products.<br>5. Company has demonstrated that it is moving beyond implementing basic human and working rights in factories/suppliers and acting on sustainable development values. |
| 4 stars | 1. Company has a published comprehensive code of conduct.<br>2. Company has independent inspectors of factories for compliance with code of conduct.<br>3. Company has a comprehensive public reporting system detailing number of factories/suppliers in developing countries and results of inspections.<br>4. Company has own fair trade scheme for all or some products. |
| 3 stars | 1. Company has a published comprehensive code of conduct.<br>2. Company has independent inspectors of factories for compliance with code of conduct.<br>3. Company has a comprehensive public reporting system detailing number of factories/suppliers in developing countries and results of inspections. |

| | |
|---|---|
| 2 stars | 1. Company has a published comprehensive code of conduct.<br>2. Company has independent inspectors of factories for compliance with code of conduct. |
| 1 star | 1. Company has a published (available to the public via Web site or shops or on products) comprehensive code of conduct. |
| ½ star | Company has a code of conduct or is developing a code of conduct. |
| # | Company without own-brand products. |
| > | Company has no operations in developing countries. |
| X | Company has no code of conduct. |

Table 9.3 Five-star ratings for department stores

| Symbol | Department Stores |
|---|---|
| 5 stars | None |
| 4 stars | None |
| 3 stars | None |
| 2 stars | None |
| 1 star | Debenhams |
| ½ star | None |
| # | Beatties |
| | Harvey Nichols |
| | Selfridges |
| > | Harrods |
| X | Allders |
| | Allders at Home |
| | Arding & Hobbs |
| | Army & Navy |
| | Arnotts |
| | Barkers |
| | Beales |
| | Bentalls |
| | Binns |
| | Bodgers |
| | Boyes Stores |
| | Broadbents & Boothroyds |
| | Denners |

D H Evans
Dickens & Jones
Dingles
Elys
Fenwick
House of Fraser
James Selby
Jenners
John Lewis
Kendals
Lewis
Liberty
Morley's
Owen Owen
Peter Jones
Rackhams
Riceman
Smith Bros
T J Hughes
Whitakers

---

Example codes of conduct from department stores are set out in the Appendix.

## Detailed survey results

The survey results are presented in the tables below:

- Retailers without own-brand products (Table 9.4).
- Retailers with no operations in developing countries (Table 9.5).
- Those retailers that have suppliers in developing countries and have a code of conduct (Table 9.6). This table summarises the contents of their codes of conduct, covering issues such as freedom to join employee associations, child labour, forced labour and violence against employees. In addition, it covers

whether the code of conduct is mandatory for all the retailer's suppliers, if compliance by suppliers to the code of conduct is checked by independent (to the retailer and the suppliers) inspectors and finally if the retailer is a member of the Ethical Trading Initiative (see Chapter 2).

- Retailers that do not have a code of conduct (Table 9.7).

**Table 9.4 Department stores without own-brand products**

| Department Stores | Parent Company |
|---|---|
| Beatties | James Beattie Plc |
| Harvey Nichols | Harvey Nichols Plc |
| Selfridges | Selfridges Plc |

**Table 9.5 Department stores with no operations in developing countries**

| Department Store | Parent Company |
|---|---|
| Harrods* | Harrods Holdings Plc |

* also developing a code of conduct

**Table 9.6 Department stores with a code of conduct**

| Department Store | Parent Company | Contents of Code of Conduct: Forced labour | Collective bargaining | Freedom of association | Health and safety | Child labour | Wages | Working hours | Equality | Job security | Harsh/inhumane treatment | Mandatory? | Independently inspected? | Member of ETI? |
|---|---|---|---|---|---|---|---|---|---|---|---|---|---|---|
| Debenhams | Debenhams Plc | X | | | X | X | X | X | X | | | X | X | |

Table 9.7 Department stores without a code of conduct

| Department Stores | Parent Company |
|---|---|
| Allders | Allders Plc |
| Allders at Home | Allders Plc |
| Arding & Hobbs | Allders Plc |
| Army & Navy | House of Fraser Plc |
| Arnotts | House of Fraser Plc |
| Barkers | House of Fraser Plc |
| Beales | Beale Plc |
| Bentalls | Bentalls Plc |
| Binns | House of Fraser Plc |
| Bodgers | Morley's Stores Ltd |
| Boyes Stores | W Boyes & Co Ltd |
| Broadbents & Boothroyds | Beale Plc |
| Denners | Beale Plc |
| D H Evans | House of Fraser Plc |
| Dickens & Jones | House of Fraser Plc |
| Dingles | House of Fraser Plc |
| Elys | Morley's Stores Ltd |
| Fenwick | Fenwick Ltd |
| House of Fraser | House of Fraser Plc |
| James Selby | Morley's Stores Ltd |
| Jenners | Jenners Princes Street Edinburgh Ltd |
| John Lewis | John Lewis Partnership Plc |
| Kendals | House of Fraser Plc |
| Lewis | Owen Owen Ltd |
| Liberty | Liberty Plc |
| Morley's | Morley's Stores Ltd |
| Owen Owen | Owen Owen Ltd |
| Peter Jones | John Lewis Partnership Plc |
| Rackhams | House of Fraser Plc |
| Riceman | Fenwick Ltd |
| Smith Bros | Morley's Stores Ltd |
| T J Hughes | T J Hughes Plc |
| Whitakers | Beale Plc |

# 10 | DIY retailers

## Introduction

Do-it-yourself (DIY) retailers range from builders' yards servicing the building trade to a cross between garden centres and home furnishing stores. The range and complexity of the products DIY retailers offer vary, with a large proportion being own-brand products and materials. The products range from paints and chemicals to wood and metal, some of which are produced in developing countries.

## Working conditions

The types of issues that arise in addition to poor wages and child labour are extremely hazardous working conditions and the dumping of hazardous waste into rivers and housing areas. Usually employees work with molten metals, high levels of dust or fumes or hazardous chemicals without any protective or venting equipment. This is exacerbated by most of the work being done in people's homes – the so-called cottage industry.

## Initiatives

B&Q has done much in this area and in its 1998 report How Green Is My Patio? and 1999 report Being a Better Trading Neighbour presents the problems of working conditions in its supplier factories. It places some targets and activities to tackle these issues in these public reports. It is commendable that B&Q has reported in this way but even by its own admission there is much to do to improve the working conditions of its suppliers. It is also a shame that few of the other retailers report such issues, with targets and activities to improve conditions. Most retailers seem not to be bothered about such issues as long as products are made at the cheapest possible price.

One of the product ranges where there has been a great deal of success is timber and wood-based products. The Forest Stewardship Council (FSC), which is made up of representatives of environmental groups, community forestry projects, indigenous organisations and local government, has established a set of 'principles and criteria' to help make sustainable forestry a reality. To date over a thousand firms have received FSC approval and there are something like 20,000 products available with FSC certification.

### *Extract from B&Q's How Can We Be Better Neighbours?*[1]

**Our trading neighbourhood**

We buy products from over 40 countries around the world. Our approach to addressing social and environmental improvements within the supply chain has been to tackle issues country by country.

*Project India*

- Hand-knotted rugs – B&Q was the first UK retailer to stock rugs that the Rugmark scheme guaranteed weren't made using exploited or illegal child labour.
- Brassware – In 1993 we started working with our suppliers of brass door furniture to improve health and safety within factory and sub-contracting casting units. This programme was extended to all Indian brassware suppliers during 1999.
- Coir doormats – An environmental and social review of entire production from coconut plantation to finishing plant identified key areas for improvement. Cleaner man-made tanks will be trialed to reduce pollution from the lagoons where the coconuts are soaked. A savings and credit scheme has been set up to improve the economic status of women beaters and spinners. During 1999, we extended Project India to include every factory we use in India. This has involved 13 suppliers and 15 factories.

*Project China*
We've started working in China applying the lessons learned in India and the Philippines. Health and safety audits of several factories have been completed including our toilet seat factory and cast iron bench factory. This year, we will be working with suppliers and factory managers to find a best practice for motivating improvements in other factories in China.

*South Africa*
At the end of 1999, we conducted a tour of factories in South Africa to help us understand environmental and social issues in our South African supply chains. We are currently working with suppliers to produce action plans for improvement where required.

**What about developed countries?**
Social problems are, of course, not just confined to developing countries. For example, homeworkers are commonly used in the UK. Homeworking caters for a need since most homeworkers prefer to work at home but we must avoid exploitation. In 1998 we introduced a Code of Practice for our suppliers using homeworkers and we are currently re-assessing its content and effectiveness through consultation with our suppliers and homeworkers.

## British DIY retailing industry

Table 10.1 highlights that the two most popular DIY retailers in the UK, ie B&Q and Homebase, have codes of conduct.[2] Homebase used to be part of the J Sainsbury Plc group, which, as seen in Chapter 13, is implementing a code of conduct into its supply chain. However, it is disappointing that with such a small number of DIY retailers only two are attempting to improve the working conditions of workers in developing countries.

Table 10.1 Most popular DIY retailer to shop at in 2000

| DIY Retailer | % of People Who Shop at Them |
|---|---|
| B&Q | 61 |
| Homebase | 33 |
| Focus Do It All | 28 |
| Wickes | 21 |
| Builders' merchants | 20 |

## DIY retailers' rankings

Table 10.2 Five-star rating system of retailers

| Symbol | Explanation |
|---|---|
| 5 stars | 1. Company has a published comprehensive code of conduct.<br>2. Company has independent inspectors of factories for compliance with code of conduct.<br>3. Company has a comprehensive public reporting system detailing number of factories/suppliers in developing countries and results of inspections.<br>4. Company has own fair trade scheme for all or some products.<br>5. Company has demonstrated that it is moving beyond implementing basic human and working rights in factories/suppliers and acting on sustainable development values. |
| 4 stars | 1. Company has a published comprehensive code of conduct.<br>2. Company has independent inspectors of factories for compliance with code of conduct.<br>3. Company has a comprehensive public reporting system detailing number of factories/suppliers in developing countries and results of inspections.<br>4. Company has own fair trade scheme for all or some products. |
| 3 stars | 1. Company has a published comprehensive code of conduct.<br>2. Company has independent inspectors of factories for compliance with code of conduct.<br>3. Company has a comprehensive public reporting system detailing number of factories/suppliers in developing countries and results of inspections. |

| | |
|---|---|
| 2 stars | 1. Company has a published comprehensive code of conduct.<br>2. Company has independent inspectors of factories for compliance with code of conduct. |
| 1 star | 1. Company has a published (available to the public via Web site or shops or on products) comprehensive code of conduct. |
| ½ star | Company has a code of conduct or is developing a code of conduct. |
| # | Company without own-brand products. |
| > | Company has no operations in developing countries. |
| X | Company has no code of conduct. |

**Table 10.3 Five-star ratings for DIY retailers**

| Symbol | DIY Retailers |
|---|---|
| 5 stars | None |
| 4 stars | None |
| 3 stars | B&Q (no independent inspections but comprehensive reporting) |
| 2 stars | None |
| 1 star | Homebase |
| ½ star | None |
| # | None |
| > | Topps Tiles |
| X | Brewer<br>Focus Do It All<br>Glyn Webb<br>Great Mills<br>J H Leekes & Sons<br>Wickes |

Example codes of conduct from DIY retailers are set out in the Appendix.

## Detailed survey results

The survey results are presented in the tables below:

- Those retailers that have suppliers in developing countries and have a code of conduct (Table 10.4). This table summarises the contents of their codes of conduct, and covers issues such as freedom to join employee associations, child labour, forced labour and violence against employees. In addition, it covers whether the code of conduct is mandatory for all the retailer's suppliers, if compliance by suppliers to the code of conduct is checked by independent (to the retailer and the suppliers) inspectors and finally if the retailer is a member of the Ethical Trading Initiative (see Chapter 2).
- Retailers without operations in developing countries (Table 10.5).
- Retailers that do not have a code of conduct (Table 10.6).

**Table 10.4 DIY retailers with a code of conduct**

| DIY Retailers | Parent Company | Contents of Code of Conduct | | | | | | | | | | | | |
|---|---|---|---|---|---|---|---|---|---|---|---|---|---|---|
| | | Forced labour | Collective bargaining | Freedom of association | Health and safety | Child labour | Wages | Working hours | Equality | Job security | Harsh/inhumane treatment | Mandatory? | Independently inspected? | Member of ETI? |
| B&Q Plc | Kingfisher Plc | X | X | X | X | X | X | X | X | | X | X | | |
| Homebase | Schroder Ventures | X | X | X | X | X | X | X | X | X | X | | | |

**Table 10.5 DIY retailers without operations in developing countries**

| DIY Retailer | Parent Company |
|---|---|
| Topps Tiles | Topps Tiles Plc |

Table 10.6 DIY retailers without a code of conduct

| DIY Retailers | Parent Company |
| --- | --- |
| Brewer | C Brewer & Sons Ltd |
| Focus Do It All | Focus Do It All Ltd |
| Glyn Webb | Glyn Webb Wallpaper Ltd |
| Great Mills | Great Mills Retail Ltd |
| J H Leekes & Sons | J H Leekes & Sons |
| Wickes | Wickes Plc |

# 11 | Electronics retailers

## Introduction

The electronics industry is still growing fast with many new products such as WAP mobile phones, digital cameras and portable computers being brought on to the market. Many of these products are produced in developing countries such as Thailand, Brazil, Malaysia and China. Of the main retailers selling electronics in the UK, Dixons has a code of conduct and Time Computers claims not to have products produced in developing countries. Comet, PC World and Tiny Computers do not have a code of conduct. This means that when you buy electronic products you need to consult the manufacturers (who often have Web sites) for information on codes of conduct.

## Electronic retailers' rankings

Table 11.1 Five-star rating system of retailers

| Symbol | Explanation |
| --- | --- |
| 5 stars | 1. Company has a published comprehensive code of conduct.<br>2. Company has independent inspectors of factories for compliance with code of conduct.<br>3. Company has a comprehensive public reporting system detailing number of factories/suppliers in developing countries and results of inspections.<br>4. Company has own fair trade scheme for all or some products.<br>5. Company has demonstrated that it is moving beyond implementing basic human and working rights in |

| | |
|---|---|
| | factories/suppliers and acting on sustainable development values. |
| 4 stars | 1. Company has a published comprehensive code of conduct.<br>2. Company has independent inspectors of factories for compliance with code of conduct.<br>3. Company has a comprehensive public reporting system detailing number of factories/suppliers in developing countries and results of inspections.<br>4. Company has own fair trade scheme for all or some products. |
| 3 stars | 1. Company has a published comprehensive code of conduct.<br>2. Company has independent inspectors of factories for compliance with code of conduct.<br>3. Company has a comprehensive public reporting system detailing number of factories/suppliers in developing countries and results of inspections. |
| 2 stars | 1. Company has a published comprehensive code of conduct.<br>2. Company has independent inspectors of factories for compliance with code of conduct. |
| 1 star | 1. Company has a published (available to the public via Web site or shops or on products) comprehensive code of conduct. |
| ½ star | Company has a code of conduct or is developing a code of conduct. |
| # | Company without own-brand products. |
| > | Company has no operations in developing countries. |
| X | Company has no code of conduct. |

Table 11.2 Five-star ratings for electronic retailers

| Symbol | Electronic retailers |
|---|---|
| 5 stars | None |
| 4 stars | None |
| 3 stars | None |

| | |
|---|---|
| 2 stars | None |
| 1 star | None |
| ½ star | Dixons |
| # | @Jakarta |
| | British Gas Energy Centres |
| | Carphone Warehouse |
| | Currys |
| | DX Communications |
| | Electricity Plus |
| | Foto Processing |
| | Klik Photopoint |
| | Mill Bros |
| | Powerhouse |
| | Richer Sounds |
| | Scottish Power |
| | Shop Electric |
| | Supasnaps |
| | Tempo |
| | The Link |
| | The Pocket Phone Shop |
| > | Time Computers |
| X | City Camera Exchange |
| | Comet |
| | Electricworld |
| | Jessop |
| | PC World |
| | Tiny |

## Detailed survey results

The survey results are presented in the tables below:

- Retailers with no own-brand products (Table 11.3).
- Retailers that do not have suppliers in developing countries (Table 11.4).
- Retailers with a code of conduct (Table 11.5).
- Retailers that do not have a code of conduct (Table 11.6).

**Table 11.3 Electronic retailers with no own-brand products**

| Electronic Retailers | Parent Company |
|---|---|
| @Jakarta | Dixons Group Plc |
| British Gas Energy Centres | Centrica Plc |
| Carphone Warehouse | The Carphone Warehouse |
| Currys | Dixons Group Plc |
| DX Communications | DX Communications |
| Electricity Plus | Scottish Power Plc |
| Foto Processing | Bowie-Castlebank Ltd |
| Klik Photopoint | Bowie-Castlebank Ltd |
| Miller Bros Ltd | Miller Bros Ltd |
| Powerhouse | Powerhouse Holdings Ltd |
| Richer Sounds | Richer Sounds Plc |
| Scottish Power | Scottish Power Plc |
| Shop Electric | Lislyn Ltd |
| Supasnaps | Supasnaps Ltd |
| Tempo | Tempo |
| The Link | Dixons Group Plc |
| The Pocket Phone Shop | The Pocket Phone Shop |

**Table 11.4 Electronic retailers with no operations in developing countries**

| Electronic Retailer | Parent Company |
|---|---|
| Time Computers | Time Group Ltd |

Table 11.5 Electronic retailers with a code of conduct

| Electronic Retailer | Parent Company | Contents of Code of Conduct | | | | | | | | | | | | |
|---|---|---|---|---|---|---|---|---|---|---|---|---|---|---|
| | | Forced labour | Collective bargaining | Freedom of association | Health and safety | Child labour | Wages | Working hours | Equality | Job security | Harsh/inhumane treatment | Mandatory? | Independently inspected? | Member of ETI? |
| Dixons | Dixons Group Plc | * | | | | | | | | | | | | |

*Code of conduct unavailable

Table 11.6 Electronic retailers without a code of conduct

| Electronic Retailers | Parent Company |
|---|---|
| City Camera Exchange | The Jessop Group Ltd |
| Comet | Kingfisher Plc |
| Electricworld | Lislyn Ltd |
| Jessop | The Jessop Group Ltd |
| PC World | Dixons Group Plc |
| Tiny | Tiny (OT Computers Ltd) |

# 12 | Financial services

## Introduction

The high street financial service providers used by consumers in the UK invest or provide loans to companies with operations or suppliers in developing countries. Obviously, the financial providers can influence these companies or their suppliers with regard to, at the very least, codes of conduct relating to working conditions. There are different types of financial service providers or 'bank retailers' providing current accounts to the public, and they have different functions and forms:[1]

- high street banks;
- building societies;
- 'incorporated' former building societies;
- Internet banking and financial services;
- supermarkets; and
- ethical banks and societies.

Table 12.1 illustrates financial service providers' shares of the current account market, with the top four banks dominating 65 per cent of the market.[2]

Table 12.1 Share of main current account market in 2000

| Financial Service Provider | % |
|---|---|
| Lloyds TSB | 26 |
| Other banks | 17 |
| Barclays | 16 |
| NatWest | 13 |
| HSBC | 10 |

| | |
|---|---|
| Halifax | 7 |
| Abbey National | 4 |
| Royal Bank of Scotland | 4 |
| Other building societies | 3 |

## Initiatives

Most building societies do not invest in companies abroad but this is becoming less significant with changing legislation and the advent of demutualisation and mergers with banks.[3] Most banks and building societies do not have a general policy for all loans and investments but some such as the Co-operative Bank, Triodos Bank and the Ecology Building Society run their businesses based on ethical policies. Investment policies can filter some of the types of organisations or activities wanting loans or investment, such as weapons manufacturers or tobacco companies. Increasingly policies are including consideration of working conditions and human rights.

Some building societies and banks are members of the UK Social Investment Forum (UKSIF), which promotes socially responsible investment. Further information is contained in the box below.[4]

*UK Social Investment Forum (UKSIF)*

Aims and objectives are:

- To inform, educate and provide a forum for discussion and debate for the membership and the public at large about issues and developments in the socially responsible investment (SRI) field.
- To promote the understanding of socially responsible investment and to encourage the development of appropriate SRI practices and vehicles, both in terms of stock exchange investment and within the wider social economy.
- To identify, encourage and help develop working models

which demonstrate the effectiveness of SRI in protecting the environment, alleviating social hardship and stimulating sustainable economic development.

- To support and encourage a greater sense of social accountability amongst investors – both corporate and individual – and by financial institutions.
- To encourage and expect high ethical standards of professional conduct from the members and the public at large.
- To initiate and publish research for required changes in legislation and company policies and practices in order to enable SRI to develop rapidly and effectively both in the UK and internationally.
- To promote co-operation with European and other international SRI organisations through the exchange of information and ideas.

Membership of the UK Social Investment Forum is open to members of the public, professional advisors and fund managers, individual and institutional investors, community organisations, and other bodies concerned with socially responsible investment.

In joining the UK Social Investment Forum, members subscribe to the following statement of principles:

- Members agree to support the work of and to disseminate information about UKSIF and the work of its members.
- Members commit to assist, either individually or with other UKSIF members, in improving the public's understanding of Socially Responsible Investment and in supporting the theory and practice of SRI, including the concepts of ethical, cause-based, environmental and green investments.
- Members endeavour to place the public interest and the interest of their clients over their own. The responsibility of UKSIF members extends not only to the individual, but to society.
- Members strive to act with a high degree of personal

integrity, maintaining honourable relationships with colleagues, clients and all those who rely on the member's professional judgement and skills.

- Members seek continually to maintain and improve their knowledge, skills and competence relevant to their profession and be diligent in the performance of their occupational duties.
- Members make an affirmative commitment to apply honest, thorough and diligent methods of research and evaluation.
- Members should obey the laws and regulations relevant to their profession and should avoid any conduct or activity that would cause unjust harm to others.
- Members should use the fact of membership in a manner consistent with the UKSIF Statement of Principles. Membership of UKSIF is not intended to endorse an individual member's or organisation's business, qualifications, values or practices.

See the table of financial service providers for members.

Web site: www.uksif.org

There are also other financial services from investment companies providing ethical investment funds such as unit trusts, investment trusts and open-ended investment companies (OEICs) (including personal pension funds, life assurance, ISAs and other products available through these funds).[5] These are available to the retail market and use ethical criteria for the selection of investments. The value of these funds at the end of 2000 stood at more than £3.7 billion.[6]

## Financial service providers' rankings

**Table 12.2 Five-star rating system of retailers**

| Symbol | Explanation |
|---|---|
| 5 stars | 1. Company has a published ethical lending policy.<br>2. Company has published ethical lending policy that covers working conditions in developing countries.<br>3. Company has a comprehensive public reporting system containing results of lending policy.<br>4. Company has positive investment policies for specific projects tackling poverty and social exclusion.<br>5. Company has demonstrated that it is moving beyond ethical investment policies and acting on sustainable development values. |
| 4 stars | 1. Company has a published ethical lending policy.<br>2. Company has published ethical lending policy that covers working conditions in developing countries.<br>3. Company has a comprehensive public reporting system containing results of lending policy.<br>4. Company has positive investment policies for specific projects tackling poverty and social exclusion. |
| 3 stars | 1. Company has a published ethical lending policy.<br>2. Company has published ethical lending policy that covers working conditions in developing countries.<br>3. Company has a comprehensive public reporting system containing results of lending policy. |
| 2 stars | 1. Company has a published ethical lending policy.<br>2. Company has published ethical lending policy that covers working conditions in developing countries. |
| 1 star | 1. Company has a published ethical lending policy. |
| ½ star | Company has an ethical lending policy. |
| > | Company does not lend to companies. |
| X | Company has no ethical lending policy. |

**Table 12.3 Five-star ratings for financial service providers**

| Symbol | Financial Service Providers |
|---|---|
| 5 stars | None |
| 4 stars | Co-operative Bank |
| | Smile |
| | Triodos Bank |
| 3 stars | None |
| 2 stars | Abbey National |
| 1 star | HSBC |
| ½ star | First Direct |
| > | Chelsea Building Society |
| | Clydesdale Bank |
| | Coventry Building Society |
| | Derbyshire Building Society |
| | Ecology Building Society |
| | Leeds & Holbeck Building Society |
| | Market Harborough Building Society |
| | Nationwide Building Society |
| | Portman Building Society |
| | Virgin one |
| | Yorkshire Building Society |
| X | Alliance & Leicester |
| | Bank of Ireland GB |
| | Bank of Scotland |
| | Bank of Wales |
| | Barclays |
| | Birmingham Midshires |
| | Bradford & Bingley |
| | Bristol & West |
| | Britannia Building Society |
| | Cheltenham & Gloucester |
| | Cumberland Building Society |
| | Direct Line Financial Services |
| | Dunfermline Building Society |
| | Egg |
| | Girobank |
| | Halifax |

Lloyds TSB
NatWest Bank
Northern Bank
Northern Rock
Royal Bank of Scotland
Skipton Building Society
Ulster Bank
West Bromwich Building Society
Woolwich
Yorkshire Bank

---

Example investment policies from financial service providers are set out in the Appendix.

## Detailed survey results

The survey results are presented in Table 12.4, and cover the following subjects:

- whether the financial service provider lends to or invests in companies;
- whether the financial service provider has an ethical lending policy and, if so, whether the policy covers working conditions;
- whether the financial service provider is a member of the Ethical Trading Initiative (ETI) (see Chapter 2) or the UK Social Investment Forum (see the box on pages 109–11);
- whether the financial service provider has an ethical investment policy.

Table 12.4 Survey results for financial service providers

| Financial Service Provider | Parent Company | Lend to/invest in companies? | Ethical lending policy? | Working conditions policy? | Member of ETI? | Member UK Social Investment Forum? |
|---|---|---|---|---|---|---|
| Abbey National | Abbey National Plc | Y | Y | Y | | |
| Alliance & Leicester | Alliance & Leicester Plc | Y | N | | | |
| Bank of Ireland GB | Bank of Ireland | Y | N | | | |
| Bank of Scotland | Bank of Scotland | Y | N | | | Y |
| Bank of Wales | Bank of Scotland | Y | N | | | Y |
| Barclays | Barclays Bank Plc | Y | N | | | Y |
| Birmingham Midshires | Halifax Plc | * | | | | |
| Bradford & Bingley | Bradford & Bingley Plc | Y | N | | | |
| Bristol & West | Bank of Ireland | Y | N | | | |
| Britannia Building Society | Britannia Building Society | * | | | | |
| Chelsea Building Society | Chelsea Building Society | N | | | | |
| Cheltenham & Gloucester | Lloyds TSB Bank Plc | Y | N | | | |
| Clydesdale Bank | National Australia Bank Group | N | | | | |
| Co-operative Bank | Co-operative Group | Y | Y | Y | Y | Y |
| Coventry Building Society | Coventry Building Society | N | | | | |
| Cumberland Building Society | Cumberland Building Society | * | | | | |
| Derbyshire Building Society | Derbyshire Building Society | N | | | | Y |
| Direct Line Financial Services | Royal Bank of Scotland Group | Y | N | | | |
| Dunfermline Building Society | Dunfermline Building Society | * | | | | |
| Ecology Building Society | Ecology Building Society | N | | | | Y |
| Egg | Prudential | Y | N | | | |
| First Direct | HSBC Bank Plc | Y | Y | N | | |
| Girobank | Alliance & Leicester Plc | Y | N | | | |
| Halifax | Halifax Plc | Y | N | | | |
| HSBC | HSBC Bank Plc | Y | Y | N | | |
| Leeds & Holbeck Building Society | Leeds & Holbeck Building Society | N | | | | |

| | | | | | | |
|---|---|---|---|---|---|---|
| Lloyds TSB | Lloyds TSB Bank Plc | Y | N | | | |
| Market Harborough Building Society | Market Harborough Building Society | N | | | | |
| Nationwide Building Society | Nationwide Building Society | N | | | | |
| NatWest Bank | Royal Bank of Scotland Group | Y | N | | | Y |
| Northern Bank | National Australia Bank Group | Y | N | | | |
| Northern Rock | Northern Rock Plc | Y | N | | | Y |
| Portman Building Society | Portman Building Society | N | | | | |
| Royal Bank of Scotland | Royal Bank of Scotland Group | Y | N | | | |
| Skipton Building Society | Skipton Building Society | * | | | | |
| Smile | Co-operative Group | Y | Y | Y | Y | Y |
| Triodos Bank | Triodos Bank | Y | Y | Y | | Y |
| Ulster Bank | Royal Bank of Scotland Group | Y | N | | | |
| Virgin one | Australian Mutual Provident Society | N | | | | |
| West Bromwich Building Society | West Bromwich Building Society | * | | | | |
| Woolwich | Barclays Bank Plc | Y | N | | | |
| Yorkshire Bank | National Australia Bank Group | Y | N | | | |
| Yorkshire Building Society | Yorkshire Building Society | N | | | | |

*information unavailable

# 13 | Food retailers

## Introduction

The six largest retailers in the UK by sales are supermarkets. In total there are only 17 national food retailers (as opposed to a hundred or so clothes retailers).[1] Food retailers not only sell the obvious but a host of other products such as drinks, clothes, household items and electrical goods. Table 13.1 gives the market shares in the industry, and shows that Tesco, Sainsbury's, Asda and Safeway account for 70 per cent of the market.[2] These retailers sell both own-brand products and individually branded products. Supermarkets have recently taken the lead on particular issues such as removing genetically modified (GM) foodstuffs from their own-brand products and introducing a range of organic products to their stores. Because food is now commonly sourced from all over the world and price competition is fierce this means that the food retailers have a large range of issues to tackle when it comes to fair and ethical trade for the different types of products they sell.

Table 13.1 Food retailer market shares in 1999

| Retailer | % |
|---|---|
| Tesco | 24.6 |
| Sainsbury's | 20.1 |
| Asda | 15.3 |
| Safeway | 10.7 |
| Wm Morrison | 4.9 |
| Somerfield | 4.7 |
| Kwik Save | 4.4 |
| Iceland | 3.4 |
| Waitrose | 1.5 |

| | |
|---|---|
| Lidl | 0.9 |
| Netto | 0.9 |
| Aldi | 0.7 |
| Co-ops | 4.4 |
| Other independents | 2.3 |
| Other convenience stores | 0.7 |
| Other multiples | 0.5 |

## Working conditions

An investigation by the BBC in 2000 showed that illegal immigrants from Eastern Europe had been employed for £5.80 per day in farms and food-processing plants that supplied own-brand produce to supermarkets including Iceland and Sainsbury's.[3] Marks & Spencer has come under criticism for sourcing clothes from a Latvian factory where staff reportedly had to work 12-hour shifts, seven days a week. Union officials stated that 10 per cent of the staff were paid 30p an hour.[4] Asda's new owner, Wal-Mart, is also famous for its abuse of workers' rights. It sources much of its clothing in the US from developing countries and was fined $205,650 for breaking child labour laws in every one of its stores in the US state of Maine.[5]

In 2001, the *Guardian* reported that 50 years ago, between 50 and 60 pence of each pound spent on food by the consumer was returned to the farmer. This figure is now 9 pence in the pound.[6] A competition report in 2000 found that supermarkets all share practices that enable them to maximise their own profits at the expense of farmers and producers.[7] In addition, the buying practices of supermarkets make it difficult for suppliers in developing countries not just to comply with codes of conduct but to survive. These practices include:[8]

- High cosmetic quality standards. Rigid standards on appearance of fresh produce are leading to large amounts of produce being rejected. This causes a large financial loss to growers and a disincentive to continue production for the export market. It reduces income for poor, small-scale farmers, and is also undesirable from an environmental viewpoint since much of the rejected produce is wasted.

- Late payments. Late payment by supermarkets creates cash flow problems for exporters and growers. They find it difficult to pay their own outgrowers on time. Small-scale outgrowers need a steady cash flow to afford the inputs that will ensure quality and maintain sustainable farming systems. Fertilisers, for instance, are a high cost and, if payment for the previous harvest is late, farmers cannot afford to purchase what is required for the following crop. Failure to apply correct amounts of fertiliser results in a poorer and inconsistent crop, whose shelf-life may also be impaired.
- 'Last-minute' orders. Supermarkets sometimes make late orders, or change orders at the last minute. Late orders force exporters to employ workers to work overnight/long hours to get the order ready in time. Reducing orders at the last minute can cause huge wastage of crops already harvested.

## Food retailers' rankings

Table 13.2 Five-star rating system of retailers

| Symbol | Explanation |
|---|---|
| 5 stars | 1. Company has a published comprehensive code of conduct. |
| | 2. Company has independent inspectors of factories for compliance with code of conduct. |
| | 3. Company has a comprehensive public reporting system detailing number of factories/suppliers in developing countries and results of inspections. |
| | 4. Company has own fair trade scheme for all or some products. |
| | 5. Company has demonstrated that it is moving beyond implementing basic human and working rights in factories/suppliers and acting on sustainable development values. |
| 4 stars | 1. Company has a published comprehensive code of conduct. |
| | 2. Company has independent inspectors of factories for compliance with code of conduct. |
| | 3. Company has a comprehensive public reporting system detailing number of factories/suppliers in developing countries and results of inspections. |

| | |
|---|---|
| | 4. Company has own fair trade scheme for all or some products. |
| 3 stars | 1. Company has a published comprehensive code of conduct.<br>2. Company has independent inspectors of factories for compliance with code of conduct.<br>3. Company has a comprehensive public reporting system detailing number of factories/suppliers in developing countries and results of inspections. |
| 2 stars | 1. Company has a published comprehensive code of conduct.<br>2. Company has independent inspectors of factories for compliance with code of conduct. |
| 1 star | 1. Company has a published (available to the public via Web site or shops or on products) comprehensive code of conduct. |
| ½ star | Company has a code of conduct or is developing a code of conduct. |
| # | Company without own-brand products. |
| > | Company has no operations in developing countries. |
| X | Company has no code of conduct. |

Table 13.3 Five-star ratings for food retailers

| Symbol | Food Retailers |
|---|---|
| 5 stars | None |
| 4 stars | Co-op |
| 3 stars | None |
| 2 stars | Sainsbury's |
| 1 star | Asda |
| | Kwik Save |
| | Safeway |
| | Somerfield |
| | Tesco |
| ½ star | Farmfoods |
| | Marks & Spencer |
| | Morrisons |
| | Thorntons |
| | Waitrose |
| # | Aldi |
| > | None |

| | |
|---|---|
| X | Budgens |
| | Iceland |
| | Lidl |
| | Netto |

Example codes of conduct from food retailers are set out in the Appendix.

## Detailed survey results

The survey results are presented in the tables below:

- Retailers with no own-brand products (Table 13.4).
- Retailers that have a code of conduct (Table 13.5). This table highlights the issues covered and also indicates if these codes of conduct are mandatory to all suppliers and if compliance is independently inspected. With regard to fair trade, the food retailers selling their own fair trade products and/or selling Fairtrade Mark products are shown. The food retailers who are members of the Ethical Trading Initiative (ETI) are also shown.
- Retailers developing a code of conduct (Table 13.6).
- Retailers with no code of conduct (Table 13.7).

Table 13.4 Food retailers with no own-brand products

| Food Retailer | Parent Company |
|---|---|
| Aldi | Aldi Gruppe |

**Table 13.5 Food retailers with a code of conduct**

| Food Retailers | Parent Company | Forced labour | Collective bargaining | Freedom of association | Health and safety | Child labour | Wages | Working hours | Equality | Job security | Harsh/inhumane treatment | Mandatory? | Independently inspected? | Member of ETI? | Fairtrade Mark products? | Own fair trade products? |
|---|---|---|---|---|---|---|---|---|---|---|---|---|---|---|---|---|
| | | **Contents of Code of Conduct** | | | | | | | | | | | | | | |
| Asda | Wal-Mart Inc | X | X | X | X | X | X | X | X | X | X | X | X | X | X | |
| Co-ops | Co-operative Group | X | | X | X | X | X | X | | X | | X | X | X | X | X |
| Farmfoods | Farmfoods Ltd | * | | | | | | | | | | X | | | | |
| Kwik Save | Somerfield Plc | X | X | X | X | X | X | X | X | X | X | | | X | | |
| Marks & Spencer | Marks & Spencer Plc | | X | X | X | X | X | X | | | | X | | X | | |
| Morrisons | Wm Morrison Supermarkets Plc | * | | | | | | | | | | | | | | |
| Safeway | Safeway Plc | X | X | X | X | X | X | X | X | X | X | | | X | X | |
| Sainsbury's | J Sainsbury Plc | X | | X | X | X | X | X | X | | X | X | pilot | X | X | |
| Somerfield | Somerfield Plc | X | X | X | X | X | X | X | X | X | X | | | X | | |
| Tesco | Tesco Plc | X | X | X | X | X | X | X | X | X | X | | | X | | |
| Waitrose | John Lewis Partnership Plc | * | | | | | | | | | | | | | | |

*code of conduct unavailable

**Table 13.6 Food retailers developing a code of conduct**

| Food Retailer | Parent Company |
|---|---|
| Thorntons | Thorntons Plc |

**Table 13.7 Food retailers with no code of conduct**

| Food Retailers | Parent Company |
|---|---|
| Budgens | Budgens Plc |
| Iceland | Iceland Group Plc |
| Lidl | Lidl (UK) |
| Netto | Dansk Supermarketed A/S |

# 14 | Footwear retailers

## Introduction

Footwear ranges from formal shoes for work to branded fashion sports shoes. The high profile brands in sport shoes such as Nike have been criticised for alleged use of child labour and forced overtime.[1] This chapter concentrates on footwear from retailers selling their own-brand footwear. This area has been largely ignored as attention has focused on high-profile sports brands.

## Working conditions

According to the *Ethical Consumer* magazine, working conditions within factories, particularly those manufacturing sports shoes, are typically very poor.[2] They are often situated in low-waged economies, and workers may be subjected to long hours, forced unpaid overtime, intimidation from management (both verbal and physical) and pitiful wages.[3] Attempts by workers to organise are at best frowned upon and at worst brutally put down.[4]

Brazil and China are two of the world's largest shoe exporters and sell millions of pairs of shoes to Britain every year as well as to other developing countries such as Indonesia, Vietnam and India.[5] This has created a downward spiral in working conditions as countries compete to produce ever-cheaper shoes.[6] This is exacerbated by the fact that little of the final price the consumer pays for the shoes goes to the workers. For example CAFOD researchers found that in Brazil workers received 4 pence in the pound.[7] In general more expensive shoes are produced in developed countries but CAFOD argues that consumers should not buy just shoes produced in developed countries because this would effectively be a boycott of shoes produced in developing countries. CAFOD goes on to express concern that a boycott would lead to job losses and greater suffering in the developing countries where there is little or no social welfare.[8]

## The footwear retailing industry

Footwear retailing sales in 2000 in the UK amounted to £3.9 billion[9] with Clarks being the most popular choice of retailer. No specialist retailers are dominating the market, as they do with other related products such as clothing and sports gear (see Table 14.1).[10] Table 14.2 summarises the retailers from which consumers bought their footwear in 2000.[11]

Table 14.1 Retail shares of UK footwear market, by type of retailer

| Type of Footwear Retailer | % of Market |
|---|---|
| Specialist shoe shops (multiples) | 27 |
| Sports shops | 16 |
| Clothing retailers | 15 |
| Variety/department stores | 14 |
| Mail order | 9 |
| Specialist shoe shops (independents) | 8 |
| Other outlets* | 11 |

* includes factory outlets, market stalls, supermarkets, etc

Table 14.2 Retailers consumers have purchased footwear from in the last year

| Specialist Retailer | % | Non-Specialist Retailer | % |
|---|---|---|---|
| Clarks | 21 | Sports/outdoor shop | 20 |
| Other shoe shops | 15 | Marks & Spencer | 11 |
| Barratts | 8 | Mail order | 10 |
| K Shoes | 6 | Department store | 9 |
| Shoe Express | 6 | Somewhere else | 8 |
| Shoefayre | 6 | Specialist clothes shops | 7 |
| Stead & Simpson | 5 | Factory outlet | 4 |

| | | | |
|---|---|---|---|
| Dolcis | 5 | Market stall | 5 |
| Discount shoe shop | 4 | Supermarkets | 3 |
| Saxone | 3 | Other variety stores | 3 |
| Shoe City/Brantano | 3 | | |
| Olivers/Timpson | 3 | | |
| Ravel | 2 | | |
| Faith Shoes | 2 | | |

## Footwear retailers' rankings

Table 14.3 Five-star rating system of retailers

| Symbol | Explanation |
|---|---|
| 5 stars | 1. Company has a published comprehensive code of conduct.<br>2. Company has independent inspectors of factories for compliance with code of conduct.<br>3. Company has a comprehensive public reporting system detailing number of factories/suppliers in developing countries and results of inspections.<br>4. Company has own fair trade scheme for all or some products.<br>5. Company has demonstrated that it is moving beyond implementing basic human and working rights in factories/suppliers and acting on sustainable development values. |
| 4 stars | 1. Company has a published comprehensive code of conduct.<br>2. Company has independent inspectors of factories for compliance with code of conduct.<br>3. Company has a comprehensive public reporting system detailing number of factories/suppliers in developing countries and results of inspections.<br>4. Company has own fair trade scheme for all or some products. |
| 3 stars | 1. Company has a published comprehensive code of conduct.<br>2. Company has independent inspectors of factories for compliance with code of conduct.<br>3. Company has a comprehensive public reporting system detailing number of factories/suppliers in developing countries and results of inspections. |
| 2 stars | 1. Company has a published comprehensive code of conduct. |

| | |
|---|---|
| | 2. Company has independent inspectors of factories for compliance with code of conduct. |
| 1 star | 1. Company has a published (available to the public via Web site or shops or on products) comprehensive code of conduct. |
| ½ star | Company has a code of conduct or is developing a code of conduct. |
| # | Company without own-brand products. |
| > | Company has no operations in developing countries. |
| X | Company has no code of conduct. |

**Table 14.4 Five-star ratings for footwear retailers**

| Symbol | Footwear Retailers |
|---|---|
| 5 stars | None |
| 4 stars | None |
| 3 stars | None |
| 2 stars | Shoefayre |
| 1 star | None |
| ½ star | Bertie |
| | Brantano Footwear |
| | Cable & Co |
| | Clarks |
| | K Shoes |
| | Nine West |
| | Pied a Terre |
| | Ravel |
| | Roland Cartier |
| | Shoe Collection |
| # | A Jones & Sons |
| | Beghins |
| | Church's |
| | Elts |
| | James Allen |
| | Russell & Bromley |
| > | Dolcis |
| X | Adesso Shoes |
| | Bacons |
| | Bally |

Barratts
Broughton Shoe Warehouse
Carvela
Faith Footwear
Famous Footwear
Hush Puppies
Jonathan James
KG
Kurt Geiger
Max Bally
Oaris
Olivers/Timpson
Peter Briggs
Saxone
Schuh – Clothing For Feet
Shelly's Shoes
Shoe Express
Shoeright
Shoestop
Stead & Simpson
Stylo Superstores
Thrifty
Tyrells

---

Example codes of conduct from footwear retailers are set out in the Appendix.

## Detailed survey results

The survey results are presented in the tables below:

- Retailers with no own-brand products (Table 14.5).
- Retailers with no operations in developing countries (Table 14.6).
- Those retailers that do have suppliers in developing countries and have a code of conduct (Table 14.7). This table summarises the contents of their codes of conduct, covering issues such as freedom to join employee associations, child labour, forced

labour and violence against employees. In addition, the table covers whether the code of conduct is mandatory for all the retailer's suppliers, if compliance by suppliers to the code of conduct is checked by independent (to the retailer and the suppliers) inspectors and finally if the retailer is a member of the Ethical Trading Initiative (see Chapter 2).

- Retailers that are developing a code of conduct (Table 14.8).
- Retailers with no code of conduct (Table 14.9).

**Table 14.5 Footwear retailers with no own-brand products**

| Footwear Retailers | Parent Company |
|---|---|
| A Jones & Sons | Church & Co Plc |
| Beghins | Church & Co Plc |
| Church's | Church & Co Plc |
| Elts | Church & Co Plc |
| James Allen | Church & Co Plc |
| Russell & Bromley | Russell & Bromley Ltd |

**Table 14.6 Footwear retailers with no operations in developing countries**

| Footwear retailer | Parent Company |
|---|---|
| Dolcis | Dolcis Ltd |

**Table 14.7 Footwear retailers with a code of conduct**

| Footwear Retailers | Parent Company | Contents of Code of Conduct | | | | | | | | | | | | |
|---|---|---|---|---|---|---|---|---|---|---|---|---|---|---|
| | | Forced labour | Collective bargaining | Freedom of association | Health and safety | Child labour | Wages | Working hours | Equality | Job security | Harsh/inhumane treatment | Mandatory? | Independently inspected? | Member of ETI? |
| Bertie | The Shoe Studio Group Ltd | | X | | X | X | X | X | X | X | | X | X | |
| Cable & Co | The Shoe Studio Group Ltd | | X | | X | X | X | X | X | X | | X | X | |

| | | | | | | | | | | | | |
|---|---|---|---|---|---|---|---|---|---|---|---|---|
| Clarks | C&J Clark International Ltd | X | | X | X | X | X | X | X | X | X | |
| K Shoes | C&J Clark International Ltd | X | | X | X | X | X | X | X | X | X | |
| Nine West | The Shoe Studio Group Ltd | X | X | X | X | X | X | X | | X | X | |
| Pied a Terre | The Shoe Studio Group Ltd | X | X | X | X | X | X | X | | X | X | |
| Ravel | C&J Clark International Ltd | X | | X | X | X | X | X | X | X | X | |
| Roland Cartier | The Shoe Studio Group Ltd | X | X | X | X | X | X | X | | X | X | |
| Shoe Collection | The Shoe Studio Group Ltd | X | X | X | X | X | X | X | | X | X | |
| Shoefayre | The Co-operative Group | X | X | X | X | X | X | | X | X | X | X |

Table 14.8 Footwear retailers developing a code of conduct

| Footwear Retailer | Parent Company |
|---|---|
| Brantano Footwear | Brantano UK Ltd |

Table 14.9 Footwear retailers without a code of conduct

| Footwear Retailers | Parent Company |
|---|---|
| Adesso Shoes | Kurt Geiger Ltd |
| Bacons | Stylo Plc |
| Bally | Bally Group (UK) Ltd |
| Barratts | Stylo Plc |
| Broughton Shoe Warehouse | Broughton Brothers Ltd |
| Carvela | Kurt Geiger Ltd |
| Faith Footwear | Faith Footwear Ltd |
| Famous Footwear | Stead & Simpson Ltd |
| Hush Puppies | Stylo Plc |
| Jonathan James | Broughton Brothers Ltd |
| KG | Kurt Geiger Ltd |
| Kurt Geiger | Kurt Geiger Ltd |
| Max Bally | Bally Group (UK) Ltd |
| Oaris | Oliver Group Plc |
| Olivers/Timpson | Oliver Group Plc |
| Peter Briggs | Stead & Simpson Ltd |
| Saxone | Stylo Plc |
| Schuh – Clothing For Feet | Schuh Ltd |
| Shelly's Shoes | Shelly's Shoes Ltd |

| | |
|---|---|
| Shoe Express | Stead & Simpson Ltd |
| Shoeright | Oliver Group Plc |
| Shoestop | Broughton Brothers Ltd |
| Stead & Simpson | Stead & Simpson Ltd |
| Stylo Superstores | Stylo Plc |
| Thrifty | Broughton Brothers Ltd |
| Tyrells | Broughton Brothers Ltd |

# 15 | Furniture retailers

## Introduction

Furniture is purchased by consumers from a variety of retailers ranging from DIY and department stores to home shopping and household retailers. Table 15.1 sets out the major retailers in this area, including those described in other chapters.[1] This chapter concentrates on retailers that only or mainly sell furniture, such as IKEA and MFI Homeworks. Furniture types range from sofas to kitchens and beds to bookshelves. Increasingly furniture is being manufactured in developing countries such as China using wood often sourced from local natural forests and cloth materials made in similar conditions to carpets and clothing. Of the furniture retailers surveyed in this chapter only 4 out of 17 had codes of conduct, again highlighting the poor record of retailers for taking their responsibilities beyond profit and into protecting human rights.

Table 15.1 Retailers used to purchase furniture in 2000 in the UK

| Retailers | % |
|---|---|
| Argos | 13 |
| IKEA | 12 |
| DIY multiples (eg B&Q, Homebase, Focus Do It All, Great Mills) | 11 |
| MFI | 8 |
| Independent specialist furniture stores | 5 |
| Department stores (eg John Lewis, Allders) | 5 |
| Mail order (eg GUS, Littlewoods, Freemans) | 5 |
| Other stores | 5 |
| Index | 4 |
| Other specialist furniture chains (eg Furnitureland, Harveys) | 3 |

| | |
|---|---|
| Marks & Spencer | 3 |
| Other variety stores (eg Bhs, Woolworths) | 3 |
| Courts | 2 |
| DFS | 2 |
| Co-op | 2 |
| Kitchen specialists (eg Magnet) | 1 |
| Bedroom specialists (eg London Bedding Company) | 1 |
| Houseware stores (eg Heal's, Habitat, The Pier) | 1 |
| Clothing retailers (eg Next, Laura Ashley) | 1 |
| Discount stores | 1 |
| Antique shops | 1 |
| Market stalls | 1 |
| Other | 10 |

## Furniture retailers' rankings

Table 15.2 Five-star rating system of retailers

| Symbol | Explanation |
|---|---|
| 5 stars | 1. Company has a published comprehensive code of conduct.<br>2. Company has independent inspectors of factories for compliance with code of conduct.<br>3. Company has a comprehensive public reporting system detailing number of factories/suppliers in developing countries and results of inspections.<br>4. Company has own fair trade scheme for all or some products.<br>5. Company has demonstrated that it is moving beyond implementing basic human and working rights in factories/suppliers and acting on sustainable development values. |
| 4 stars | 1. Company has a published comprehensive code of conduct.<br>2. Company has independent inspectors of factories for compliance with code of conduct.<br>3. Company has a comprehensive public reporting system detailing number of factories/suppliers in developing countries and results of inspections.<br>4. Company has own fair trade scheme for all or some products. |
| 3 stars | 1. Company has a published comprehensive code of conduct. |

| | |
|---|---|
| | 2. Company has independent inspectors of factories for compliance with code of conduct.<br>3. Company has a comprehensive public reporting system detailing number of factories/suppliers in developing countries and results of inspections. |
| 2 stars | 1. Company has a published comprehensive code of conduct.<br>2. Company has independent inspectors of factories for compliance with code of conduct. |
| 1 star | 1. Company has a published (available to the public via Web site or shops or on products) comprehensive code of conduct. |
| ½ star | Company has a code of conduct or is developing a code of conduct. |
| # | Company without own-brand products. |
| > | Company has no operations in developing countries. |
| X | Company has no code of conduct. |

Table 15.3 Five-star ratings for furniture retailers

| Symbol | Furniture Retailers |
|---|---|
| 5 stars | None |
| 4 stars | None |
| 3 stars | None |
| 2 stars | None |
| 1 star | None |
| ½ star | Courts<br>Habitat<br>IKEA<br>MFI Homeworks |
| # | None |
| > | Magnet, CP Hart |
| X | DFS<br>Dolphin<br>Furnitureland<br>Furniture Village<br>Kitchens Direct<br>Moben<br>Multiyork<br>Portland |

ScS
Sharps
Sofa Workshop
The London Bedding Company

Example codes of conduct from furniture retailers are set out in the Appendix.

## Detailed survey results

The survey results are presented in the tables below:

- Retailers with no operations in developing countries (Table 15.4).
- Those retailers that have suppliers in developing countries and have a code of conduct (Table 15.5). This table summarises the contents of their codes of conduct, covering issues such as freedom to join employee associations, child labour, forced labour and violence against employees. In addition, it covers whether the code of conduct is mandatory for all the retailer's suppliers, if compliance by suppliers to the code of conduct is checked by independent (to the retailer and the suppliers) inspectors and finally if the retailer is a member of the Ethical Trading Initiative (see Chapter 2).
- Retailers without a code of conduct (Table 15.6).

Table 15.4 Furniture retailers with no operations in developing countries

| Furniture Retailer | Parent Company |
| --- | --- |
| Magnet, CP Hart | Magnet Ltd |

## Table 15.5 Furniture retailers with a code of conduct

| Furniture retailers | Parent Company | Contents of Code of Conduct: Forced labour | Collective bargaining | Freedom of association | Health and safety | Child labour | Wages | Working hours | Equality | Job security | Harsh/inhumane treatment | Mandatory? | Independently inspected? | Member of ETI? |
|---|---|---|---|---|---|---|---|---|---|---|---|---|---|---|
| Courts | Courts Plc | | X | X | X | X | X | X | X | X | | X | X | |
| Habitat | Habitat UK Ltd | | X | | | | X | | | | | | | |
| IKEA | IKEA Ltd | | X | X | X | X | X | X | | X | | X | X | |
| MFI Homeworks | MFI Furniture Group Plc | | | | | X | X | X | | | | | X | |

## Table 15.6 Furniture retailers without a code of conduct

| Furniture Retailers | Parent Company |
|---|---|
| DFS | DFS Furniture Company Plc |
| Dolphin | Homeform Group Plc |
| Furnitureland | Furnitureland Ltd |
| Furniture Village | Furniture Village Plc |
| Kitchens Direct | Homeform Group Plc |
| Moben | Homeform Group Plc |
| Multiyork | Multiyork Furniture Ltd |
| Portland | Homeform Group Plc |
| ScS | ScS Upholstery Plc |
| Sharps | Homeform Group Plc |
| Sofa Workshop | The Sofa Workshop Ltd |
| The London Bedding Company | Furniture Village Plc |

# 16 | Health and beauty retailers

## Introduction

Health and beauty retailers vary enormously in size. They offer a wide variety of products from outlets ranging from local chemists to supermarkets. Chemists are often part of a national or international company and are increasingly selling own-brand products such as soap and paracetamol. Supermarkets and large chains are attempting to dominate the market by taking over local pharmacy licences to sell medicines. This is with the aim of enticing customers into their shops to buy other health and beauty products. The result of this practice is that local community chemists are being pushed out of the market (see Table 16.1[1]). Other well-known retail chains that sell health and beauty products (but not medicines) include The Body Shop and Lush.

**Table 16.1 Retail shares of UK toiletries and cosmetics market, 1999**

| Retailers | % |
|---|---|
| Boots the Chemist | 29.2 |
| Superdrug | 10.9 |
| Other chemists/drugstores | 4.1 |
| Tesco | 14.4 |
| Sainsbury's | 9.4 |
| Asda | 9.0 |
| Safeway | 5.3 |
| Other grocers | 7.0 |
| Department/variety stores | 4.0 |
| Direct sell (including Avon) | 3.1 |
| The Body Shop | 2.7 |
| Other specialist health and beauty retailers | 0.4 |
| Other | 0.5 |

## Initiatives

The star in this sector is of course The Body Shop, which is renowned for its environmental and social campaigns and activities. These range from recycled and returnable packaging and biodegradable ingredients to its own fair trading scheme, called community trading. This scheme trades directly with small communities around the world providing favourable prices and support.

### *The Body Shop International's Community Trade scheme*[2]

**What is Community Trade?**

The Community Trade programme is a special purchasing programme that is the result of The Body Shop's commitment to support long-term sustainable trading relationships with communities in need. The goal of Community Trade is to help create livelihoods, and to explore a trade-based approach to supporting sustainable development by sourcing ingredients and accessories directly from socially and economically marginalised producer communities.

**The message of Community Trade?**

Community Trade can provide a vehicle for community and individual development. It's one way that The Body Shop can use its knowledge, creativity and purchasing power to directly benefit communities throughout the world. Working with The Body Shop provides suppliers with access to a market which can serve as a training ground and a gateway to other markets and customers. The Body Shop Community Trade programme is a journey and an adventure. We believe we are firmly on the right track. We hope that, in due course, the successes will speak for themselves and, most important of all, that the communities we trade with will fully achieve their aspiration for economic independence and social progress.

**Why Community Trade?**

The Body Shop Mission Statement is 'to dedicate our business to the pursuit of social and environmental change' and 'to tirelessly work to narrow the gap between position and practice'. Our Community Trade programme aims at long-term, sustainable relationships and is one way of using trade as a mechanism for communities to benefit through employment, income, skills development and social initiatives. Community Trade is very much a partnership. This partnership is designed to produce results which fit in with a community's own development goals. The partnership is based on trust, respect and an understanding that we buy good quality products at a fair price which covers production, wages and also enables an investment in the community and the future. It is about far more than exchange of goods and money – it is about working with people.

**Criteria for Community Trade**

In 1994 The Body Shop developed a set of guidelines to ensure that potential Community Trade partnerships have the greatest chance of fulfilling a community's goals. Within these guidelines, information is collected in five areas:

1. Community organisation
   We seek to work with organisations which already exist to represent the interests of the social group concerned. These might be an association of women, a farming co-operative, a tribal council, a group of homeless people in an urban setting or even a more conventional business that has stakeholder representation way above the norm for that country. In this way, our purchasing power serves to strengthen organisations which represent collective interests.
2. Community in need
   We seek to work with groups who would normally have limited opportunities, limited resources, limited access to education, limited health care and limited outlets for their goods. By targeting disadvantaged groups we hope to improve their opportunities.

3. Benefits
   It is vital that our trade benefits the people who actually produce the goods we buy but not just on an economic level. We are looking for organisations that encourage worker participation, leadership, training – primarily for women. Suppliers have a work force that are socially, as well as economically, benefiting.
4. Commercial viability
   The business must be commercially viable which means that price, quality, capacity and availability must all be carefully considered.
5. Environmental sustainability
   The commercial activity has to meet The Body Shop standards for environmental and animal protection.

**Success**

Success for The Body Shop Community Trade programme can be measured by the increase in the volume of raw materials and accessories purchased, and the community benefits that have resulted. However, as Anita and Gordon Roddick have said, 'How do we measure human development? Where are the instruments that are capable of measuring the search for new awareness and greater strength in organisations?'

The Body Shop is committed to the growth of its Community Trade programme. During the last year, 27 new products were launched containing ingredients sourced from Community Trade suppliers, bringing the total number to 96. Purchases of raw materials and accessories from Community Trade suppliers totalled £3.3 million for the year, compared with £3.6 million in 1999. The Body Shop trades with 37 supplier groups in 23 countries. 'Before Kuapa Kokoo Ltd, we had to wait a long time for payments and we were cheated by the purchasing clerks at the weighing scales. Now we are paid on time, we are paid extra, there are no problems with the weighing scales, the society members determine how Kuapa Kokoo Ltd trades with the farmers and at the end of the year Kuapa Kokoo

Ltd has to account to the farmers themselves. We have never experienced this before' – A cocoa farmer member of Kuapa Kokoo Union.

Since 1989 we have been sourcing paper products from General Paper Industries in Nepal. They have set up an organisation which promotes AIDS awareness, offers scholarships to enable girls to go to school and replants barren hillsides with sustainable shrubs.

Now that's something else to celebrate!

**Lessons learnt**

The Body Shop is not pretending that there haven't been difficulties along the way. This has been a grand experiment, a new venture for a global retailer – there were no text books telling us how to ethically source ingredients for our products. But where there have been difficulties, we have persevered and worked with communities to find solutions. We've made mistakes, such as over-estimating customer interest in Community Trade products, and we have faced criticism, but Community Trade is and will remain a fundamental part of the way The Body Shop does business. More importantly, this history of involvement has strengthened The Body Shop conviction that Community Trade is a valid proposition, and it does make a difference to the people it touches.

The benefits are across the board. Community Trade may only be a small part of our business but the effects are great for all those involved:

- For The Body Shop: the Community Trade programme is a practical expression of our broader social goals. 'As a buyer, you're seeing what you can provide in the way of livelihoods, but you're also seeing the ripple effects, the contribution to community and that's about self-esteem. That's the core of what these economic development initiatives are all about' – Anita Roddick.

- For community-based producer organisations: the Community Trade Programme supports them in their efforts to develop their economies and communities in ways they have chosen. 'In my community, every day the trust among the men and women increases. In the meetings they (men) were the only ones who talked. Now it seems that things are changing because it is us, the women, who talk the most now. It is nice to see how the women are waking up after so many years of being asleep' – A member of the Nahñu Indians, Mexico.
- For customers: Community Trade products provide customers with an opportunity to use their purchasing power in ways that support these communities while receiving a good quality product. At the same time, they become informed about the source of the ingredients in the products on the shelves and the accessories available.
- For the business world: Community Trade provides a practical example of ethical trading and an opportunity for other companies to meet the needs of a growing section of society calling for better standards of global trade.

**Wider issues of fair trade**

For The Body Shop, Community Trade represents part of our commitment to global fair trade. We aim to conduct all our trade according to our Fair Trade principles. We have a Fair Trade department which oversees this in operation – and which drives the Community Trade programme. We are committed to the following goals:

- We aim to ensure that human and civil rights are respected throughout our business activities.
- We will promote animal protection.
- We will use environmentally sustainable resources wherever technically and economically viable.
- Our trading relationships will be commercially viable and mutually beneficial.

## Health and beauty retailers' rankings

Table 16.2 Five-star rating system of retailers

| Symbol | Explanation |
|---|---|
| 5 stars | 1. Company has a published comprehensive code of conduct.<br>2. Company has independent inspectors of factories for compliance with code of conduct.<br>3. Company has a comprehensive public reporting system detailing number of factories/suppliers in developing countries and results of inspections.<br>4. Company has own fair trade scheme for all or some products.<br>5. Company has demonstrated that it is moving beyond implementing basic human and working rights in factories/suppliers and acting on sustainable development values. |
| 4 stars | 1. Company has a published comprehensive code of conduct.<br>2. Company has independent inspectors of factories for compliance with code of conduct.<br>3. Company has a comprehensive public reporting system detailing number of factories/suppliers in developing countries and results of inspections.<br>4. Company has own fair trade scheme for all or some products. |
| 3 stars | 1. Company has a published comprehensive code of conduct.<br>2. Company has independent inspectors of factories for compliance with code of conduct.<br>3. Company has a comprehensive public reporting system detailing number of factories/suppliers in developing countries and results of inspections. |
| 2 stars | 1. Company has a published comprehensive code of conduct.<br>2. Company has independent inspectors of factories for compliance with code of conduct. |
| 1 star | 1. Company has a published (available to the public via Web site or shops or on products) comprehensive code of conduct. |
| ½ star | Company has a code of conduct or is developing a code of conduct. |
| # | Company without own-brand products. |
| > | Company has no operations in developing countries. |
| X | Company has no code of conduct. |

**Table 16.3 Five-star ratings for health and beauty retailers**

| Symbol | Health and Beauty Retailers |
|---|---|
| 5 stars | None |
| 4 stars | The Body Shop International* |
| 3 stars | None |
| 2 stars | National Co-operative Chemists |
| 1 star | None |
| ½ star | Boots the Chemist |
| # | None |
| > | Moss Chemists |
| X | Body Care |
| | Graham's Toiletries |
| | Hills |
| | Lloyds Chemists |
| | Lloyds Supersave |
| | Lloydspharmacy |
| | Lush |
| | Peel Street Pharmacy |
| | Savers Health & Beauty |
| | Superdrug |
| | UniChem |

* no independent inspections, some reporting and integration of sustainable development values

Example codes of conduct from health and beauty retailers are set out in the Appendix.

## Detailed survey results

The survey results are presented in the tables below:

- Retailers that do not have suppliers in developing countries (Table 16.4).
- Those retailers that do have suppliers in developing countries and have a code of conduct (Table 16.5). This table summarises the contents of their codes of conduct, covering issues such as freedom to join employee associations, child labour, forced

labour and violence against employees. In addition, it covers whether the code of conduct is mandatory for all the retailer's suppliers, whether compliance by suppliers to the code of conduct is checked by independent (to the retailer and the suppliers) inspectors and finally whether the retailer is a member of the Ethical Trading Initiative (see Chapter 2).

- Retailers without a code of conduct (Table 16.6).

**Table 16.4 Health and beauty retailers with no operations in developing countries**

| Health and Beauty Retailer | Parent Company |
| --- | --- |
| Moss Chemists | Alliance-UniChem |

**Table 16.5 Health and beauty retailers with a code of conduct**

| Health & Beauty Retailers | Parent Company | Contents of Code of Conduct | | | | | | | | | | | | | |
| --- | --- | --- | --- | --- | --- | --- | --- | --- | --- | --- | --- | --- | --- | --- | --- |
| | | Forced labour | Collective bargaining | Freedom of association | Health and safety | Child labour | Wages | Working hours | Equality | Job security | Harsh/inhumane treatment | Mandatory? | Independently inspected? | Member of ETI? | Own fair trade products? |
| Boots the Chemist | The Boots Company | X | | X | X | X | X | X | X | | X | X | | | |
| National Co-operative Chemists | National Co-operative Chemists | X | | X | X | X | X | X | | X | | X | X | X | |
| The Body Shop | The Body Shop International | X | X | X | X | X | X | X | X | X | X | X | | X | X |

**Table 16.6 Health and beauty retailers without a code of conduct**

| Health and Beauty Retailers | Parent Company |
| --- | --- |
| Body Care | Bodycare (Health & Beauty) |
| Graham's Toiletries | Bodycare (Health & Beauty) |
| Hills | Lloyds Pharmacy Ltd |

| | |
|---|---|
| Lloyds Chemists | Lloyds Pharmacy Ltd |
| Lloyds Supersave | Lloyds Pharmacy Ltd |
| Lloydspharmacy | Lloyds Pharmacy Ltd |
| Lush | Lush Ltd |
| Peel Street Pharmacy | Lloyds Pharmacy Ltd |
| Savers Health & Beauty | Savers Health & Beauty Plc |
| Superdrug | Superdrug Stores Plc |
| UniChem | Alliance-UniChem |

# 17 | Home shopping

## Introduction

Home shopping covers all retailing sectors from clothes to financial service providers. Consumers can access home shopping in a number of ways. Using the post and telephone is common, as is door-to-door sales and group selling (for example Tupperware parties). In addition, Internet shopping is becoming increasingly popular.

Table 17.1 illustrates the main home shopping companies by size of sales.[1] Table 17.2 summarises the main catalogues from the main home shopping companies.[2] Many of the home shopping brands are hybrids of the high street retailers or vice versa. It is interesting to note that, in general, only the home shopping brands that have a high street presence have a code of conduct. Obviously much is still to be done for the other half of the home shopping brands. Issues of ethical and fair trade for the different types of goods are covered in the other chapters.

Retailers whose main activities are high street retailing but have a home shopping service (for example many of the clothing retailers) are not included here but are covered in the relevant chapters.

Table 17.1 Major home shopping retailers' sales (1998)

| Home Shopping Retailers | Sales (£ million) |
|---|---|
| GUS | 2,076.8 |
| Littlewoods | 1,533.6 |
| Freemans | 509.6 |
| Grattan | 499.7* |
| Empire Stores | 365.6 |
| N Brown | 317.9 |
| Flying Flowers | 45.3 |
| Total | 5,348.5 |

* 1997

Table 17.2 Main catalogues from home shopping retailers (1998)

| Company | Agency | Direct |
|---|---|---|
| N Brown | | Ambrose Wilson |
| | | Bury Boot & Shoe |
| | | Candid |
| | | Classic Combination |
| | | Fashion World |
| | | Fifty Plus |
| | | Heather Valley |
| | | J D Williams |
| | | Oxendales |
| | | Sander & Kay |
| | | Sartor |
| | | Shoe Tailor |
| | | Special Collection |
| | | Whitfords |
| Empire Stores | Empire | Anne Weyburn |
| | | Cyrillus |
| | | Daxon |
| | | La Redoute |
| | | Taillissime |
| | | Vertbaudet |
| Freemans | Freemans | One to One |
| Grattan | Grattan | Curiosity Shop |
| | Look Again | Kaleidoscope |
| | | Sensations |
| | | The Collection |
| GUS | Great Universal | Home Free |
| | Kays | Innovations |
| | Choice | McCord |
| Littlewoods | Littlewoods | Index Extra |
| | Peter Craig | |
| | Janet Fraser | |

## Home shopping companies' ratings

**Table 17.3 Five-star rating system of retailers**

| Symbol | Explanation |
|---|---|
| 5 stars | 1. Company has a published comprehensive code of conduct. |
| | 2. Company has independent inspectors of factories for compliance with code of conduct. |
| | 3. Company has a comprehensive public reporting system detailing number of factories/suppliers in developing countries and results of inspections. |
| | 4. Company has own fair trade scheme for all or some products. |
| | 5. Company has demonstrated that it is moving beyond implementing basic human and working rights in factories/suppliers and acting on sustainable development values. |
| 4 stars | 1. Company has a published comprehensive code of conduct. |
| | 2. Company has independent inspectors of factories for compliance with code of conduct. |
| | 3. Company has a comprehensive public reporting system detailing number of factories/suppliers in developing countries and results of inspections. |
| | 4. Company has own fair trade scheme for all or some products. |
| 3 stars | 1. Company has a published comprehensive code of conduct. |
| | 2. Company has independent inspectors of factories for compliance with code of conduct. |
| | 3. Company has a comprehensive public reporting system detailing number of factories/suppliers in developing countries and results of inspections. |
| 2 stars | 1. Company has a published comprehensive code of conduct. |
| | 2. Company has independent inspectors of factories for compliance with code of conduct. |
| 1 star | 1. Company has a published (available to the public via Web site or shops or on products) comprehensive code of conduct. |
| ½ star | Company has a code of conduct or is developing a code of conduct. |
| # | Company without own-brand products. |
| > | Company has no operations in developing countries. |
| X | Company has no code of conduct. |

Table 17.4 Five-star ratings for home shopping companies

| Symbol | Home Shopping Companies |
|---|---|
| 5 stars | None |
| 4 stars | Traidcraft |
| 3 stars | None |
| 2 stars | Dorothy Perkins |
| | Hawkshead |
| | Racing Green |
| 1 star | Burlington |
| | Choice* |
| | Great Universal* |
| | Index Extra |
| | Innovations* |
| | Janet Fraser |
| | John Moores |
| | Kays* |
| | Lands' End |
| | Littlewoods Hampers |
| | Marshall Ward* |
| | Morses* |
| | Peter Craig |
| ½ star | Andre de Brett |
| | Avon |
| | Cyrillus |
| | Damart |
| | Daxon |
| | Empire |
| | La Redoute |
| | Miller |
| | Next Directory |
| | Studio |
| | Vert Baudet |
| | WebbIvory |
| # | None |
| > | None |
| X | Ace |

Ambrose Wilson
Amway
Betterware
Candid
Classic Combination
Eddie Bauer
Farepak Hampers
Fashion World
Freemans
Grattan
Home Farm Hampers
J D Williams
Kaleidoscope
Kleeneze
Lakeland
Look Again
QVC The Shopping Channel

* independent inspections but poor code of conduct

Example codes of conduct from home shopping companies are set out in the Appendix.

## Detailed survey results

The survey results are presented in the tables below:

- Those retailers that do have suppliers in developing countries and have a code of conduct (Table 17.5). This table summarises the contents of their codes of conduct, covering issues such as freedom to join employee associations, child labour, forced labour and violence against employees. In addition, it covers whether the code of conduct is mandatory for all the retailer's suppliers, if compliance by suppliers to the code of conduct is checked by independent (to the retailer and the suppliers) inspectors and finally if the retailer is a member of the Ethical Trading Initiative (see Chapter 2).
- Retailers without a code of conduct (Table 17.6).

Table 17.5 Home shopping companies with a code of conduct

| Home Shopping Company | Parent Company | Contents of Code of Conduct | | | | | | | | | | | | |
|---|---|---|---|---|---|---|---|---|---|---|---|---|---|---|
| | | Forced labour | Collective bargaining | Freedom of association | Health and safety | Child labour | Wages | Working hours | Equality | Job security | Harsh/inhumane treatment | Mandatory? | Independently inspected? | Member of ETI? |
| Andre de Brett | Thermawear Ltd | * | | | | | | | | | | X | | |
| Avon | Avon Cosmetics Ltd | * | | | | | | | | | | X | X | |
| Burlington | Littlewoods Home Shopping | X | X | X | X | X | X | X | X | X | X | X | | X |
| Choice | Great Universal Stores Plc | X | X | X | | X | | | X | X | | | | |
| Cyrillus | Empire Stores Group (Redcats) | + | | | | X | | | X | | | | | |
| Damart | Thermawear Ltd | * | | | | | | | | | | | | |
| Daxon | Empire Stores Group (Redcats) | + | | | | X | | | X | | | | | |
| Dorothy Perkins | Arcadia | X | | X | X | X | X | X | X | | X | X | X | |
| Empire | Empire Stores Group (Redcats) | + | | | | X | | | X | | | | | |
| Great Universal | Great Universal Stores Plc | X | X | X | | X | | | X | X | | | | |
| Hawkshead | Arcadia | X | | X | X | X | X | X | X | | X | X | X | |
| Index Extra | Littlewoods Home Shopping | X | X | X | X | X | X | X | X | X | X | X | | X |
| Innovations | Great Universal Stores Plc | X | X | X | | X | | | X | X | | | | |
| Janet Fraser | Littlewoods Home Shopping | X | X | X | X | X | X | X | X | X | X | X | | X |
| John Moores | Littlewoods Home Shopping | X | X | X | X | X | X | X | X | X | X | X | | X |
| Kays | Great Universal Stores Plc | X | X | X | | X | | | X | X | | | | |

| | | | | | | | | | | | | | | |
|---|---|---|---|---|---|---|---|---|---|---|---|---|---|---|
| Lands' End | Lands' End Direct Merchants | X | | X | X | X | X | | X | | X | X | | |
| La Redoute | Empire Stores Group (Redcats) | + | | | | X | | | X | | | | | |
| Littlewoods Hampers | Littlewoods Home Shopping | X | X | X | X | X | X | X | X | X | X | X | | X |
| Marshall Ward | Great Universal Stores Plc | X | X | X | | X | | | X | X | | | | |
| Miller | Fine Art Developments Plc | X | | | X | X | X | | | | | X | | |
| Morses | Great Universal Stores Plc | X | X | X | | X | | | X | X | | | | |
| Next Directory | Next Directory | X | X | X | X | X | X | X | X | X | X | | | |
| Peter Craig | Littlewoods Home Shopping | X | X | X | X | X | X | X | X | X | X | X | | X |
| Racing Green | Arcadia | X | | X | X | X | X | X | X | | X | X | X | |
| Studio | Fine Art Developments Plc | X | | | X | X | X | | | | | X | | |
| Traidcraft | Traidcraft | X | X | X | X | X | X | X | X | X | X | X | X | X |
| Vert Baudet | Empire Stores Group (Redcats) | + | | | | X | | | X | | | | | |
| WebbIvory | Fine Art Developments Plc | X | | | X | X | X | | | | | X | | |

* code of conduct unavailable

+ complies with ILO standards and guidelines but unspecified

**Table 17.6 Home shopping companies with no code of conduct**

| Home Shopping Company | Parent Company |
|---|---|
| Ace | Fine Art Developments Plc |
| Ambrose Wilson | N Brown Group Plc |
| Amway | Amway (UK) Ltd |
| Betterware | Betterware UK Ltd |
| Candid | N Brown Group Plc |
| Classic Combination | N Brown Group Plc |
| Eddie Bauer | Grattan Plc |
| Farepak Hampers | Kleeneze Plc |

| | |
|---|---|
| Fashion World | N Brown Group Plc |
| Freemans | Freemans Plc |
| Grattan | Grattan Plc |
| Home Farm Hampers | Kleeneze Plc |
| J D Williams | N Brown Group Plc |
| Kaleidoscope | Grattan Plc |
| Kleeneze | Kleeneze Plc |
| Lakeland | Lakeland Ltd |
| Look Again | Grattan Plc |
| QVC The Shopping Channel | QVC Ltd |

# 18 | Household retailers

## Introduction

Housewares range from kitchenware and cookware to household products such as lighting. They are becoming increasingly available in most retailers because of their affordability and 'add-on' sales value for the host retailers. This chapter concentrates on retailers that principally sell housewares. Table 18.1 illustrates the retailers that consumers bought housewares from in 1999.[1] As with DIY and home shopping retailers, the range of products available in this sector is large and much of it is made in developing countries.

Table 18.1 Customers purchasing houseware by retailer in 1999

| Retailers | % |
|---|---|
| Argos | 16 |
| Woolworths | 12 |
| DIY superstore | 12 |
| IKEA | 11 |
| Bhs | 8 |
| Marks & Spencer | 8 |
| John Lewis | 7 |
| Boots | 7 |
| Debenhams | 6 |
| Gift shop | 5 |
| Craft shop/craft fair | 5 |
| Market stall | 5 |
| Other department store | 4 |
| Other general housewares shop | 4 |
| Tesco | 4 |
| Discount store | 4 |

| | |
|---|---|
| Mail order/direct | 4 |
| Habitat | 3 |
| MFI Homeworks | 3 |
| The Reject Shop | 3 |
| Hardware shop | 3 |
| Sainsbury's | 3 |
| Other supermarket | 3 |
| Next | 2 |
| The Pier | 2 |
| Furniture/soft furnishings/linen shop | 2 |
| Cargo | 1 |
| Kitchen shop | 1 |
| Elsewhere | 10 |
| Have not bought any in the last 12 months | 31 |
| Don't know | 1 |

## Initiatives

Argos, Index, Marks & Spencer and Past Times have codes of conduct, while a newcomer to the UK, MUJI, is developing one. It is disappointing that the second largest company in this sector, Woolworths, has not developed a code of conduct. Littlewoods Index has gone furthest to implement its code of conduct. The other companies have patchy coverage of the issues and do not publicly report progress.

## Household retailers' rankings

Table 18.2 Five-star rating system of retailers

| Symbol | Explanation |
|---|---|
| 5 stars | 1. Company has a published comprehensive code of conduct.<br>2. Company has independent inspectors of factories for compliance with code of conduct.<br>3. Company has a comprehensive public reporting system detailing number of factories/suppliers in developing countries and results of inspections. |

| | |
|---|---|
| | 4. Company has own fair trade scheme for all or some products.<br>5. Company has demonstrated that it is moving beyond implementing basic human and working rights in factories/suppliers and acting on sustainable development values. |
| 4 stars | 1. Company has a published comprehensive code of conduct.<br>2. Company has independent inspectors of factories for compliance with code of conduct.<br>3. Company has a comprehensive public reporting system detailing number of factories/suppliers in developing countries and results of inspections.<br>4. Company has own fair trade scheme for all or some products. |
| 3 stars | 1. Company has a published comprehensive code of conduct.<br>2. Company has independent inspectors of factories for compliance with code of conduct.<br>3. Company has a comprehensive public reporting system detailing number of factories/suppliers in developing countries and results of inspections. |
| 2 stars | 1. Company has a published comprehensive code of conduct.<br>2. Company has independent inspectors of factories for compliance with code of conduct. |
| 1 star | 1. Company has a published (available to the public via Web site or shops or on products) comprehensive code of conduct. |
| ½ star | Company has a code of conduct or is developing a code of conduct. |
| # | Company without own-brand products. |
| > | Company has no operations in developing countries. |
| X | Company has no code of conduct. |

**Table 18.3 Five-star ratings of household retailers**

| Symbol | Household Retailers |
|---|---|
| 5 stars | None |
| 4 stars | None |
| 3 stars | None |
| 2 stars | None |
| 1 star | Argos* |
| | Littlewoods Index |

| | |
|---|---|
| | Marks & Spencer |
| ½ star | MUJI |
| | Past Times |
| # | Trago Mills |
| > | None |
| X | QD Stores |
| | Woolworths |

* has independent inspections but poor coverage in code of conduct

Example codes of conduct from household retailers are set out in the Appendix.

## Detailed survey results

The survey results are presented in the tables below:

- Retailers with no own-brand products (Table 18.4).
- Those retailers that do have suppliers in developing countries and have a code of conduct (Table 18.5). This table summarises the content of their codes of conduct, covering issues such as freedom to join employee associations, child labour, forced labour and violence against employees. In addition, it covers whether the code of conduct is mandatory for all the retailer's suppliers, if compliance by suppliers to the code of conduct is checked by independent (to the retailer and the suppliers) inspectors and finally if the retailer is a member of the Ethical Trading Initiative (see Chapter 2).
- Retailers that are developing a code of conduct (Table 18.6).
- Retailers that do not have a code of conduct (Table 18.7).

Table 18.4 Household retailers with no own-brand products

| Household Retailer | Parent company |
|---|---|
| Trago Mills | Trago Mills Ltd |

## Table 18.5 Household retailers with a code of conduct

| Household Retailers | Parent Company | Forced labour | Collective bargaining | Freedom of association | Health and safety | Child labour | Wages | Working hours | Equality | Job security | Harsh/inhumane treatment | Mandatory? | Independently inspected? | Member of ETI? |
|---|---|---|---|---|---|---|---|---|---|---|---|---|---|---|
| | | **Contents of Code of Conduct** | | | | | | | | | | | | |
| Argos | GUS | | | | X | X | X | | X | | | X | X | |
| Littlewoods Index | The LittlewoodsX Organisation | X | X | X | X | X | X | X | X | X | X | | X | |
| Marks & Spencer | Marks & Spencer Plc | | X | X | X | X | X | X | | | | X | | X |
| Past Times | Historical Collections Group Ltd | X | | | | X | X | | | | X | | | |

## Table 18.6 Household retailers developing a code of conduct

| Household Retailer | Parent Company |
|---|---|
| MUJI | MUJI |

## Table 18.7 Household retailers without a code of conduct

| Household Retailers | Parent Company |
|---|---|
| QD Stores | QD Stores Ltd |
| Woolworths | Woolworths Plc |

# 19 | Jewellers

## Introduction

One of the longest-established retailing trades depends on gold and diamonds mined in some of the most volatile and exploitative areas of the world. A total of 85 per cent of world gold production is used for jewellery.[1] Profitable jewellers tend to have some of the highest net margins of any retail sector.[2] Table 19.1 summarises the major jewellers' sales.[3]

Table 19.1 Major jewellers' sales (1998)

| Jewellers | Sales (£ million) |
|---|---|
| Signet | 352.4 |
| Asprey Group | 216.9* |
| Goldsmiths | 79.9 |
| F Hinds | 42.6* |
| Adlestones | 33.2* |
| Fred Hill | 21.6 |
| Total | 746.6 |

* 1997

## Working conditions

The jewellery trade often props up oppressive regimes, with workers frequently working in dangerous conditions for low wages.[4] In Indonesia the largest gold mine in the world exists, producing $7.2 million worth of gold per day (along with 110,000 tonnes of waste including cyanide effluent).[5] Here indigenous land claims and workers' rights have little importance and the multinational corporations' owners are not obliged to provide adequate housing and facilities.[6] In South Africa the legacy of apartheid is not being addressed adequately, with labour conditions, inspection and enforcement remaining poor.[7] Diamond mining likewise creates dangerous and low-paid jobs often in oppressive regimes[8] and has played a part in the civil wars in parts of Africa, including Angola and Sierra Leone.[9]

The jewellers below mostly purchase gold and diamonds through international markets such as Amsterdam rather than direct from the mines. It is therefore unsurprising that none of the jewellers surveyed has an ethical sourcing policy. The gold and diamond industry can be compared to the coffee industry in this sense. As with the coffee industry, the consumer can however purchase jewellery that has been fairly traded. At the moment this only extends to gems purchased through two companies, Salon Gems (USA) and Fair Diamonds (Germany). A mining cooperative in Lesotho (southern Africa) is helped with equipment such as scales, and a cutters' cooperative in India has concentrated on trying to ensure that adults are paid a fair wage, so that children do not have to work.[10] Both companies return a percentage (25 to 50 per cent) of the price to the producers.

It is disappointing that only a few jewellers surveyed for this book have started to develop a code of conduct. The majority have not started to think about tackling the poor working conditions that the gold and diamonds they sell are mined and processed in by trying to source direct or by forcing the multinational organisations (who own most of the mines) to improve working conditions. Some action is being taken on the issue of 'conflict diamonds' (diamonds sold by rebel movements to fund military campaigns) by the International Diamond Manufacturers' Association and the World Federation of Diamond Bourses (bourses being trade associations). These two organisations have agreed a system of voluntary certification for rough diamonds. This will entail the identification of the country of origin of uncut stones with a new international diamond organisation monitoring the trade. Unfortunately this scheme is only as good as the diamond mining country's border controls and the reality is that many of these countries are involved in civil unrest.

## Jewellers' rankings

Table 19.2 Five-star rating system of retailers

| Symbol | Explanation |
|---|---|
| 5 stars | 1. Company has a published comprehensive code of conduct.<br>2. Company has independent inspectors of factories for compliance with code of conduct.<br>3. Company has a comprehensive public reporting system detailing number of factories/suppliers in developing countries and results of inspections.<br>4. Company has own fair trade scheme for all or some products.<br>5. Company has demonstrated that it is moving beyond implementing basic human and working rights in factories/suppliers and acting on sustainable development values. |
| 4 stars | 1. Company has a published comprehensive code of conduct.<br>2. Company has independent inspectors of factories for compliance with code of conduct.<br>3. Company has a comprehensive public reporting system detailing number of factories/suppliers in developing countries and results of inspections.<br>4. Company has own fair trade scheme for all or some products. |
| 3 stars | 1. Company has a published comprehensive code of conduct.<br>2. Company has independent inspectors of factories for compliance with code of conduct.<br>3. Company has a comprehensive public reporting system detailing number of factories/suppliers in developing countries and results of inspections. |
| 2 stars | 1. Company has a published comprehensive code of conduct.<br>2. Company has independent inspectors of factories for compliance with code of conduct. |
| 1 star | 1. Company has a published (available to the public via Web site or shops or on products) comprehensive code of conduct. |
| ½ star | Company has a code of conduct or is developing a code of conduct. |
| # | Company without own-brand products. |
| > | Company has no operations in developing countries. |
| X | Company has no code of conduct. |

Table 19.3 Five-star ratings for jewellers

| Symbol | Jewellers |
| --- | --- |
| 5 stars | None |
| 4 stars | None |
| 3 stars | None |
| 2 stars | None |
| 1 star | None |
| ½ star | Ernest Jones |
| | Goldsmiths |
| | H Samuel |
| | Leslie Davis |
| # | Asprey & Garrard |
| | Half Price Jewellers |
| > | None |
| X | Adlestones |
| | Beaverbrooks |
| | Bow Bangles |
| | Claire's Accessories |
| | F Hinds |
| | Mappin & Webb |
| | Northern Goldsmiths |
| | Walker & Hall |
| | Warren James |
| | Watches of Switzerland |

Example codes of conduct from jewellers are set out in the Appendix.

## Detailed survey results

The survey results are presented in the tables below:

- Retailers that do not sell own-brand products (Table 19.4).
- Retailers developing a code of conduct (Table 19.5).
- Retailers without a code of conduct (Table 19.6).

Table 19.4 Jewellers with no own-brand products

| Jewellers | Parent Company |
|---|---|
| Asprey & Garrard | Asprey & Garrard Ltd |
| Half Price Jewellers | HPJ UK Ltd |

Table 19.5 Jewellers developing a code of conduct

| Jewellers | Parent Company |
|---|---|
| Ernest Jones | Signet Group Plc |
| Goldsmiths | Goldsmith Group Ltd |
| H Samuel | Signet Group Plc |
| Leslie Davis | Signet Group Plc |

Table 19.6 Jewellers without a code of conduct

| Jewellers | Parent Company |
|---|---|
| Adlestones | Beaverbrooks the Jewellers Ltd |
| Beaverbrooks | Beaverbrooks the Jewellers Ltd |
| Bow Bangles | Claire's Accessories (UK) Ltd |
| Claire's Accessories | Claire's Accessories (UK) Ltd |
| F Hinds | F Hinds |
| Mappin & Webb | Watches of Switzerland Ltd |
| Northern Goldsmiths | Goldsmith Group Ltd |
| Walker & Hall | Goldsmith Group Ltd |
| Warren James | Warren James (Jewellers) Ltd |
| Watches of Switzerland | Watches of Switzerland Ltd |

# 20 | Sports retailers

## Introduction

Most sports goods in the UK are manufactured in developing countries. Not surprisingly, therefore, there has been a range of campaigns against some of the big brand names such as Nike and Adidas. Many of the retailers in the UK do not sell own-brand products but do sell other branded products such as Nike and Adidas. Of the ones that do sell own-brand products, only the Blacks Leisure Group and JJB Sports have a formal code of conduct. This makes clear that ethical trade international campaigns have neglected retailers' own-brand products and have instead concentrated on brand products. Table 20.1 sets out the retailers from which consumers buy their sports goods.[1] It can be seen that own-brand sports wear accounts for about 30 to 40 per cent of the market.

The survey in this chapter concentrates on retailers mainly selling sports goods – other types of retailers are covered in other chapters. Retailers with own-brand sports goods should learn from the experiences of Nike and Adidas and implement codes of conduct before international attention widens to include them.

Table 20.1 Retailers used by buyers of sports goods in 2000

| Sports Retailers | % |
|---|---|
| JJB Sports | 38 |
| Local independent sports shop (excl Intersport) | 22 |
| Allsports | 15 |
| JD Sports | 15 |
| Mail order | 15 |
| Somewhere else | 13 |

| | |
|---|---|
| Other multiple sports shop chain | 12 |
| Sports Division | 11 |
| Marks & Spencer | 10 |
| Footwear shop | 10 |
| Millets | 8 |
| Intersport | 7 |
| Other variety store (eg Bhs, Littlewoods) | 7 |
| Department store | 7 |
| Factory outlet | 7 |
| Club shop (excl football) | 6 |
| Market stall | 6 |
| Clothing shop | 6 |
| C&A | 5 |
| Catalogue showroom (eg Argos, Index) | 5 |
| Bought from abroad on holiday | 5 |
| Blacks, First Sport or Active Venture | 3 |
| Internet | 2 |
| Bought second-hand | 2 |
| Supermarket | * |
| Football club shop | * |

* figures not available

## Sports retailers' rankings

**Table 20.2 Five-star rating system of retailers**

| Symbol | Explanation |
|---|---|
| 5 stars | 1. Company has a published comprehensive code of conduct.<br>2. Company has independent inspectors of factories for compliance with code of conduct.<br>3. Company has a comprehensive public reporting system detailing number of factories/suppliers in developing countries and results of inspections.<br>4. Company has own fair trade scheme for all or some products.<br>5. Company has demonstrated that it is moving beyond implementing basic human and working rights in factories/suppliers and acting on sustainable development values. |

| | |
|---|---|
| 4 stars | 1. Company has a published comprehensive code of conduct.<br>2. Company has independent inspectors of factories for compliance with code of conduct.<br>3. Company has a comprehensive public reporting system detailing number of factories/suppliers in developing countries and results of inspections.<br>4. Company has own fair trade scheme for all or some products. |
| 3 stars | 1. Company has a published comprehensive code of conduct.<br>2. Company has independent inspectors of factories for compliance with code of conduct.<br>3. Company has a comprehensive public reporting system detailing number of factories/suppliers in developing countries and results of inspections. |
| 2 stars | 1. Company has a published comprehensive code of conduct.<br>2. Company has independent inspectors of factories for compliance with code of conduct. |
| 1 star | 1. Company has a published (available to the public via Web site or shops or on products) comprehensive code of conduct. |
| ½ star | Company has a code of conduct or is developing a code of conduct. |
| # | Company without own-brand products. |
| > | Company has no operations in developing countries. |
| X | Company has no code of conduct. |

**Table 20.3 Five-star ratings of sports retailers**

| Symbol | Sports Retailers |
|---|---|
| 5 stars | None |
| 4 stars | None |
| 3 stars | None |
| 2 stars | None |
| 1 star | JJB Sports |
| ½ star | Blacks Outdoor |
| | Field and Trek |
| | First Sport |
| | Free Spirit |
| | Millets |

| | |
|---|---|
| | O'Neills |
| | Pure Woman |
| | YHA Adventure Shops |
| # | Allsports |
| | American Golf Discount |
| | Ath-Leisure |
| | Cotsworld |
| | Ellis Brigham Mountain Sports |
| | Gilesports |
| | JD Footwear |
| | JD Junior |
| | JD Sports |
| | JD Woman |
| | Nevisport |
| | The Outdoor People |
| | Wilderness Ways |
| > | None |
| X | Famous Army Stores |
| | Footlocker |
| | Intersport GB |
| | Lillywhites |
| | Outdoor Venture |
| | Sports Connection* |
| | The Bike Chain |
| | Work and Leisure |

* no own-brand products but have some product specifications specific to their company

Example codes of conduct from sports retailers are set out in the Appendix.

## Detailed survey results

The survey results are presented in the tables below:

- Retailers without own-brand products (Table 20.4).
- Those retailers that do have suppliers in developing countries and have a code of conduct (Table 20.5). This table summarises

the contents of their codes of conduct, covering issues such as freedom to join employee associations, child labour, forced labour and violence against employees. In addition, it covers whether the code of conduct is mandatory for all the retailer's suppliers, if compliance by suppliers to the code of conduct is checked by independent (to the retailer and the suppliers) inspectors and finally if the retailer is a member of the Ethical Trading Initiative (see Chapter 2).

- Retailers without a code of conduct (Table 20.6).

**Table 20.4 Sports retailers with no own-brand products**

| Sports Retailers | Parent Company |
|---|---|
| Allsports | Allsports Retail Ltd |
| American Golf Discount | American Golf |
| Ath-Leisure | JD Sports Plc |
| Cotsworld | Cotsworld Outdoor Ltd |
| Ellis Brigham Mountain Sports | Ellis Brigham Ltd |
| Gilesports | Gilesports Plc |
| JD Footwear | JD Sports Plc |
| JD Junior | JD Sports Plc |
| JD Sports | JD Sports Plc |
| JD Woman | JD Sports Plc |
| Nevisport | Nevisport Ltd |
| The Outdoor People | Cotsworld Outdoor Ltd |
| Wilderness Ways | Nevisport Ltd |

**Table 20.5 Sports retailers with a code of conduct**

| Sports Retailers | Parent Company | Forced labour | Collective bargaining | Freedom of association | Health and safety | Child labour | Wages | Working hours | Equality | Job security | Harsh/inhumane treatment | Mandatory? | Independently inspected? | Member of ETI? |
|---|---|---|---|---|---|---|---|---|---|---|---|---|---|---|
| | | Contents of Code of Conduct | | | | | | | | | | | | |
| Blacks Outdoor | Blacks Leisure Group Plc | * | | | | | | | | | | | | |
| Field and Trek | Field and Trek Plc | # | | | | | | | | | | | | |
| First Sport | Blacks Leisure Group Plc | * | | | | | | | | | | | | |
| Free Spirit | Blacks Leisure Group Plc | * | | | | | | | | | | | | |
| JJB Sports | JJB Sports Plc | X | X | X | X | X | X | X | X | | X | X | | |
| Millets | Blacks Leisure Group Plc | * | | | | | | | | | | | | |
| O'Neills | Blacks Leisure Group Plc | * | | | | | | | | | | | | |
| Pure Woman | Blacks Leisure Group Plc | * | | | | | | | | | | | | |
| YHA Adventure Shops | YHA Adventure Shops Plc | + | | | | | | | | | | | | |

* code of conduct unavailable

# try to be socially responsible but too small to implement a code of conduct

+ inspections but no formal code of conduct

**Table 20.6 Sports retailers without a code of conduct**

| Sports Retailers | Parent Company |
|---|---|
| Famous Army Stores | Famous Army Stores Ltd |
| Footlocker | Footlocker |
| Intersport GB | Intersport |
| Lillywhites | Lillywhites Ltd |
| Outdoor Venture | Famous Army Stores Ltd |
| Sports Connection | Sports Connection |
| The Bike Chain | YHA Adventure Shops Plc |
| Work and Leisure | Famous Army Stores Ltd |

# 21 | Toy retailers

## Introduction

The devastating truth about the manufacture of toys is that children in the developed world can be playing with toys that were made by other children in developing countries. Toys are big business and most of the retailers selling mostly toys sell their own-brand products. Table 21.1 shows that these retailers control approximately 30 per cent of the UK market.[1] Household retailers and catalogue showrooms have a similar share of the market. The type of toys and games is illustrated in Table 21.2, which shows that babies are the top target for retailers.[2]

Table 21.1 Market share by sales of retailer types in 2000

| Toy Retailers | % |
|---|---|
| Toy shops | 28 |
| Household retailers | 24 |
| Catalogue showrooms | 22 |
| Mail order | 7 |
| Superstores | 6 |
| Department stores | 5 |
| Others | 8 |

Table 21.2 UK retail sales of toys and games by type in 2000

| Type of Toy | % |
|---|---|
| Infant/pre-school | 17 |
| Games and puzzles | 14 |
| Activity toys | 14 |

| | |
|---|---|
| Dolls | 10 |
| Plush (soft toys) | 9 |
| Male action | 8 |
| Vehicles | 7 |
| Ride-ons | 5 |
| Others | 16 |

## Initiatives

Toy retailers seem to have done little to improve working conditions in developing countries and it is noteworthy that the worldwide brand Toys 'R' Us does not even have a code of conduct. This is particularly disappointing because it is an international brand selling millions of pounds worth of toys. The British Toy and Hobby Association (BTHA) and International Council of Toy Industries (ICTI) claim that manufacturers have to implement a code of conduct to be members of their associations. The downside is that the BTHA and ICTI do not monitor compliance but instead put the onus on the members to monitor their own activities.

The codes of conduct from the two organisations are set out in the boxes below.

### *British Toy and Hobby Association (BTHA) Code of Practice*[3]

Each member of the BTHA must sign the following form:

I/We undertake to the best of my/our ability to uphold the prestige of the Association and to further its objects for the welfare of the membership and the good name of the industry and trade as a whole, to use our best endeavours to comply with the Association's Vendor and Subcontractor Code of Conduct and declare my/our willingness to abide by the following code of practice as a condition of my/our membership of the Association:

1. I/We agree to market only products that conform to

BS5665/BS EN 71 and to exercise due diligence in regard to the safety of my/our products.

2. I/We agree to deal promptly with any enquiries as to the safety of my/our products and take effective action where appropriate; the Association will be notified immediately of any allegation by an enforcement authority that my/our products contravene the toy safety regulations.
3. I/We understand that a successful prosecution under the toy safety regulations will be regarded by the Association as a breach of this code and may render me/us liable to investigation under the BTHA complaints procedure.
4. I/We declare that I/we do not market counterfeit toys/hobbies and I/we understand that a judgement against me/us whether brought privately or otherwise for copyright or trade mark infringement may render me/us liable to investigation under the BTHA complaints procedure.
5. I/We undertake that all my/our advertising of toys in whatever form is legal, decent, honest and truthful and is in conformity with both the ITC's advertising code, which governs television and radio, and the British Code of Advertising Practice, which controls the majority of all other advertising.
6. I/We undertake that any toy gun, imitation or replica firearm modelled on a firearm designed or produced since 1898 is marked in accordance with the BTHA code for such product.
7. I/We understand that the Association reserves the right to refer breaches of this code to the independently constituted Complaints Committee which will report to the Council of the Association with recommendations as to the action to be taken.
8. I/We understand that wilful breaches of the code may lead to my/our expulsion from the Association, the denial of space at the British International Toy & Hobby Fair and the cancellation of the Lion Mark licence.

The members of the British Toy & Hobby Association (BTHA) have long recognised that they have a duty to ensure lawful, fair, safe and healthy working conditions for those employed in the contract manufacture of toys. To discharge this duty, BTHA members use their best efforts to construct supply agreements and/or working arrangements with vendors which require and maintain such conditions. Specific matters on which BTHA members require vendors' compliance are as follows.

**1. Labour**

The members of BTHA believe in the fair treatment and lawful compensation of workers. Accordingly, we believe that no forced, indentured or underage labour should be utilised to produce toys, wholly or in part. That means that employees must show up for work voluntarily, not be put at risk of harm and be fairly compensated all in accordance with the prevailing local laws. And we believe that due diligence should be exercised to ensure compliance.

Therefore, the BTHA Council recommends that, in those circumstances deemed appropriate, BTHA members will ensure:

- a) That on site inspections be conducted regularly at all facilities used to produce toys and toys' components, including the facilities of contractors and subcontractors, to determine whether any forced, indentured or underage labour is employed.
- b) That contractors and subcontractors certify that no forced, indentured or underage workers are employed to produce goods, wholly or in part.
- c) That, when appropriate, letters of credit include among the conditions of payment a certification by the supplier that no forced, indentured or underage labour was used to produce the covered merchandise or any parts thereof.
- d) That contracts state the furnishing of merchandise made in whole or in part by forced, indentured or underage labour

is a breach of contract for which the contract may be cancelled and damages assessed.

- e) That contracts for merchandise not covered by a letter of credit require the presentation of a signed and dated certificate stating that no forced, indentured or underage labour was used to produce the covered merchandise or any parts thereof.
- f) That local legislation on underaged labour is complied with in all cases.

**2. Working conditions**

The BTHA also believes that toys should be manufactured in a safe, hygienic working environment. Its members will, therefore, avoid using vendors where working conditions are unacceptably poor and will seek to ensure, principally through continuing dialogue with its vendors and an open attitude towards worker representation, that:

- a) Factory working conditions are well ventilated, with comfortable, well lit work stations.
- b) Fire exits are adequate and well identified and employees are trained for emergency evacuation, if required. The use of safety equipment and instruction should be emphasised.
- c) Professional medical assistance should be available with specified employees trained for emergency needs.
- d) Employee living quarters, food, clothing allowance or other provision should be adequate to meet the standards of the job.
- e) Business will not be provided to supplier vendors who subject employees to unhealthy, unsafe conditions or employ unreasonable mental or physical disciplinary practices.
- f) Vendors will be encouraged to establish education or training programmes for employees in basic health and hygiene.

**3. Other**

BTHA members will also do their best to ensure that:

- a) All vendors and subcontractors comply with the national laws of the country in which the business is being conducted. Such legislation is to include, but is not limited to, building safety, fire code rules, employment standards, employee health and safety regulation.
- b) Employee working hours should be governed by local standards but are not to be more than 60 hours per week for full-time employment. Each employee should have at least one day off during every 7 day working week.
- c) Part-time or temporary employment will be governed by local and national regulations. Hours worked on a temporary basis should not exceed those for full employment.
- d) Employees should be paid in accordance with local and/or national laws and will be paid overtime as earned in accordance with such legislation.

This code will be administered to direct contractors, who in turn will be required to supervise their subcontractors in the same terms.

*The International Council of Toy Industries (ICTI) Code of Business Practices*[4]

The International Council of Toy Industries (ICTI), an association of associations, is committed on behalf of its member companies to the operation of toy factories in a lawful, safe, and healthful manner. It upholds the principles that no underage, forced, or prison labour* should be employed; that no one is denied a job because of gender, ethnic origin, religion, affiliation or association, and that factories comply with laws protecting the environment. Supply agreements with firms manufacturing on behalf of ICTI members must also provide for adherence to these principles.

The role of ICTI is to inform, educate and survey its members so that individual member companies can adhere to its Code of Business Practices. As an association, it also acts to encourage local and national governments to enforce wage and hour laws and factory health and safety laws.

Specific operating conditions that member companies are expected to meet and obtain contractor agreement in advance are as follows:

- Labour
  a. that working hours per week, wages and overtime pay practices comply with the standards set by law or, in the absence of a law, address humane, safe and productive working conditions;
  b. that no one under the legal minimum age is employed in any stage of toy manufacturing; that a minimum age of 14 applies in all circumstances, but notwithstanding the foregoing, that C138 Minimum Age Convention (1973) and C182 Worst Forms of Child Labour Convention (1999) of the International Labour Organisation apply;
  c. that no forced or prison labour is employed*, that workers are free to leave once their shift ends, and that guards are posted only for normal security reasons;
  d. that all workers are entitled to sick and maternity benefits as provided by law;
  e. that all workers are entitled to freely exercise their rights of employee representation as provided by local law.
- The workplace
  a. that toy factories provide a safe working environment for their employees and comply with or exceed all applicable local laws concerning sanitation and risk protection;
  b. that the factory is properly lighted and ventilated and that aisles and exits are accessible at all times;
  c. that there is adequate medical assistance available in emergencies, and that designated employees are trained in first aid procedures;

d. that there are adequate and well-identified emergency exits, and that all employees are trained in emergency evacuation;
e. that protective safety equipment is available and employees are trained in its use;
f. that safeguards on machinery meet or exceed local laws;
g. that there are adequate toilet facilities which meet local hygiene requirements, and that they are properly maintained;
h. that there are facilities or appropriate provisions for meals and other breaks;
i. if a factory provides housing for its employees, it will ensure that dormitory rooms and sanitary facilities meet basic needs, are adequately ventilated and meet fire safety and other local laws;
j. that no mental or physical disciplinary practices are employed.

- Compliance
a. The purpose of this Code is to establish a standard of performance, to educate, and to encourage commitment to responsible manufacturing, not to punish.
b. To determine adherence, ICTI member companies will evaluate their own facilities as well as those of their contractors. They will examine all books and records and conduct on-site inspections of the facilities, and request that their contractors follow the same practices with subcontractors.
c. An annual statement of compliance with this Code must be signed by an officer of each manufacturing company or contractor.
d. Contracts for the manufacture of toys should provide that a material failure to comply with the Code or to implement a corrective action plan on a timely basis is a breach of contract for which the contract may be cancelled.
e. Because of the great diversity in the kinds of toys manufactured and the manufacturing methods used, as well as the

wide range in factory sizes and numbers of employees, three annexes are attached to this Code to provide guidelines for determining compliance. A rule of reason must be used to determine applicability of the annex provisions.
f. This Code should be posted or available for all employees in the local language.

* Many countries recognise that prison labour is essential to the rehabilitation process. This provision prohibits the exportation of prison-made goods to countries that prohibit or restrict the importation of such goods.

## Toy retailers' rankings

**Table 21.3 Five-star rating system of retailers**

| Symbol | Explanation |
|---|---|
| 5 stars | 1. Company has a published comprehensive code of conduct. |
| | 2. Company has independent inspectors of factories for compliance with code of conduct. |
| | 3. Company has a comprehensive public reporting system detailing number of factories/suppliers in developing countries and results of inspections. |
| | 4. Company has own fair trade scheme for all or some products. |
| | 5. Company has demonstrated that it is moving beyond implementing basic human and working rights in factories/suppliers and acting on sustainable development values. |
| 4 stars | 1. Company has a published comprehensive code of conduct. |
| | 2. Company has independent inspectors of factories for compliance with code of conduct. |
| | 3. Company has a comprehensive public reporting system detailing number of factories/suppliers in developing countries and results of inspections. |
| | 4. Company has own fair trade scheme for all or some products. |
| 3 stars | 1. Company has a published comprehensive code of conduct. |

| | |
|---|---|
| | 2. Company has independent inspectors of factories for compliance with code of conduct. |
| | 3. Company has a comprehensive public reporting system detailing number of factories/suppliers in developing countries and results of inspections. |
| 2 stars | 1. Company has a published comprehensive code of conduct. |
| | 2. Company has independent inspectors of factories for compliance with code of conduct. |
| 1 star | 1. Company has a published (available to the public via Web site or shops or on products) comprehensive code of conduct. |
| ½ star | Company has a code of conduct or is developing a code of conduct. |
| # | Company without own-brand products. |
| > | Company has no operations in developing countries. |
| X | Company has no code of conduct. |

**Table 21.4 Five-star ratings of toy retailers**

| Symbol | Toy Retailers |
|---|---|
| 5 stars | None |
| 4 stars | None |
| 3 stars | None |
| 2 stars | Disney Store |
| 1 star | None |
| ½ star | Early Learning Centre |
| | Hamleys |
| | House of Toys |
| | Toy Stack |
| # | Beatties |
| | Electronics Boutique, GAME |
| > | Studio Stores |
| X | Toys 'R' Us |

Example codes of conduct from toy retailers are set out in the Appendix.

## Detailed survey results

The survey results are presented in the tables below:

- Retailers with no own-brand products (Table 21.5).
- Retailers with no operations in developing countries (Table 21.6).
- Those retailers that do have suppliers in developing countries and have a code of conduct (Table 21.7). This table summarises the contents of their codes of conduct, covering issues such as freedom to join employee associations, child labour, forced labour and violence against employees. In addition, it covers whether the code of conduct is mandatory for all the retailer's suppliers, if compliance by suppliers to the code of conduct is checked by independent (to the retailer and the suppliers) inspectors and finally if the retailer is a member of the Ethical Trading Initiative (see Chapter 2).
- Retailers without a code of conduct (Table 21.8).

**Table 21.5 Toy retailers with no own-brand products**

| Toy Retailers | Parent Company |
|---|---|
| Beatties | Beatties of London Ltd |
| Electronics Boutique, GAME | The Electronics Boutique Plc |

**Table 21.6 Toy retailers with no operations in developing countries**

| Toy Retailer | Parent Company |
|---|---|
| Studio Stores | Warner Bros Studio Stores Ltd |

Table 21.7 Toy retailers with a code of conduct

| Toy Retailers | Parent Company | Forced labour | Collective bargaining | Freedom of association | Health and safety | Child labour | Wages | Working hours | Equality | Job security | Harsh/inhumane treatment | Mandatory? | Independently inspected? | Member of ETI? |
|---|---|---|---|---|---|---|---|---|---|---|---|---|---|---|
| | | Contents of Code of Conduct | | | | | | | | | | | | |
| Disney Store | The Disney Stores Ltd | X | X | X | X | X | X | X | X | | X | X | X | |
| Early Learning Centre | Early Learning Centre | X | | | X | X | X | | | | | X | | |
| Hamleys | Hamleys of Regent Street Ltd | X | | X | X | X | X | X | X | | X | X | | |
| House of Toys | Hamleys of Regent Street Ltd | X | | X | X | X | X | X | X | | X | X | | |
| Toy Stack | Hamleys of Regent Street Ltd | X | | X | X | X | X | X | X | | X | X | | |

Table 21.8 Toy retailers without a code of conduct

| Toy Retailer | Parent Company |
|---|---|
| Toys 'R' Us | Toys 'R' Us Ltd |

# 22 | Summary of retailers' rankings

This chapter collates all the retailers' rankings into one table providing a one-stop reference for which retailers have, and which retailers do not have, a code of conduct. All retailers were ranked using the criteria set out in Table 22.1 except the financial service providers, which used the criteria in Table 22.2.

Figure 22.1 (below) summarises the proportions of retailers in the different categories of five-star ratings and clearly illustrates that the majority of the retailers – 75 per cent of all retailers or 89 per cent of retailers with own-brand products produced in developing countries – are below the '2 stars' category. This means that the majority of retailers do not have a code of conduct or are developing one or have one but without independent assurance of implementation. This shows a lack of concern by retailers about the working conditions under which their products are produced that at best shows ignorance of the problems and at worst is pure exploitation.

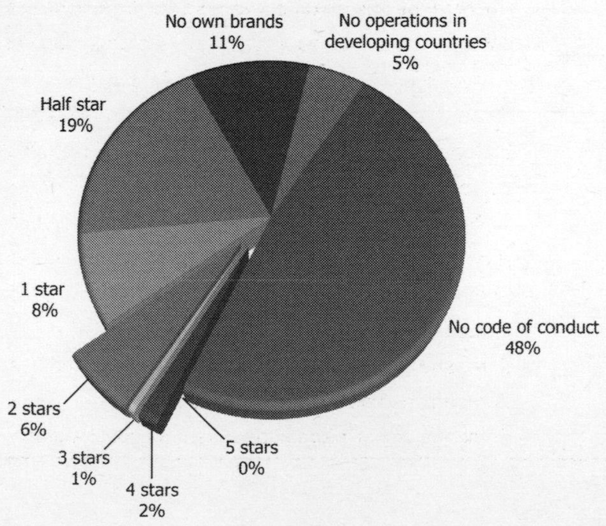

**Table 22.1 Criteria for retailers' rankings except financial service providers**

| Symbol | Explanation |
|---|---|
| 5 stars | 1. Company has a published comprehensive code of conduct.<br>2. Company has independent inspectors of factories for compliance with code of conduct.<br>3. Company has a comprehensive public reporting system detailing number of factories/suppliers in developing countries and results of inspections.<br>4. Company has own fair trade scheme for all or some products.<br>5. Company has demonstrated that it is moving beyond implementing basic human and working rights in factories/suppliers and acting on sustainable development values. |
| 4 stars | 1. Company has a published comprehensive code of conduct.<br>2. Company has independent inspectors of factories for compliance with code of conduct.<br>3. Company has a comprehensive public reporting system detailing number of factories/suppliers in developing countries and results of inspections.<br>4. Company has own fair trade scheme for all or some products. |
| 3 stars | 1. Company has a published comprehensive code of conduct.<br>2. Company has independent inspectors of factories for compliance with code of conduct.<br>3. Company has a comprehensive public reporting system detailing number of factories/suppliers in developing countries and results of inspections. |
| 2 stars | 1. Company has a published comprehensive code of conduct.<br>2. Company has independent inspectors of factories for compliance with code of conduct. |
| 1 star | 1. Company has a published (available to the public via Web site or shops or on products) comprehensive code of conduct. |
| ½ star | Company has a code of conduct or is developing a code of conduct. |
| # | Company without own-brand products. |
| > | Company has no operations in developing countries. |
| X | Company has no code of conduct. |
| Δ | Company wants information to remain confidential. |

Table 22.2 Criteria for ranking financial service providers

| Symbol | Explanation |
|---|---|
| 5 stars | 1. Company has a published ethical lending policy. |
| | 2. Company has published ethical lending policy that covers working conditions in developing countries. |
| | 3. Company has a comprehensive public reporting system containing results of lending policy. |
| | 4. Company has positive investment policies for specific projects tackling poverty and social exclusion. |
| | 5. Company has demonstrated that it is moving beyond ethical investment policies and acting on sustainable development values. |
| 4 stars | 1. Company has a published ethical lending policy. |
| | 2. Company has published ethical lending policy that covers working conditions in developing countries. |
| | 3. Company has a comprehensive public reporting system containing results of lending policy. |
| | 4. Company has positive investment policies for specific projects tackling poverty and social exclusion. |
| 3 stars | 1. Company has a published ethical lending policy. |
| | 2. Company has published ethical lending policy that covers working conditions in developing countries. |
| | 3. Company has a comprehensive public reporting system containing results of lending policy. |
| 2 stars | 1. Company has a published ethical lending policy. |
| | 2. Company has published ethical lending policy that covers working conditions in developing countries. |
| 1 star | 1. Company has a published ethical lending policy. |
| ½ star | Company has an ethical lending policy. |
| > | Company does not lend to companies. |
| X | Company has no ethical lending policy. |

**Table 22.3 The collated retailers' rankings**

| Symbol | Retailers | |
|---|---|---|
| 5 stars | None | |
| 4 stars | Co-op | Smile |
| | Co-operative Bank | Traidcraft |
| | The Body Shop International | Triodos Bank |
| 3 stars | B&Q | C&A |
| 2 stars | Abbey National | Principles |
| | Burton | Principles Menswear |
| | Disney Store | Racing Green |
| | Dorothy Perkins | Sainsbury's |
| | Evans | Shoefayre |
| | Hawkshead | Timberland |
| | Littlewoods | Top Man |
| | Miss Selfridge | Top Shop |
| | National Co-operative | Wade Smith |
| | Chemists | Wallis |
| | Primark | Warehouse |
| 1 star | Argos | Lands' End |
| | Asda | Littlewoods Hampers |
| | Burlington | Littlewoods Index |
| | Choice | Marks & Spencer |
| | Debenhams | (clothes and household) |
| | Gap | Marshall Ward |
| | Great Universal | Monsoon |
| | Homebase | Morses |
| | HSBC | New Look |
| | Index Extra | Original Levi Stores |
| | Innovations | Outfit |
| | Janet Fraser | Peter Craig |
| | JJB Sports | Safeway |
| | John Moores | Somerfield |
| | Kays | Tesco |
| | Kwik Save | |
| ½ star | Adams | Benetton |
| | Andre de Brett | Bertie |
| | Avon | Blacks Outdoor |

Blazer
Boots the Chemist
Brantano Footwear
Cable & Co
Clarks
Courts
Cyrillus
Damart
Daxon
Diesel
Dixons
Early Learning Centre
Edinburgh Woollen Mill
Empire
Ernest Jones
Etam
Farmfoods
Field and Trek
First Direct
First Sport
Free Spirit
French Connection
Goldsmiths
H Samuel
Habitat
Hamleys
House of Toys
Hugo Boss
IKEA
Jaeger
K Shoes
La Redoute
Laura Ashley
Leslie Davis
Mackays
Marks & Spencer (food)
Matalan
MFI Homeworks
Miller
Millets
Morrisons
Moss Bros
Mothercare
MUJI
Next
Next Directory
Nine West
Oasis
O'Neills
Past Times
Peacock's
Pied a Terre
Pure Woman
Ravel
River Island
Roland Cartier
Shoe Collection
Studio
Ted Baker
The Suit Company
Thermawear
Thorntons
Thrifty
Toy Stack
Vert Baudet
Viyella
Waitrose
WebbIvory
YHA Adventure Shops

#

@Jakarta
A Jones & Sons
Aldi
Allsports
American Golf Discount
Asprey & Garrard

Ath-Leisure
Beatties
Beghins
British Gas Energy Centres
Carphone Warehouse
Church's
Cotsworld
Currys
DX Communications
Electricity Plus
Electronics Boutique, GAME
Ellis Brigham Mountain Sports
Elts
Foto Processing
Gilesports
Half Price Jewellers
Harvey Nichols
James Allen
JD Footwear
JD Junior
JD Sports
JD Woman
Klik Photopoint
Mill Bros
Nevisport
Powerhouse
Richer Sounds
Russell & Bromley
Scottish Power
Selfridges
Shop Electric
Supasnaps
Tempo
The Link
The Outdoor People
Trago Mills
Wilderness Way

> Chelsea Building Society
Clydesdale Bank
Coventry Building Society
Derbyshire Building Society
Dolcis
Ecology Building Society
Giorgio Armani
Harrods
Leeds & Holbeck Building Society
Magnet, CP Hart
Market Harborough Building Society
Moss Chemists
Nationwide Building Society
Portman Building Society
Studio Stores
Thomas Pink
Time Computers
Topps Tiles
Virgin one
Yorkshire Building Society

X Ace
Adesso Shoes
Adlestones
Alexon
Allders
Allders at Home
Alliance & Leicester
Allied Carpets
Ambrose Wilson
Amway

Arding & Hobbs
Army & Navy
Arnotts
Austin Reed
Bacons
Bally
Bank of Ireland GB
Bank of Scotland
Bank of Wales
Barclays
Barkers
Barratts
Bay Trading
Beales
Beaverbrooks
Bentalls
Betterware
Bhs
Binns
Birmingham Midshires
Bodgers
Body Care
Bon Marché
Bow Bangles
Boyes Stores
Bradford & Bingley
Brewer
Bristol & West
Britannia Building
Society
Broadbents &
Boothroyds
Broughton Shoe
Warehouse
Budgens
Candid
Carpetland
Carpetworld
Carvela
Cheltenham &
Gloucester
City Camera Exchange
Claire's Accessories
Classic Combination
Comet
Cumberland Building
Society
Dash
Denners
DFS
D H Evans
Dickens & Jones
Dingles
Direct Line Financial
Services
DKNY
Dolphin
Dunfermline Building
Society
Eastex
Eddie Bauer
Egg
Electricworld
Elys
Emporio Armani
Esprit
F Hinds
Faith Footwear
Famous Army Stores
Famous Footwear
Farepak Hampers
Fashion World
Fenwick
Focus Do It All
Footlocker
Freemans

Furnitureland
Furniture Village
General George
Girobank
Glyn Webb
Graham's Toiletries
Grattan
Great Mills
Gucci
Halifax
Hills
Hobbs
Home Farm Hampers
House of Fraser
Hush Puppies
Iceland
Intersport GB
J D Williams
J H Leekes & Sons
James Selby
Jenners
Jessop
Jigsaw
John Lewis
Jonathan James
Kaleidoscope
Kendals
KG
Kitchens Direct
Kleeneze
Kurt Geiger
Lakeland
Lewis
Liberty
Lidl
Lillywhites
Lloyds Chemists
Lloyds Supersave

Lloyds TSB
Lloydspharmacy
Look Again
Lush
Mappin & Webb
Mark One
Max Bally
Moben
Morley's
Multiyork
NatWest Bank
Netto
Northern Bank
Northern Goldsmiths
Northern Rock
Olivers/Timpson
Outdoor Venture
Owen Owen
PC World
Peel Street Pharmacy
Peter Briggs
Peter Jones
Polo Ralph Lauren
Portland
QD Stores
QVC The Shopping
Channel
Rackhams
Riceman
Royal Bank of Scotland
Savers Health & Beauty
Saxone
Schuh Clothing For
Feet
ScS
Sharps
Shelly's Shoes
Shoe Express

Shoeright
Shoestop
Skipton Building Society
Smith Bros
Sofa Workshop
Sports Connection
Stead & Simpson
Stylo Superstores
Superdrug
T J Hughes
The Bike Chain
The London Bedding Company
Thrifty
Tie Rack
Tiny
Toys 'R' Us
UniChem
Walker & Hall
Warren James
Watches of Switzerland
Tyrells
Ulster Bank
West Bromwich Building Society
Whitakers
Wickes
Woolwich
Woolworths
Work and Leisure
Yorkshire Bank
Yves Saint Laurent

Δ Carpet Depot
Carpetright
Harris Carpets

# 23 | Resources

## Useful books, Web sites and organisations

*Poverty*

ActionAid, UK, www.actionaid.org
Cafod, UK, www.cafod.org.uk
Christian Aid, UK, www.christian-aid.org.uk
Oxfam, UK, www.oxfam.org.uk
Save the Children, UK, www.savethechildren.org.uk
World Development Movement, UK, www.wdm.org.uk

*Globalisation*

Ellwood, W (2001) *The No-nonsense Guide to Globalisation*, New Internationalist Publications, Oxford
Fair Trade Watch, US, www.fairtradewatch.org
Student Alliance to Reform Corporations, US, www.corpreform.org

*Governments*

Department for International Development, UK Government, www.dfid.gov.uk
European Commission – Trade, http://europa.eu.int/comm/trade/index_en.htm
International Labour Organisation, www.ilo.org
United Nations, www.un.org
United Nations Development Programme, www.undp.org
World Bank, www.worldbank.org
World Trade Organisation, www.wto.org

*Working conditions and human rights*

Amnesty International, www.amnesty.org
Anti-Slavery, UK, www.antislavery.org

Clean Clothes Campaign, Europe, www.cleanclothes.org
Global March Against Child Labour, UK, www.globalmarch.org
Labour Behind the Label (LBL), UK, www.labourbehindthelabel.org
National Labour Committee, US, www.nlcnet.org
One World not Three, www.oneworldnotthree.com
UNITE! (Union of Needletrades, Industrial and Textile Employees) Sweatshop Campaign, US, www.uniteunion.org/sweatshops/index.htm
United Students Against Sweatshops (USAS), US, www.umich.edu/~sole/usassy1/about/

*International standards*

Fairtrade Mark, UK, www.fairtrade.org.uk
RUGMARK, www.rugmark.net
SA8000, www.cepaa.org
UN Global Compact, www.unglobalcompact.org

*Fair trade*

Brown, M B (1993) *Fair Trade – Reform and Realities in the International Trading System*, Zed Books, London
Litterell, M A and Marsha, A D (1999) *Social Responsibility in the Global Market – Fair Trade of Cultural Products*, SAGE Publications, Thousand Oaks, California
Ransom, D (2001) *The No-nonsense Guide to Fair Trade*, New Internationalist Publications, Oxford
Banana Link, www.bananalink.org.uk
Équiterre, Canada, www.equiterre.qc.ca
European Fair Trade Association, www.eftafairtrade.org
Fairtrade Federation, US, www.fairtradefederation.org
Fairtrade Foundation, UK, www.fairtrade.org.uk
Fairtrade Labelling Organisations International, www.fairtrade.net
International Federation for Alternative Trade, www.ifat.org
Traidcraft, UK, www.traidcraft.co.uk

*Ethical trade*

Ethical Trading Initiative, UK, www.ethicaltrade.org
Fair Labor Association, US, www.fairlabor.org

Global Alliance, US, www.theglobalalliance.com
Interfaith Centre on Corporate Responsibility (ICCR), US, www.iccr.org
Tea Sourcing Partnership, www.teasourcingpartnership.org.uk

*Ethical shopping*
Ethical Junction, www.ethical-junction.org
Get Ethical, www.getethical.com
Traidcraft, www.traidcraft.co.uk
Business initiatives
British Toy & Hobby Association, www.btha.co.uk
Business for Social Responsibility, US, www.bsr.org
Business Impact, www.business-impact.org.uk
Corporate Social Responsibility Forum, UK, www.pwblf.org
Institute of Business Ethics, www.ibe.org.uk
UK Social Investment Forum, www.uksif.org

*News and information*
Corporate Watch, www.corpwatch.org
*Ethical Consumer* magazine, www.ethicalconsumer.org
Ethical Investment Research Services, www.eiris.org
Ethical Junction, www.ethical-junction.org
*Ethical Performance* newsletter, www.ethicalperformance.com
Natural Resources and Ethical Trade Programme, www.nri.org/NRET/
New Consumer, www.newconsumer.org
*New Internationalist*, www.newint.org
No Logo, www.nologo.org
Oneworld, www.oneworld.net
Philippine Resource Centre, UK, www.prc.dircon.co.uk
Pure Modern Lifestyles, www.greenguideonline.com/pure_intro.cfm

*Sustainable tourism*
worldsurface.com, www.worldsurface.com

# Appendix

## Example codes of conduct from clothes retailers

### *The C&A Code of Conduct for the Supply of Merchandise*[1]

**Introduction**
'The C&A Code of Conduct for the Supply of Merchandise' describes the standards of business conduct which we see as fundamental in our dealings with merchandise suppliers. Although our dealings with suppliers often take place in cultures which are different from our own and which have a different set of norms and values, certain standards are universally valid and must apply to all our commercial activities.

**Supplier relationships**
We seek to develop long-term business relationships with our suppliers who should have a natural respect for our ethical standards in the context of their own particular culture. Our relationships with suppliers are based on the principle of fair and honest dealings at all times and in all ways. We specifically require our suppliers to extend the same principle of fair and honest dealings to all others with whom they do business including employees, sub-contractors and other third parties. For example, this principle also means that gifts or favours cannot be offered nor accepted at any time.

**Legal aspects and intellectual property rights**
We will always comply fully with the legal requirements of the countries in which we do business and our suppliers are required to do likewise at all times. The Intellectual Property Rights of third parties will be respected by all concerned.

**Employment conditions**

In addition to the general requirement that all suppliers will extend the principle of fair and honest dealings to all others with whom they do business, we also have specific requirements relating to employment conditions based on respect for fundamental human rights. These requirements apply not only to production for C&A but also to production for any other third party.

- The use of child labour is absolutely unacceptable.
- Workers must not be younger than the legal minimum age for working in any specific country and not less than 14 years, whichever is the greater.
- We will not tolerate forced labour or labour which involves physical or mental abuse or any form of corporal punishment.
- Under no circumstances will the exploitation of any vulnerable individual or group be tolerated.
- Wages and benefits must be fully comparable with local norms, must comply with all local laws and must conform with the general principle of fair and honest dealings.
- Suppliers must ensure that all manufacturing processes are carried out under conditions which have proper and adequate regard for the health and safety of those involved.

**Environmental aspects**

The realisation of environmental standards is a complex issue – especially in developing countries. It therefore needs to be continuously reviewed within the limits of what is achievable per country. We will work with our suppliers to help them to meet our joint obligations towards the environment.

**Freedom of association**

C&A recognises and respects the freedom of employees to choose whether or not to associate with any group of their own choosing, as long as such groups are legal in their own country. Suppliers must not prevent or obstruct such legitimate activities.

Disclosure and inspection

We require suppliers to make full disclosure to us of all facts and circumstances concerning production and use of sub-contractors. All

C&A suppliers are obliged to make their sub-contractors aware of, and comply with, the C&A Code of Conduct. Additionally, our suppliers are required to authorise SOCAM, the auditing company appointed by C&A, to make unannounced inspections of any manufacturing facility at any time.

### Monitoring

So that this Code and the requirements it sets out have real meaning, we will ensure that standards of compliance on the part of our own employees and suppliers are actively audited and monitored and are an integral part of the day-to-day management process. We will maintain all necessary information systems and on-site inspection facilities to achieve this objective.

### Sanctions

Where we believe that a supplier has breached the requirements set out in this Code either for C&A production or for any other third party, we will not hesitate to end our business relationship including the cancellation of outstanding orders. We also reserve the right to take whatever other actions are appropriate and possible.

### Corrective plans

Where business has been suspended due to an infringement of the C&A Code of Conduct, the business relationship may only be re-established after a convincing Corrective Plan has been submitted by the supplier and approved by C&A.

### Awareness and training

We will take all necessary steps to ensure that our employees and suppliers are made fully aware of our standards and requirements. We will take all necessary actions to promote full understanding and co-operation with the aims and objectives of this Code.

### Development of the code

This document is an update of the 'C&A Code of Conduct for the Supply of Merchandise' published in May 1996, which it supersedes. Whilst accepting the need for continuity and consistency, we continue to recognise that this Code must be developed over time in the light of practical experience and changing circumstances. We will continue to ensure that the Code is reviewed on a regular basis and revised where appropriate.

## *Arcadia Group Supplier Code of Conduct*[2]

When customers buy our goods we want them to be confident that they have been produced under acceptable conditions. That means the goods must have been produced:

- lawfully, through fair and honest dealing;
- without exploiting the people who made them;
- in decent working conditions; and
- without damaging the environment.

In this code, the 'supplier' means the supplier, the manufacturer or any other person involved in supplying goods to our companies.

We have asked our suppliers to follow this code. The code is backed-up by a process of self-evaluation and independent inspections. It is designed to be fair, achievable, easy to check, and to promote the ongoing development of our suppliers.

### Legal requirement

At all times, our suppliers must meet the legal requirements of the countries in which they are working.

### Employment

*Wages, working hours, entitlements and deductions*

Suppliers must meet the local laws on conditions such as minimum wages, hours of work, overtime and deductions (International Labour Organisation (ILO) Conventions 1, 26, 95, 131 and Recommendation 85).

- If no laws apply, the conditions for workers must be at least as good as the usual terms for workers in the area doing the same type of work.
- Suppliers must give workers wage slips that they can easily understand.
- Any deductions must be at a rate that is fair and reasonable by local standards.
- Overtime must be voluntary.

*Employing children*

Suppliers must not employ children, other than under the ILO Convention number 138 and Recommendation number 146, which define a child as a person younger than 15 years old.

- Apprenticeships and education-related work are acceptable as long as the child is not being exploited, there is no risk to the child's health, education and development, and parental permission is obtained (Article 32 of the United Nations Convention of the Rights of the Child).
- Suppliers must check every worker's documents to confirm their date of birth. If no official documents are available, suppliers must take all reasonable and appropriate steps to check the child's age.

*Forced labour*

People must not be forced to work by threatening them with a penalty (ILO Conventions 29 and 105).

- Suppliers must not use forced labour, prison labour or bonded labour.

*Discriminatory practices*

Suppliers must not use or threaten their workers with physical punishment or any form of mental or verbal abuse.

*Discrimination*

Suppliers must employ and deal with all their employees fairly and without discrimination (ILO Convention 111 and Recommendation 111).

- Suppliers must treat everyone fairly, regardless of their race, religion, sex or disability.

Freedom of association

Suppliers must not prevent workers from joining legal associations (ILO Conventions 87 and 98).

*Health, safety and welfare*

Under ILO Convention 155 and Recommendation 164, suppliers must provide a safe place to work and must meet all local laws relating to health, safety and welfare in the workplace.

This also applies to any accommodation provided for workers.

- Suppliers must appoint a senior manager who is responsible for the health, safety and welfare of employees, and suppliers must do all they reasonably can to prevent accidents and injury.
- Suppliers must prepare health and safety procedures and regularly train their workers in these procedures.
- Suppliers must regularly test these procedures.
- There must be satisfactory lighting and ventilation.
- Clean drinking water must be provided.
- There must be satisfactory toilet facilities.

**Environment**

Suppliers must dispose of all the waste that is created in their factory in line with local laws, or in a way that will not harm the environment or the local population.

**Monitoring and inspecting**

Suppliers are responsible for making sure that everyone in the supply chain knows about and complies with this code of conduct.

- Suppliers must keep records to show that they are carrying out regular reviews and checks.
- Arcadia Group staff or representatives may visit factories without warning to carry out inspections.
- Suppliers must provide all the information we ask for to check that the code is being followed.
- Arcadia Group will keep this information confidential.

## *Marks & Spencer Global Sourcing Principles*[3]

**Introduction**

For many years Marks & Spencer has sought to ensure that our goods are produced in good working conditions. This supports our core principles of providing our own workforce with meaningful jobs and providing customers with high quality products. We and our suppliers have found from experience that when people are treated with respect, in decent working conditions and fair rates of pay, then both they and their companies benefit from increased commitment and productivity. Customers benefit too from goods offering better quality and value.

Achieving this objective has come through the development of agreed standards between ourselves and suppliers, a regular pattern of visits and a policy of continual improvement – backed up by strict sanctions when standards are not met.

Increasing global expansion and international competition have brought new challenges. As a major retailer selling diverse product ranges under our own exclusive brand in more than thirty countries, Marks & Spencer now works with many different suppliers from around the world.

Most of our suppliers have suppliers of their own, who in turn may themselves be supplied by others. It would be impossible for us to control the working conditions of each of the vast number of people who contribute in some way to what eventually becomes a Marks & Spencer product. However, we are determined to do what we can to ensure adherence to the principles that we believe in. We have therefore published our company-wide Global Sourcing Principles.

These principles clearly require all our direct suppliers – ie those with whom we directly contract for both goods and services – to ensure their facilities accord with what we believe to be acceptable standards, and to be continually improving. We enforce these principles firmly among direct suppliers and encourage their implementation further down the supply chain.

**Luc Vandevelde**

Marks & Spencer takes great care in choosing the companies who supply us directly with goods and services and with whom we aim to build long term partnerships. From the start we require each supplier to implement our Global Sourcing Principles, which establish a minimum acceptable entry standard. But as our business relationship develops, we expect the supplier steadily to raise standards and improve working conditions, taking account of internationally recognised standards.

**Supplier's responsibility**

Together with each supplier we establish a set of standards, which includes specifications appropriate to the industries and countries producing the goods. It is the supplier's responsibility to achieve and maintain these standards.

**Workforce rights**

The people working for our suppliers are to be treated with respect, and their health, safety and basic human rights are to be protected and promoted. Each supplier must, as a minimum, fully comply with all relevant local and national laws and regulations, particularly with regard to:

- Working hours and conditions, rates of pay and terms of employment.
- Minimum age of employment.

Moreover, whatever the local regulations, workers should normally be at least 15 years old; as a norm, they should be free to join lawful trade unions or workers' associations.

**Production sites and labelling**

Suppliers of goods must agree with us in advance the production site or sites to be used for each order and no subcontracting of our orders from these agreed locations is allowed. All goods must be labelled with their country of origin.

**Regular assessment**

All production sites are to be regularly visited and assessed by our suppliers and by our own staff. Together we will strive for continual improvement.

**Environmental responsibility**

At the very least, suppliers must meet all relevant local and national regulations. In addition, we expect them steadily to improve their environmental performance by aiming to comply with international standards.

**Dedicated production units**

Once we have established significant levels of business with a supplier, we expect that supplier to produce our goods in units, and with workers, dedicated to Marks & Spencer orders.

**Commitment to extending principles through the supply chain**

We expect our suppliers to adopt similar principles in dealing with those who, in turn, supply them.

Suppliers must not only apply these principles at all times, but must also be able to show they are doing so. We will take action against suppliers who do not comply, which may involve cancelling our orders and ceasing to trade.

## *Gap Inc. Code of Vendor Conduct*[4]

This Code of Vendor Conduct applies to all factories that produce goods for Gap Inc. or any of its subsidiaries, divisions, affiliates or agents ('Gap Inc.').

While Gap Inc. recognises that there are different legal and cultural environments in which factories operate throughout the world, this Code sets forth the basic requirements that all factories must meet in order to do business with Gap Inc. The Code also provides the foundation for Gap Inc.'s ongoing evaluation of a factory's employment practices and environmental compliance.

As a condition of doing business with Gap Inc., each and every factory must comply with this Code of Vendor Conduct. Gap Inc. will continue to develop monitoring systems to assess and ensure compliance. If Gap Inc. determines that any factory has violated this Code, Gap Inc. may either terminate its business relationship or require the factory to implement a corrective action plan. If corrective action is advised but not taken, Gap Inc. will suspend placement of future orders and may terminate current production.

### I. General principle

Factories that produce goods for Gap Inc. shall operate in full compliance with the laws of their respective countries and with all other applicable laws, rules and regulations.

- A. The factory operates in full compliance with all applicable laws, rules and regulations, including those relating to labour, worker health and safety, and the environment.
- B. The factory allows Gap Inc. and/or any of its representatives or agents unrestricted access to its facilities and to all relevant records at all times, whether or not notice is provided in advance.

**II. Environment**

Factories must comply with all applicable environmental laws and regulations. Where such requirements are less stringent than Gap Inc.'s own, factories are encouraged to meet the standards outlined in Gap Inc.'s statement of environmental principles.

- A. The factory has an environmental management system or plan.
- B. The factory has procedures for notifying local community authorities in case of accidental discharge or release or any other environmental emergency.

**III. Discrimination**

Factories shall employ workers on the basis of their ability to do the job, not on the basis of their personal characteristics or beliefs.

- A. The factory employs workers without regard to race, colour, gender, nationality, religion, age, maternity or marital status.
- B. The factory pays workers wages and provides benefits without regard to race, colour, gender, nationality, religion, age, maternity or marital status.

**IV. Forced labour**

Factories shall not use any prison, indentured or forced labour.

- A. The factory does not use involuntary labour of any kind, including prison labour, debt bondage or forced labour by governments.
- B. If the factory recruits foreign contract workers, the factory pays agency recruitment commissions and does not require any worker to remain in employment for any period of time against his or her will.

**V. Child labour**

Factories shall employ only workers who meet the applicable minimum legal age requirement or are at least 14 years of age, whichever is greater. Factories must also comply with all other applicable child labour laws. Factories are encouraged to develop lawful workplace apprenticeship programs for the educational benefit of their workers, provided that all participants meet both Gap Inc.'s minimum age standard of 14 and the minimum legal age requirement.

- A. Every worker employed by the factory is at least 14 years of age and meets the applicable minimum legal age requirement.
- B. The factory complies with all applicable child labour laws, including those related to hiring, wages, hours worked, overtime and working conditions.
- C. The factory encourages and allows eligible workers, especially younger workers, to attend night classes and participate in work-study programs and other government-sponsored educational programs.
- D. The factory maintains official documentation for every worker that verifies the worker's date of birth. In those countries where official documents are not available to confirm exact date of birth, the factory confirms age using an appropriate and reliable assessment method.

**VI. Wages and hours**

Factories shall set working hours, wages and overtime pay in compliance with all applicable laws. Workers shall be paid at least the minimum legal wage or a wage that meets local industry standards, whichever is greater. While it is understood that overtime is often required in garment production, factories shall carry out operations in ways that limit overtime to a level that ensures humane and productive working conditions.

- A. Workers are paid at least the minimum legal wage or the local industry standard, whichever is greater.
- B. The factory pays overtime and any incentive (or piece) rates that meet all legal requirements or the local industry standard, whichever is greater. Hourly wage rates for overtime must be higher than the rates for the regular work shift.
- C. The factory does not require, on a regularly scheduled basis, a work week in excess of 60 hours.
- D. Workers may refuse overtime without any threat of penalty, punishment or dismissal.
- E. Workers have at least one day off in seven.
- F. The factory provides paid annual leave and holidays as required by law or which meet the local industry standard, whichever is greater.
- G. For each pay period, the factory provides workers an

understandable wage statement which includes days worked, wage or piece rate earned per day, hours of overtime at each specified rate, bonuses, allowances and legal or contractual deductions.

**VII. Working conditions**

Factories must treat all workers with respect and dignity and provide them with a safe and healthy environment. Factories shall comply with all applicable laws and regulations regarding working conditions. Factories shall not use corporal punishment or any other form of physical or psychological coercion. Factories must be sufficiently lighted and ventilated, aisles accessible, machinery maintained, and hazardous materials sensibly stored and disposed of. Factories providing housing for workers must keep these facilities clean and safe.

*Factory*

- A. The factory does not engage in or permit physical acts to punish or coerce workers.
- B. The factory does not engage in or permit psychological coercion or any other form of non-physical abuse, including threats of violence, sexual harassment, screaming or other verbal abuse.
- C. The factory complies with all applicable laws regarding working conditions, including worker health and safety, sanitation, fire safety, risk protection, and electrical, mechanical and structural safety.
- D. Work surface lighting in production areas – such as sewing, knitting, pressing and cutting – is sufficient for the safe performance of production activities.
- E. The factory is well ventilated. There are windows, fans, air conditioners or heaters in all work areas for adequate circulation, ventilation and temperature control.
- F. There are sufficient, clearly marked exits allowing for the orderly evacuation of workers in case of fire or other emergencies. Emergency exit routes are posted and clearly marked in all sections of the factory.
- G. Aisles, exits and stairwells are kept clear at all times of work in process, finished garments, bolts of fabric, boxes and

all other objects that could obstruct the orderly evacuation of workers in case of fire or other emergencies. The factory indicates with a 'yellow box' or other markings that the areas in front of exits, fire fighting equipment, control panels and potential fire sources are to be kept clear.

- H. Doors and other exits are kept accessible and unlocked during all working hours for orderly evacuation in case of fire or other emergencies. All main exit doors open to the outside.
- I. Fire extinguishers are appropriate to the types of possible fires in the various areas of the factory, are regularly maintained and charged, display the date of their last inspection, and are mounted on walls and columns throughout the factory so they are visible and accessible to workers in all areas.
- J. Fire alarms are on each floor and emergency lights are placed above exits and on stairwells.
- K. Evacuation drills are conducted at least annually.
- L. Machinery is equipped with operational safety devices and is inspected and serviced on a regular basis.
- M. Appropriate personal protective equipment – such as masks, gloves, goggles, ear plugs and rubber boots – is made available at no cost to all workers and instruction in its use is provided.
- N. The factory provides potable water for all workers and allows reasonable access to it throughout the working day.
- O. The factory places at least one well-stocked first aid kit on every factory floor and trains specific staff in basic first aid. The factory has procedures for dealing with serious injuries that require medical treatment outside the factory.
- P. The factory maintains throughout working hours clean and sanitary toilet areas and places no unreasonable restrictions on their use.
- Q. The factory stores hazardous and combustible materials in secure and ventilated areas and disposes of them in a safe and legal manner.

*Housing (if applicable)*

- A. Dormitory facilities meet all applicable laws and regulations related to health and safety, including fire safety, sanitation, risk protection, and electrical, mechanical and structural safety.

- B. Sleeping quarters are segregated by sex.
- C. The living space per worker in the sleeping quarters meets both the minimum legal requirement and the local industry standard.
- D. Workers are provided their own individual mats or beds.
- E. Dormitory facilities are well ventilated. There are windows to the outside or fans and/or air conditioners and/or heaters in all sleeping areas for adequate circulation, ventilation and temperature control.
- F. Workers are provided their own storage space for their clothes and personal possessions.
- G. There are at least two clearly marked exits on each floor, and emergency lighting is installed in halls, stairwells and above each exit.
- H. Halls and exits are kept clear of obstructions for safe and rapid evacuation in case of fire or other emergencies.
- I. Directions for evacuation in case of fire or other emergencies are posted in all sleeping quarters.
- J. Fire extinguishers are placed in or accessible to all sleeping quarters.
- K. Hazardous and combustible materials used in the production process are not stored in the dormitory or in buildings connected to sleeping quarters.
- L. Fire drills are conducted at least every six months.
- M. Sleeping quarters have adequate lighting.
- N. Sufficient toilets and showers or mandis are segregated by sex and provided in safe, sanitary, accessible and private areas.
- O. Potable water or facilities to boil water are available to dormitory residents.
- P. Dormitory residents are free to come and go during their off-hours under reasonable limitations imposed for their safety and comfort.

### VIII. Freedom of association

Workers are free to join associations of their own choosing. Factories must not interfere with workers who wish to lawfully and peacefully associate, organise or bargain collectively. The decision whether or not to do so should be made solely by the workers.

- A. Workers are free to choose whether or not to lawfully organise and join associations.
- B. The factory does not threaten, penalise, restrict or interfere with workers' lawful efforts to join associations of their choosing.

## *Etam's Group Sourcing Policy*[5]

Etam's Supplier and Delivery Manual is issued to every supplier working with us and sets out clear terms and conditions of trade to which suppliers sign a declaration to abide.

The terms and conditions clearly state our policy of working with reputable suppliers and manufacturers who have acceptable working conditions and practices, and that we will not buy goods from any which are unethical. This policy is broken down further, detailing policies with regard to:

- Supplier responsibility
- Child labour
- Health and safety
- Forced labour
- Discipline
- Discrimination

Etam are committed to this policy and will terminate any breach of these conditions immediately.

## *Primark*

Primark source many of their garments from developing countries.

We trade with all our suppliers against a strict, written code of conduct. This code stipulates the conditions laid down in the United Nations Charter governing international economic and social cooperation with specific reference to workers' rights and social conditions (ref chapter IX, Article 55).

In addition all regional and local law regarding workers' rights, minimum wage and working conditions must be complied with.

With regard to quality and safety of products supplied, these must comply with UK and Eire consumer protection law and Primark's own comprehensive specifications for the type of garment being supplied.

It is Primark policy to deal directly with all its manufacturing partners and all aspects of this code are therefore regularly audited by our buyers during site visits. In addition to this independent audits are carried out on our behalf by professional quality auditors.

## *Timberland's Guiding Principles for Choosing Business Partners*

**Human rights**

We recognise the value of diverse peoples, cultures and perspectives. And while we recognise and respect the cultural differences that exist throughout the world, we are committed to work only with partners who choose their employees based on their ability to do the job, not on their personal beliefs or individual characteristics.

We are committed to doing business only with partners whose employees are offered the opportunity to be contributors in a work environment that is safe and non-discriminatory, and who recognise the right of employees to freely associate and bargain collectively. This environment must be free of harassment, abuse, retribution for grievances, and corporal punishment. Further specific guidelines include:

- Voluntary employment: We will not do business with partners whose employees' presence is anything other than voluntary. This specifically prohibits all forms of prison labour, indentured labour, or any other forms of forced labour.
- Child labour: We will not work with partners who use the labour of children. We define 'child' as younger than 15 years of age (or 14 where the local law allows) or younger than the compulsory age for school attendance.
- Compensation: We will do business only with partners who provide wages and benefits that at a minimum meet all applicable laws governing minimum wage and legally mandated benefits. In addition to compensating for regular work hours, partners must provide compensation to employees for overtime hours at a premium rate (as is legally required by

all applicable local laws) or minimally at a rate at least equal to their regular hourly wage.

- Pay practices: We will seek partners who do not apply conditional employment practices, such as training wages, pre-employment fees and deposits, or any other practices that effectively lower a worker's pay below legal minimum wage.
- Working hours: We will seek partners whose employees' work schedule (excluding appropriately compensated overtime) is not more than 48 hours per six-day period. Our partners must ensure that employees do not exceed 60 hours (inclusive of overtime) in a given week or 12 hours in a given day. Employees shall not work more than 6 days consecutively.
- Health and safety: We will seek business partners who provide, and will support, their employees with a safe and healthy work environment and who make a significant effort toward continuous improvement of that environment. When applicable, we will seek partners who provide residential environments that are safe and healthy.

### Environmental requirements

We will actively seek business partners who share our commitment to the environment. We will favour partners who aggressively work to preserve, protect and restore the natural environment, by such means as energy conservation, reduction and proper disposal of waste, environmental restoration and public disclosure.

### Compliance with applicable laws

We will do business only with partners that comply with both the letter and the spirit of applicable legal requirements.

### Right of review

We will conduct ongoing reviews to measure our compliance, and the compliance of our business partners, with these guiding principles. We require full and open access to the facilities and operations involved in our business relationships.

## Example codes of conduct from department stores

### *Debenhams Sourcing Policy*

Our suppliers, manufacturers, or any persons involved in supplying goods to the Debenhams Group must meet the conditions of our sourcing policy, as set out in our Supplier Handbook.

Where any supplier, manufacturer or any other person involved in supplying goods to the Debenhams Group does not make the goods, they must ensure that the manufacturer who does, also keeps to these conditions.

The Debenhams Group will only work with reputable suppliers and manufacturers who have acceptable working conditions and practices.

The Debenhams Group will not buy goods from any supplier or manufacturer who has unacceptable working practices or conditions.

We regularly review our sourcing policy to make sure that it remains relevant.

**What is Debenhams' policy in respect of wages, hours and entitlements for their suppliers' employees?**
Our suppliers must keep to local laws on conditions such as minimum wages, overtime, hours of work and sick pay. If no laws apply, the conditions suppliers impose upon their workers must not be less favourable than the normal terms in their area for workers doing the same type of work.

**What is Debenhams' policy in respect of child labour?**
Our suppliers must not employ children for manufacturing goods. For this purpose a child is any person who is younger than the normal school-leaving age.

Legitimate apprenticeships or education-related work are acceptable as long as the children are not being exploited and there is no risk to the children's health or safety.

**What is Debenhams' Health and Safety policy for its suppliers' workforce?**
Our suppliers must provide a safe place of work and keep to all local laws relating to health and safety in the workplace.

**What is Debenhams' policy on forced labour practices?**
Our suppliers must not use forced labour in the workplace.

Our suppliers and their representatives must not use, or threaten their workers with any physical punishment, or dominate or restrain workers by force, authority or threats.

**What is Debenhams' policy on discrimination?**
Our suppliers must treat everyone fairly when choosing and dealing with their workers. They must not treat any person less favourably because of their race, religion or sex.

## Example codes of conduct from DIY retailers

### *Summary of B&Q's Code of Conduct*[6]

(The full version is 18 pages.)

B&Q has developed a code of conduct which outlines the way in which we would like the factories and workplaces in our supply chains to be managed. The standards set out in the code are based on our own experience and cover the following key issues:

- Slave labour
- Freedom of assembly and association
- Health and safety and hygiene
- Child labour
- Wages and benefits
- Hours of work
- Discrimination
- Accommodation
- Supply chain management
- Environment

The Code of Conduct covers all our suppliers. However, we know from experience that many of our suppliers are not yet able to fully meet the Code and it may take them some time to do so.

The people making our products in the UK and around the world are our trading neighbours – we depend on them just as they depend on us. Buying globally makes commercial sense for us and gives people in our supply chains the opportunity to participate in the market economy and to build a better life for themselves. However, this only works if supply chains are managed so that everyone benefits. We have witnessed the opportunities, and the downsides, of globalisation in our supply chains from Papua New Guinea to the Philippines.

In our bid to develop supply chains which benefit us all, we will work with suppliers who are committed to a process of continuous improvement, in order to come into line with the Code over an agreed timescale.

The commitment and the actions of our suppliers will be examined and monitored as part of QUEST, our existing supplier assessment process. Each supplier will be required to produce an action plan, demonstrating how they will move towards compliance with the code. They must keep appropriate records to demonstrate improvement and we will agree appropriate timescales with each supplier. Cooperation with this process is a requirement of supplying B&Q.

**The bottom line**

Our approach is one of engagement with suppliers. For this to work, factory managers must show commitment to our aims and values. We will not buy from factories where management practices indicate an absence of commitment ie where workers are subject to unacceptable treatment (by the country standard), as set out below.

B&Q will not buy from suppliers where:

- Forced, bonded or involuntary labour is used.
- There is a culture of physical abuse and verbal intimidation.
- It is unrealistic that the factory can improve its standards.
- Safe, unlocked and unblocked fire escapes are not accessible from all parts of the factory or accommodation.
- Accommodation is located in the same building as the factory, production or materials store.
- Women are required to submit to pregnancy testing or forced to have abortions.

## *Homebase's code of conduct*[7]

These Principles have been developed by Homebase to set out our understanding of the responsibility we share with suppliers for certain social matters. Whilst they have general application the Principles have been drafted with particular reference to our trade with companies in developing countries. Supported by the Code of Practice, they are an expression of the social values we share with our partner companies and provide a basis for our trading relationship.

### Fair trading

In the conduct of its business Homebase will deal openly and fairly with suppliers, adhere to contract terms and avoid the exercise of undue pressure.

### Protection of children

Children may only be employed in circumstances which fully safeguard them from potential exploitation, which protect them from moral or physical hazard and long term damage to health and which do not disrupt their education.

### Health and safety

Policies and procedures for health and safety will be established which are appropriate to the industry. In the absence of legal requirements these will reflect a clear awareness of obvious hazards and a general regard for the well-being of employees. Such policies and procedures will apply also to any living accommodation provided in association with employment.

### Equal opportunities

Whilst being sensitive to cultural differences we expect the development of equal opportunities in employment without discrimination on race, religion and gender or other arbitrary basis.

### Freedom of association

Employees shall be free to join lawful associations; forced labour or coercion at work is unacceptable.

Remuneration

Pay will not be lower than that required by local law or, in the absence of law, that paid generally within the industry. It will also have regard to what is needed to maintain family life above subsistence level.

## Example investment policies from financial service providers

### *The Co-operative Bank – Our Ethical Policy*[8]

Following extensive consultation with our customers, with regard to how their money should and should not be invested, our position is as follows.

Human rights

We will not invest in or provide financial services to:

- any regime or organisation which oppresses the human spirit or takes away the rights of the individual;
- manufacturers of torture equipment or other equipment that is used in the violation of human rights.

The arms trade

We will not invest in or provide financial services to any business involved in the:

- manufacture
- sale
- licensed production
- brokerage

of armaments to any country which has an oppressive regime.

Trade and social involvement

We will seek to support and encourage:

- the business of organisations which promote the concept of fair trade;
- business customers and suppliers to take a pro-active stance on ethical sourcing with any Third World suppliers they may use;

- organisations participating in the UK social economy eg co-operatives, credit unions and charities;
- suppliers whose activities are compatible with our Ethical Policy.

In addition, our customers' money will not be used to finance any of the following activities:

- we will ensure that our financial services are not exploited for the purpose of money laundering relating to the proceeds of drug trafficking, terrorism and other serious crime;
- we will avoid investment and currency trading in developing countries which does not support productive purposes;
- we will not participate in currency speculation which consciously damages the economies of sovereign states;
- we will not invest in or provide financial services to tobacco product manufacturers.

Ecological impact

We will encourage business customers to take a pro-active stance on the environmental impact of their own activities and will invest in companies that avoid repeated damage to the environment.

In line with the principles of our Ecological Mission Statement we will not invest in any business or organisation that, as a core activity, relies on:

- the extraction or production of fossil fuels, which contribute to problems such as global climate change and acid rain;
- the manufacture of unnatural chemicals which may contribute to problems such as ozone depletion, or which may accumulate in nature;
- the unsustainable harvest of natural resources such as timber clearance, which leads to deforestation.

Animal welfare

We will not invest in, or provide financial services to, organisations involved in the following activities:

- animal testing of cosmetic or household products or their ingredients;
- exploitative factory farming methods;

- blood sports, which involve the use of animals or birds to catch, fight or kill each other;
- fur farming and the trade in animal fur.

**Customer consultation**

- We will regularly re-appraise customers' views on these and other issues and develop our ethical stance accordingly.
- From time to time we seek to represent our customers' views on the issues contained within our Ethical Policy and other ethical issues.
- On occasion we will make decisions on specific business ethical issues not included in our Ethical Policy.

## *Triodos Bank*[9]

Triodos Bank lends exclusively to projects with clear social and environmental objectives which meet real needs.

Our lending process and assessment starts with a consideration of whether a project meets these qualitative criteria. If we are satisfied on these points, we then assess the project's finances, viability and security in a similar way to other banks. We try to apply our criteria flexibly, and if we don't think we can help you, we will tell you as soon as possible to save you time and expense.

We are especially active in four main sectors: charity, community, the environment and social business. This covers a wide range of ventures including:

- Social businesses – co-operatives, organic food retailing and distribution, employment creation, fair trade.
- Environmental initiatives – conservation, recycling, renewable energy, organic agriculture, sustainable transport, building restoration.
- Charities – special needs education and services, complementary therapies and health care, the arts, education, spiritual groups.
- Community projects – social housing, community services, local investment, voluntary groups.

## *Abbey National Group Statement on Ethical Investment Guidelines*[10]

Abbey National has in place guidelines to ensure that the Company considers ethical concerns when making investments.

The guidelines build on Abbey National's statement of ethical principles, 'How We Do Business', which affirms the Company's commitment to upholding high ethical standards in its relationships with all stakeholders, including regulators, customers, employees, shareholders, business partners and the community.

### Principles

Abbey National's ethical investment guidelines set out broad principles which guide the Company's decisions:

- Adherence to high standards of corporate governance and ethics.
- Consideration of the social impact of the Company's activities.
- Case-by-case ethical screening of investments.

### Procedure

Abbey National has a procedure in place for ensuring that appropriate screening of investment opportunities takes place. Individual business units within Abbey National are responsible for referring any proposals which may conflict with the Company's ethical standards to the Group Risk Director, who initiates review of the proposal by Executive Directors.

### Areas of ethical concern

The guidelines highlight a number of areas where the Company exercises special care when assessing investment proposals. These areas include:

- Investments where there are concerns about a company's or government's adherence to international human rights treaties and protocols.
- Companies or projects operating in the defence sector.
- Activities which pose a high degree of risk to the environment.
- Activities which could have an adverse impact on public health,

including production of tobacco products.
- Investments which could involve mistreatment of animals.
- Companies involved in the production or dissemination of pornographic materials.

## *HSBC – Responsible Financing*[11]

Wherever we operate, we play a constructive, responsible role in aligning our objectives with those of the local community.

HSBC believes that personal freedom flourishes best in an environment of economic growth and opportunity. We support free trade and investment because they are avenues for the creation of jobs and for the improvement of living standards. Every country and territory where we operate has its own character, history and aspirations; a single standard for their progress would be difficult to devise.

HSBC retains a pioneering spirit, promoting international trade and constructive engagement through its business activities.

We take a careful and limited approach to the financing of sales of defence equipment. We ensure that the vendor's government and other relevant authorities have granted the necessary licences and approvals. Every potential transaction is considered on individual merit and in consultation with colleagues in the country and region where the equipment may be destined.

We do not participate in financing the manufacture or export of landmines. We have assisted organisations which support the victims of anti-personnel landmines. It is not possible, however, for any financial institution involved in commercial lending to give an absolute assurance that none of its customers is an indirect supplier of component parts of landmines or other military equipment.

Specific lending and investment policies are confidential but comply with these standards.

## *Alliance & Leicester Group*

The Alliance & Leicester Group (which includes Girobank and Alliance & Leicester Group Treasury plc) invests funds wisely and prudently and follows the highest standards of business ethics and, as a general rule, only holds assets and investments in the United Kingdom. It is our policy to lend only to respected institutions and as a matter of ethical policy not to deal knowingly with businesses involved in any illicit activities, such as money laundering, or with foreign regimes which violate human rights. The Group and its subsidiaries would therefore immediately withdraw its offer of services to any organisation in breach of national or international law or financial service regulations.

## Example codes of conduct from food retailers

### *Asda – The Code of Practice*

---

1. Employment is freely chosen
    - 1.1 There is no forced, bonded or involuntary prison labour.
    - 1.2 Workers are not required to lodge deposits or their identity papers with their supplier and are free to leave their employer after reasonable notice.

2. Freedom of association and the right to collective bargaining are respected
    - 2.1 Workers without distinction have the right to join or form trade unions of their own choosing and to bargain collectively.
    - 2.2 The supplier must adopt an open attitude towards the activities of trade unions and their organisational activities.
    - 2.3 Workers' representatives are not discriminated against and have access to carry out their representative functions in the workplace.
    - 2.4 Where the right to freedom of association and collective bargaining are restricted under law, the supplier should facilitate, and not hinder, the development of parallel means for independent and free association and bargaining.

3. Working conditions are safe and hygienic
    - 3.1 A safe and hygienic working environment shall be provided, bearing in mind the prevailing knowledge of the industry and of any specific hazards. Adequate steps shall be taken to

prevent accidents and injury to health arising out of, associated with, or occurring in the course of work, by minimising, so far as is reasonably practicable, the causes of hazards inherent in the working environment.

- 3.2 Workers shall receive regular and recorded health and safety training, and such training shall be repeated for new or reassigned workers.
- 3.3 Access to clean toilet facilities and to potable water, and, if appropriate sanitary facilities for food storage shall be provided.
- 3.4 Accommodation, where provided, shall be clean, safe and meet the basic needs of the workers.
- 3.5 The supplier shall assign responsibility for health and safety to a senior management representative.

4. Child labour shall not be used
   - 4.1 There shall be no new recruitment of child labour.
   - 4.2 The supplier shall develop or participate in and contribute to policies and programmes which provide for the transition of any child found to be performing child labour to enable her or him to attend and remain in quality education until no longer a child; 'child' and 'child labour' is defined at the end.
   - 4.3 Children and young persons under 18 shall not be employed at night or under hazardous conditions.
   - 4.4 These policies and procedures shall conform to the provisions of the relevant ILO standards.

5. Living wages are paid
   - 5.1 Wages and benefits paid for a standard working week meet, at a minimum, national legal standards or industry benchmark standards, whichever is higher. In any event wages should always be enough to meet basic needs and to provide some discretionary income.
   - 5.2 All workers shall be provided with written and understandable information about their working conditions in respect to wages before they start work and about the particulars of their wages for the pay period concerned each time they are paid.
   - 5.3 Deductions from wages as a disciplinary measure shall not

be permitted nor shall any deductions from wages not provided for by national law be permitted without the expressed permission of the worker concerned. All disciplinary measures shall be recorded.

6. Working hours are not excessive
   - 6.1 Working hours comply with national laws and benchmark industry standards, whichever affords greater protection.
   - 6.2 In any event workers shall not on a regular basis be required to work in excess of 48 hours per week and shall be provided with at least one day off for every 7 days on average. Overtime shall be voluntary, shall not exceed 12 hours per week, shall not be demanded on a regular basis and shall be compensated at a premium rate.

7. No discrimination is practised
   - 7.1 There shall be no discrimination in hiring, compensation or access to training, promotion, termination or retirement based on race, caste, national origin, religion, age, disability, gender, marital status, sexual orientation, union membership or political affiliation.
   - 7.2 Maternity and paternity rights must be upheld in accordance with current national legislation.

8. Regular employment is provided
   - 8.1 To every extent possible work performed must be on the basis of a recognised employment relationship established through national law and practice.
   - 8.2 Obligations to workers under labour or social security laws and regulations arising from the regular employment relationship shall not be avoided through the use of labour-only contracting, sub-contracting, or home-working arrangements, or through apprenticeship schemes where there is no real intent to impart skills or provide regular employment, nor shall any such obligations be avoided through the excessive use of fixed term contracts of employment.

9. **No harsh or inhumane treatment is allowed**
   - 9.1 Physical abuse or discipline, the threat of physical abuse, sexual or other harassment and verbal abuse or other forms of intimidation shall be prohibited.

10. **Immigration law and compliance**
    - 10.1 Only workers with a legal right to work shall be employed or used by the supplier.
    - 10.2 All workers including Employment Agency staff, must be validated by the supplier for their legal right to work by reviewing original documentation (not photocopies) before they are allowed to commence work. Procedures which demonstrate compliance with these validations must be implemented.
    - 10.3 Employment Agencies must only supply workers registered with them.
    - 10.4 Suppliers must regularly audit Employment Agencies from whom they obtain workers to monitor compliance with this policy.

## *Safeway*[12]

**Working practices in developing countries**

Safeway was one of the first supermarkets to stock Cafédirect coffee and other products from the Fairtrade range which ensures that third world producers and workers receive a better deal. Safeway has traditionally audited a number of working practices when visiting suppliers and is now looking more closely at this issue in order to identify the best ways of encouraging further change.

**Ethical purchasing**

Safeway has a vital role to play in upholding social, environmental and employment conditions and determining suitable courses of action if these are not acceptable – whether withdrawing our contract or encouraging the supplier to make the necessary changes.

For example, in 1992, Safeway became the first major food retailer to carry the fairly traded Cafédirect coffee. This has since been extended to include Percol coffee and Clipper tea. At the end of 1997,

Safeway helped launch the Ethical Trading Initiative with other businesses and non-governmental bodies. Its aim is to develop a framework that will help govern the way business organises its trade with developing countries.

## *Sainsbury's Codes of Conduct*[13]

Application and monitoring

This Code of Practice sets out how the Principles, which of necessity are described in general terms, are to be applied in the ordinary course of business by Sainsbury's Supermarkets and their suppliers.

Sainsbury's representatives will be looking to work positively with suppliers towards a general compliance with the Principles as amplified by the Code of Practice. Monitoring of performance will be incorporated into the normal monitoring and inspection process carried out by the staff of Sainsbury's Supermarkets and their representatives. Availability of records and full access to premises and staff will be important in demonstrating compliance. Suppliers who employ agents or subcontractors will be expected to take responsibility for these aspects of performance as they do for any other aspect of contract compliance.

Specific lapses in performance will be taken up as part of the normal control arrangements. Where it becomes apparent that the Principles and Code of Practice are not being achieved in substance, suppliers will be expected to work with Sainsbury's representatives to achieve an agreed standard. This will be done in a spirit of partnership but Sainsbury's would not expect to continue doing business with companies that are unwilling to work towards such improvements.

**Fair trading**

Clear terms and conditions will be agreed at the commencement of each contract. These will include product specification and payment terms. Suppliers will have to respond to the highly competitive environments in which Sainsbury's and Homebase trade. Sainsbury's and Homebase will not make undue use of their size to bring unfair pressure on suppliers.

The importance of complying with product safety standards must be understood.

**Protection of children**

Special care is needed in the employment of children. Where children are employed due consideration must be given to their age, the hours worked, rates of pay, safety and impact on education. The ILO Conventions on child employment should be the standard.

Establishing a child's age may be difficult where there is no legal system of verification; the employer has a responsibility to make proper enquiry into the child's age and to maintain a record.

Where children are employed the employer must comply with all applicable child labour law including those relating to schooling, hiring, wages, hours worked, overtime and working conditions.

It is expected that the employer will encourage eligible younger workers to attend classes or participate in work study or other government sponsored educational programmes.

Where it is traditional for whole families to work the nature of the work undertaken by children must be clearly understood and appropriate to their age.

Children should not be allowed to work at night.

**Health and safety**

*General*

Employers are expected to provide a safe working place and ensure that the local laws relating to health and safety in the workplace are adhered to. If living accommodation and facilities are provided health and safety requirements apply equally to these. Furthermore, employee representatives should be involved in the development of standards appropriate to the workplace.

*Factories, farms and plantations*

These must comply with all relevant national laws relating to working conditions including health and safety, sanitation, fire safety and electrical, mechanical and structural safety.

There must be sufficient ventilation and light. This could include windows, fans, air conditioners or heaters, as appropriate, in order to provide adequate ventilation, circulation and temperature control to all areas.

Machinery should be well maintained, inspected and equipped with operational safety devices.

Employees should be trained in the use of personal safety equipment; essential equipment should be available free of charge.

*Fire safety*

Attention should be given to the following:

- Fitting fire alarms to each floor with emergency lighting above exits and stairways.
- Accessibility of aisles and clearly marked emergency exits which should be unlocked during working hours and free from debris.
- Ready availability of fire extinguishers and other appropriate fire fighting equipment which should be easily accessible and regularly maintained.
- Evidence that evacuation drills are conducted.
- Hazardous and combustible materials must be stored securely, in well ventilated areas and disposed of in a safe and legal manner.

Health

- Employees should have reasonable access to potable water throughout the day.
- Every factory floor should be provided with one well-stocked first aid kit.
- Procedures to deal with serious injuries requiring medical attention must be in place.
- Sufficient clean and sanitary toilet areas, with no unreasonable restrictions on their use, must be in place.

Accommodation

- Accommodation or dormitory facilities provided for staff must be kept clean and safe, maintained in a good condition and meet all relevant health and safety regulations and the local industry standard.
- There should be sufficient space for sleeping and toilets to allow segregation by gender or family group.
- Potable water should be provided or facilities to boil water should be accessible.
- Mats and beds and personal storage areas for clothing and per-

sonal possessions should be available for each employee.

- Facilities must have adequate lighting, be well ventilated and, as appropriate, have windows to the outside, air conditioners and/or heaters in all sleeping areas to provide adequate circulation, ventilation and temperature control; there will be proper fire precautions.
- Dormitory residents must have freedom of movement during their off-work hours (subject to limitations imposed for their safety and comfort).

Equal opportunities

- In applying the general principle full account must be taken of cultural and other factors in the country concerned.
- People with similar skills should receive equal treatment.
- There should be no discrimination in relation to access to jobs or training.

Freedom of association

- Employees must be free within the law to join unions or associations of their choosing without fear of intimidation or discrimination.
- Employers should not use any forced labour.
- Employers shall not engage in or permit physical acts to punish or coerce employees, neither will the employer allow psychological coercion or any other form of non-physical abuse.

Remuneration

*Hours of work and wages*

- Working hours, wages, overtime pay and holiday entitlements should be set in compliance with all applicable laws pertaining, not only to the country, but also to each industry sector.
- Normal working hours should not exceed those recommended by International Labour Organisation standards (a maximum of 48 hours per week with up to 12 hours of occasional overtime).
- Wages should be paid promptly in cash, cheque or direct to the worker's bank or other mutually agreed method which does

not use company tokens.

- The employer should provide employees with an understandable statement of their remuneration and keep records of payment.
- Employers should not avoid their legal obligations to employees through the unjustified use of temporary contracts or insistence on self employed status.

*Overtime*

It is accepted that overtime is often required in a variety of industry sectors. Overtime should not be excessive; where it is necessary the rate of pay or incentive rates must meet all legal requirements or higher local industry standard.

*Time-off/holiday entitlement*

- Employees should have on average at least one day off in seven.
- Employers should provide paid annual leave and holidays as required by law or higher local industry standard.

## *Tesco*[14]

Tesco is working with suppliers to improve conditions, not just for employees, but their families too. Housing, schools, creches, medical and recreational facilities are just some of the improvements made as a result. While it is impossible to shape and influence the working practices of entire cultures and economies around the world, Tesco believes it has an important part to play in providing an incentive for change. Only those companies who agree to abide by Tesco policies on workplace heath, safety and employment can become approved Tesco suppliers.

Among these policies are those which insist upon:

- Adherence to local labour laws, especially minimum age requirements.
- A fair pay for all, at rates that are reasonable within the local economy.
- Many other employment practices are also covered by Tesco

policies, which often impose standards far exceeding legal requirements.

All of these policies are monitored continually by Tesco staff, who carry out rolling programmes of inspection, both in Britain and abroad, to ensure that suppliers continue to maintain, develop and improve standards. Any supplier found to have broken these terms, or to have fallen below the ethical standards required by Tesco, may have their contracts cancelled immediately.

## *Waitrose*

Waitrose prides itself on its approach to responsible sourcing, and this is summarised in the constitution of the John Lewis Partnership as follows: 'The Partnership's relationships with its suppliers must be based, as with customers, on honesty, fairness, courtesy and promptness. It looks for a similar attitude throughout its supply chains. In particular, the Partnership expects its suppliers to obey the law and to respect the well-being of their employees, their local communities and the environment.'

Since the earliest inception of the Ethical Trading Initiative, Waitrose has participated constructively in numerous meetings and has commented extensively on draft documentation. We are participating in ETI pilots, and remain fully supportive of its aims and ambitions. We have also employed an ethical trade consultant to help develop our own policies and systems for supplier evaluation and monitoring. We are not prepared at present to sign up to the ETI until we feel there is a clearer consensus about the base code of practice across the corporate, NGO and union sectors.

A vital part of our approach is the Waitrose Responsible Sourcing Code of Practice. This is designed to ensure that our own trading principles are echoed in our dealings with suppliers, and they in turn with their employees. We have worked in co-operation and partnership with suppliers to achieve a relevant and workable code. Additionally, we have consulted external organisations such as Christian Aid, the Ethical Trading Initiative, The Fairtrade Foundation, the Council for Economic Priorities, the International

Labour Office (a body of the United Nations), Amnesty International and the Organisation for Economic Co-operation and Development's guidelines for multinational enterprises.

Commitment to the code flows from policy determined by the Waitrose Managing Committee, guided by the Responsible Sourcing Steering Committee. Policy affects the development of inspection and monitoring systems, determines agreement on processes for corrective actions or sanctions, and heightens awareness and understanding of Responsible Sourcing within our business.

## Example codes of conduct from footwear retailers

### *Clarks Employment Conditions – Code of Practice*

Since its foundation in 1825, Clarks has enjoyed a high reputation for the humane and progressive treatment of their direct employees, and the open, honest and honourable way that it conducts its business relationships.

This Code of Practice lists the minimum requirements that Clarks expect from their immediate suppliers and their sub-contractors. Any failure to comply with the conditions of this Code of Practice either by a primary supplier or their sub-contractors could lead to the cancellation of orders and legal action to seek compensation for any damage caused to the Clarks business by the failure to comply.

We expect suppliers to make a significant effort to continuously improve the working conditions of their workforce.

1. Forced labour: We recognise the right of individuals to choose the work that they wish to do. No forced labour of any description should be used.
2. Equality of treatment: Workers should have access to jobs and training on equal terms irrespective of gender, age, race, colour, political opinion, religion or social origin. Physical harassment or psychological oppression particularly of women workers must not be tolerated.
3. Wages: Pay should be in cash or into a bank account direct to the workers promptly and in full. Information relating to wages should be available to workers in an understand-

able form. Wages should equal or exceed industry averages or legal minima and be at least sufficient for basic needs.

4. Working hours: Normal hours should not exceed 48 per week. Under normal circumstances, overtime should be voluntary, should not exceed 12 hours per week and should be paid according to national legislation. Workers should have at least 24 consecutive hours of rest per week and paid leave in line with national legislation.
5. Health and safety: Suppliers should provide free protective clothing and equipment and comply with internationally recognised health and safety standards. Workers and their organisation should be consulted, trained and allowed to investigate safety issues. Factories must have adequate fire exits and fire-prevention facilities. Dormitories, warehouses and workshops must be in separate buildings.
6. Security of employment: Suppliers should endeavour to employ workers long-term on the basis of negotiated, legal, written contracts. Employers should give at least as much notice to employees, as they demand from them. All the provisions of this code should apply to part-time, short-term and casual workers.
7. Social security: Suppliers should ensure that workers are included in all appropriate state or private security provisions, especially invalidity benefit, injury benefit and old-age benefit.
8. Employment of children: No children under 14 (or the legal minimum or school leaving age if higher) should be newly recruited. Children under 18 should not work at night or in hazardous conditions.

## *The Shoe Studio Group – Standards for Contractors and Suppliers*

The Shoe Studio Group Ltd and its wholly owned subsidiaries are committed to legal compliance and ethical business practice in all of our operations world-wide. We choose suppliers and contractors who we believe share that commitment. We require our suppliers and contractors to comply with all applicable laws and regulations of the country, or countries, in which they are conducting business. Our standards are summarised as follows.

### Child labour

Contractors and suppliers must not use child labour, defined under the age of 14, or higher if the country of manufacture requires compulsory education beyond 14 years of age.

### Wages/benefits

Employees must be compensated for all hours worked, at rates that meet the national minimum standards or local industry standards, whichever is higher. Overtime must be compensated at legally mandated rates, or at a rate at least equal to the regular hourly wage. Employees must be provided all legally mandated benefits.

### Working hours/days off

On a regular basis, employees shall not be required to work more than the lesser of 60 hours per week, including overtime, or the amount specified by the applicable labour code. Workers shall have at least one day of rest in every seven.

### Health and safety – workplace and housing

Health, safety and other workplace environment conditions must meet all applicable laws and regulations, including those for housing where provided.

### Forced labour

Our contractors and suppliers must not utilise forced labour, prison labour or other compulsory labour. Or purchase materials from suppliers using forced labour, prison labour or compulsory labour.

### Discrimination

Contractors and suppliers must not discriminate against employees or potential employees in employment practices, including hiring, wages, benefits, advancement, disciplinary procedures, termination or retirement, on the basis of gender, race, religion, age, disability, nationality, political opinion, sexual orientation, ethnic origin, maternity or marital status.

**Environment**

Contractors and suppliers must adhere to all applicable laws regarding the protection and preservation of the environment.

**Disciplinary practices**

The Shoe Studio Group Ltd will not utilise contractors or suppliers who use corporate punishment or any form of mental or physical coercion or harassment.

**Freedom of association**

Employees should be free to join organisations of their own choice. Employees should not be subject to intimidation or harassment in the exercise of their right to join, or to refrain from joining any organisation.

**Customs compliance**

Contractors and suppliers must respect all applicable laws regarding the importance and transhipment of merchandise into the United Kingdom, Ireland or the EEC.

**Subcontracting**

Contractors and suppliers may not subcontract any operation in the manufacturing process without prior written consent from The Shoe Studio Group Ltd. Any subcontractor must be able to meet the criteria set forth above.

**Inspections: record keeping by contractor/supplier – verification by The Shoe Studio Group Ltd**

In order for The Shoe Studio Group Ltd to monitor compliance with these standards:

1. Contractors and suppliers must permit representatives of The Shoe Studio Group Ltd complete and free access to employees, the workplace and workers' housing (where applicable); and
2. Contractors and suppliers must keep and maintain thorough records of employment actions, hours worked, wages

paid, charges to workers for housing and meals (where applicable), and other relevant records. All such records must be made available to representatives of The Shoe Studio Group Ltd upon request.

### *Schuh*

As a fashion footwear retailer we purchase the majority of our product range from a number of wholesale distributors and suppliers, and rely on the policies of individual brand partners to ensure that their own practices are in keeping with acceptable fair trading regulations. As an equal opportunities employer ourselves with a commitment to best practice in all aspects of our business activity, we make a concerted effort to work with brand suppliers who we believe share our views in this issue. We do have a small percentage of our own brand product produced in developing countries; however, due to the minimal volume of these products, we are currently unable to effectively monitor the compliance of an ethical trading policy. Like many, we are consciously aware of the plight of individuals in countries that do not offer workers the protection we are fortunate to enjoy within the United Kingdom. We, like the majority of retailers, work within the normal regulations concerning employment as set out by the European Labour Laws.

## Example codes of conduct from furniture retailers

### *Habitat*

Habitat's sourcing policy is to only use woods that are not endangered and are abundant. We substitute softwood for hardwood whenever the nature of the timber is not fundamental to the product. When using tropical woods we constantly aim to verify the forest management regime from which the timber came. We also support the principles of the Forest Stewardship Council.

Habitat employees visit all manufacturers in the Far East and the Indian Sub-Continent approximately twice a year. This is to ensure that child slave labour is not employed on any of our products. However we cannot provide a complete assurance with regard to bonded labour because of the hold of an adult over a child. All vendors are certainly aware that should a child be found to be working illegally, we would re-source immediately.

Habitat trade responsibly throughout the world. We pay the best price we can for merchandise, but not a price that cannot be sustained by the vendor. Many of the vendors whom we have traded with over the years have expanded with us and thus created employment for local people. We also ensure no intermediaries take a financial 'cut' from our business by always ordering from and paying the actual manufacturer.

Habitat uses the minimum of display packaging and we also recycle all corrugated cartons to have them recycled into our main carrier bags and catalogue.

## *MFI's Ethical Policy*

MFI responded to a letter containing the following questions:

1. Are your own brand products produced in developing countries?
2. Do you have a Code of Conduct?
3. Is the Code of Conduct mandatory for your suppliers?
4. Do you have independent inspectors for compliance to the Code of Conduct?

'Schreiber Furniture Ltd and Hygena Ltd are wholly owned subsidiaries of MFI Furniture Group Plc and they, together with a smaller subsidiary, Hygena Components Ltd, produce between 55 and 60% of the goods that are sold in MFI Furniture Centres Ltd stores. In practice, Hygena/Schreiber will manufacture the kitchen and bedroom furniture and our factories in the North of England produce the kitchen and bedroom carcasses and some of the door and drawer fronts. Traditionally when we experiment by introducing a new range, we will buy in the door and drawer fronts from one of the leading Italian manufacturers and if it proves popular ie there is a large volume of doors to be made we will then start to make them ourselves. The Hygena factories also make ovens and hobs, stainless steel and resin sinks and the plastic and metal components that are required in the kitchens and bedrooms that we sell eg shelf supports, metal components etc.

Some of the items that we buy in such as lighting and stools do emanate from the Far East and we are currently investigating the possibility of sourcing some kitchen doors in Vietnam. Turning now to your specific questions the answers are as follows:

1. Some, but not all; overall the percentage from the developing countries in terms of turnover is very small ie less than 2%.
2. We do have an ethical trading policy but it is not in writing. The reason for this is that with only four buyers it was never thought worthwhile reducing it to writing. However, we are expanding the buying department and I am currently attempting to draft a suitable policy. I have examined various policies prepared eg by the Ethical Trading Organisation and I do not think we will have any difficulty complying. You may be interested to know that MFI was a founder member of the Worldwide Fund 95 Group. In 1996 we commissioned SGS Inspection Services to visit all our suppliers throughout the world to audit the origin of materials supplied to MFI. Although we continue to support the objectives of WWF we felt compelled to resign from the organisation because it was impossible to effectively audit the origin of all timber. The reason for this is that occasionally timber is bought on the spot and you can never guarantee its origin. Since then the WWF initiative has in effect been replaced by the Forest Stewardship Council which enables companies to purchase certified material.
3. The Policy is mandatory for all our suppliers in that MFI would not consider purchasing goods or services without asking to see the supplier's H&S Policy Statement, Environmental Statement and Sourcing Policy and establishing that all employees are properly remunerated and work in suitable conditions and are not under age. It is difficult to be precise because no two situations are exactly

the same. However, the point I am trying to get across is that if a supplier had all the appropriate documentation but in principle ignored it then MFI would not want to do business with them. If another supplier failed to comply with one or two of our requirements we would rather work with them to bring them up to the required standard instead of refusing to purchase from them.

4. All our buyers visit our suppliers' factories on a regular basis and report following each visit.'

## *An extract from Courts plc Ethical Trading Policy Supplier Requirements for Safety, Quality, Legal, Environmental and Social Issues, Section 3 (Social)*

We shall ensure that the merchandise we source is obtained from manufacturers who maintain satisfactory working conditions and at a minimum, comply fully with all legal requirements and the labour, health and safety standards of those countries in which production takes place. We oppose the exploitation of child labour and exploitation of workers in general and we support a fair and reasonable reward for workers comparable with the local norms in the countries of production.

We recognise that our customers are concerned about price, quality, convenience and safety of the goods we supply and increasingly the internal corporate practices that we operate. We support the principle of supplier companies operating to internationally agreed standards and codes of labour practice.

### Supplier standards

We are committed to supporting the International Standard SA8000 for Social Accountability as a minimum standard for our suppliers. We are working with our suppliers to promote best practice in the local industry norms.

We expect our suppliers to support these minimum standards:

- 3.1 Employment choice. Employment is freely chosen and there is no forced labour. Workers are not required to pay deposits nor have identity papers as a condition of employment.

- 3.2 Child labour. There should be no child labour. Normally 15 years of age unless local minimum age law is set at a lower age. No child under the age of 14 years should be employed in any circumstances regardless of local conditions.
- 3.3 Working environment. Suppliers must provide a safe and hygienic working environment bearing in mind the prevailing knowledge of the industry and any specific hazards. There should be supplies of potable water, access to clean toilet facilities, any applicable safety equipment and necessary training given.
- 3.4 Freedom of association. Freedom of association and the right to collective bargaining are respected and workers without distinction shall have the right to join or form trade unions without fear of reprisals.
- 3.5 Discrimination. No discrimination is practised on the basis of race, caste, national origin, religion, age, disability, gender, marital status, sexual orientation, union membership or political affiliation.
- 3.6 Treatment of staff. Harsh or inhumane treatment is forbidden; no corporal punishment, mental or physical coercion or verbal abuse is allowed.
- 3.7 Working hours. A maximum 48-hour working week shall be operated with at least one day off for every 7 working day period. Overtime shall be voluntary, shall not exceed 12 hours per week and pre-paid at a premium rate.
- 3.8 Wages. Wages should meet national, legal or industry benchmark standards, whichever is higher. Wages should be sufficient to meet basic needs and provide some discretionary income.

## *IKEA – Our Responsibility*[15]

We at IKEA want our customers to be aware that our products are manufactured in a responsible way. We have firmly stated our views and policies relating to working environment, child labour and environmental awareness to our suppliers in a code of conduct: 'The IKEA Way on Purchasing Home Furnishing Products'. We respect different cultures and we are aware that working conditions vary between countries. However, wherever our suppliers are located, we have certain fundamental requirements: the working place shall be safe and protection against noise, dust and dangerous machinery shall exist and all employees shall be treated fairly and well.

Child labour is an unacceptable part of the reality of today. It occurs in a number of the countries where we make our purchases. Our attitude is to always see to the best interests of the child in what we do.

Our operations affect our planet and its resources. Environmental questions and questions as to how we use our resources efficiently are therefore an important part of our operations. Together with our suppliers we are continually working to improve the environment. Many of our suppliers already have well implemented environmental management systems in place, while others are only beginning. A large proportion of the raw materials for our furniture consist of wood or wood fibre. It is vitally important for us that the forests from which our raw materials come are managed and logged in a responsible way. As a minimum requirement, we insist that the wood in our solid wood furniture does not originate from intact natural forests, if not specially certified.

**Extract from 'The IKEA Way on Purchasing Home Furnishing Products'**

*Working conditions*

IKEA expects its suppliers to respect fundamental human rights, to treat their workforce fairly and with respect.

Suppliers must:

- Provide a healthy and safe working environment,
- Pay the legal minimum wage or the local industry standard and compensate for overtime,
- If housing facilities are provided, ensure reasonable privacy, quietness and personal hygiene.

Suppliers must not:

- Make use of child labour,
- Make use of forced or bonded labour,
- Discriminate,
- Use illegal overtime,
- Prevent workers from associating freely with any workers,

association or group of their choosing or collective bargaining,
- Accept any form of mental or physical disciplinary action, including harassment.

## Example codes of conduct from health and beauty retailers

### *The Body Shop International – Trading Charter*[16]

We aim to achieve commercial success by meeting our customers' needs by the provision of high quality, good value products with exceptional service and relevant information which enables customers to make informed and responsible choices.

Our trading relationships of every kind – with customers, franchisees and suppliers – will be commercially viable, mutually beneficial and based on trust and respect.

We aim to ensure that human and civil rights, as set out in the Universal Declaration of Human Rights, are respected throughout our business activities. We will establish a framework based on this declaration to include criteria for workers' rights embracing a safe, healthy working environment, fair wages, no discrimination on the basis of race, creed, gender or sexual orientation, or physical coercion of any kind.

We will support long term, sustainable relationships with communities in need. We will pay special attention to those minority groups, women and disadvantaged peoples who are socially and economically marginalised.

We will use environmentally sustainable resources wherever technically and economically viable. Our purchasing will be based on a system of screening and investigation of the ecological credentials of our finished products, ingredients, packaging and suppliers.

We will promote animal protection throughout our business activities. We are against animal testing in the cosmetics and toiletries industry. We will not test ingredients or products on animals, nor will we commission others to do so on our behalf. We will use our purchasing power to stop suppliers animal testing.

We will institute appropriate monitoring, auditing and disclosure mechanisms to ensure our accountability and demonstrate our compliance with these principles.

## *Alliance-UniChem*

Alliance-UniChem responded to a letter containing the following questions:

1. Are your own brand products produced in developing countries?
2. Do you have a Code of Conduct?
3. Is the Code of Conduct mandatory for your suppliers?
4. Do you have independent inspectors for compliance to the Code of Conduct?

1. Our own-brand medicine products are sourced from manufacturers approved by the European Union or European member states and licensed for the production of medicines under codes of practice and guidelines laid down by national or European regulation. We therefore accept this as a suitable standard with regard to the conditions under which these products are manufactured. To my knowledge the bulk of these products are produced within the European Union or by one of two large manufacturers in India who are recognised as fully licensed and reputable suppliers.
2. Our own-brand non-medical products are sourced on the whole from manufacturers with whom we have long-standing relationships and whom we believe to be ethical and responsible. However, I acknowledge that to date I am unaware of a formal sourcing policy with regard to the ethical compliance of these manufacturers.
3. Supplier agreements with all our manufacturers to establish minimum requirements under our products must be made. However, as indicated, I am unaware that we have a central policy for this.

We do maintain a strict policy that no own-brand product of either Moss or UniChem is animal tested. This policy cannot be applied to the branded products of pharmaceutical companies that we sell, as you will be aware, as part of the standard licensing requirements for pharmaceuticals in Europe includes clinical testing which, in most instances, incorporates some element of animal testing. As a full-line wholesaler we have a legal and moral obligation to supply patients with the medicines they require. However, as I have stated, our own-brand products for both Moss and UniChem are not normally tested (including our own-brand medicines) as we have no own-brand medicine product which has not already been awarded a licence while being manufactured by one of the international drug companies. We therefore simply manufacture to a recognised standard and are not required to undertake additional testing beyond standard quality control.

## *The Boots Company – Code of Conduct for Ethical Trading*

The Boots Company is committed to sourcing quality merchandise and developing partnerships with suppliers who share common principles of fair and honest trading.

We require the same principles to be adopted by all those involved in the supply of merchandise to The Boots Company and its subsidiaries at all times.

We are committed to ensuring that the merchandise we source is obtained only from manufacturers who maintain satisfactory working conditions and as a minimum comply fully with all legal requirements and the labour, health and safety standards of those countries in which production takes place.

The following code of conduct applies to all our business dealings:

- We oppose the exploitation of child labour and will not trade with manufacturers employing children under the age permitted in the countries concerned.
- We oppose the exploitation of workers in general and we will not tolerate forced labour or labour which involves physical or mental abuse or the exploitation of any vulnerable group.
- We support a fair and reasonable reward for workers which must be fully comparable with local norms including minimum wage criteria where applicable. All terms and conditions of

employment must be compatible with the principles of fair and honest trading and have due regard to the welfare of individuals.

- Suppliers must ensure that all manufacturing processes are carried out under conditions which have proper and adequate regard for health and safety of those concerned.

We will take all reasonable and practical steps, including factory inspectors and audits, to ensure that our required standards are being met by all our suppliers and in turn by their subcontractors.

We will only trade with those who comply fully with our policy and in the event of any failure to do so, we reserve the right to end the business relationship and cancel outstanding orders. We do however recognise that in the event of non-compliance, withdrawal of our business may cause severe hardship to those employed and will therefore work with our suppliers to achieve compliance before severing the relationship.

## Example codes of conduct from home shopping companies

### *Avon*

Avon beauty products are manufactured by Avon in a number of manufacturing facilities around the world while non-beauty items are sourced with carefully selected third party manufacturers. It is a key principle for Avon that all activities are undertaken within clear guidelines, supporting the highest standards of business operation.

Social accountability standards are in place relating to workforce and working conditions at Avon and at our suppliers, and each Avon facility globally is responsible for the implementation of procedures, communications, training and monitoring compliance. Purchasing contracts for components, ingredients etc are required to contain reference to compliance by suppliers as a condition to doing business with Avon. Independent auditing bodies have been appointed to support this process.

## *Betterware's policy on child labour*

At Betterware we make every effort to use UK based manufacturers for our goods. Indeed many of our products are sourced locally. However, in order to satisfy our customers' demands for variety and low prices, we do have to obtain products from other parts of the world, including the Far East, from time to time. In doing this, we are the same as the vast majority of retailers in the UK.

We conduct most of our Far Eastern business via an agency company based in Hong Kong, with whom we have traded for many years. This company seeks to ensure, on our behalf, that all the Chinese manufacturers who sell us goods conform to the highest ethical standards, in line with best practice and as operated by many large UK companies.

Our trading relationship with these independent manufacturers should not be construed as any sort of expression, positive or negative, of attitudes to the state.

## *Empire Stores Group – extract from 'Aims and Ethics'*

In relation to our suppliers:

- We will have an open and honest approach to potential and existing suppliers, ensuring equality of treatment.
- We will seek to develop long-term trading relationships, based on mutual trust.
- We will expect our suppliers to offer the best conditions as to price, quality and service for our markets.
- We will pay our suppliers on time.
- We will not use the purchasing power of the Group unscrupulously.
- We will not disclose to third parties any confidential information concerning our relationship and dealings with suppliers.
- We will avoid sourcing from manufacturers where labour (eg child labour) is exploited contrary to the rules and guidelines of the International Labour Organisation.
- We will expect all suppliers to comply with the above standards.

## *Lands' End – Standards of Business Conduct*

As direct merchants, we go anywhere in the world to find partners who are able to give us the best combination of quality, price and service that will allow us to deliver honest value to our customers. In this global environment, we take an interest in the standards of our business partners around the world.

In developing this policy, we have sought to use standards that are appropriate to diverse cultures and encourage workers to take pride in their work. We have found that these standards result in higher quality working environments and in higher quality products.

Compliance with our standards is a condition for becoming and remaining a business partner of Lands' End. If Lands' End has determined that any business partner has violated its Standards of Business Conduct, we will either require the business partner to implement a corrective action plan or terminate the business relationship. If corrective action is advised but not taken, Lands' End will suspend placement of future orders and may terminate current production.

In all of our dealings with our partners, we comply with our own Lands' End Code of Conduct and the Foreign Corrupt Practices Act. We take special care in selecting partners who follow fair, decent and legal labour practices, agree to our Standards of Business Conduct, and are dedicated to producing a quality product.

### Employment practices

- Child labour: Workers or other children present in a facility can be no less than the legal minimum working age in the host country and no less than 16, whichever is greater, except that workers can be 14 years old provided that they are enrolled in a school sponsored program which at a minimum combines work with schooling.
- Wages and benefits: Workers must be paid wages and benefits which at a minimum comply with any applicable law and match the prevailing local industry practices.

- Forced or compulsory labour: Forced or compulsory labour, as well as use of corporal punishment will not be tolerated.
- Discrimination: Workers should be employed based on their ability to perform the job, rather than discriminating on the basis of race, creed, gender, politics, or other personal characteristics or beliefs.
- Freedom of association: There shall be no unlawful interference with the right of workers to choose, or not to choose, to affiliate with legally sanctioned organisations or associations.
- Inducements: Business partners may not offer or extend gifts or financial awards for the purpose of influencing any employee or representative of Lands' End in any manner.

**Working conditions**

A safe and healthy work environment must be provided. Business partners who provide residential facilities for their workers must keep those facilities clean and safe.

**Environment**

Business partners should share our concern for the environment and adhere to their local and national laws regarding the protection and preservation of the environment.

**Intellectual property**

Business partners must respect the significance of and support the protection of the trade secrets, patents, trademarks, and copyrighted works of Lands' End and other companies.

**Legal requirements**

Business partners should be in compliance with all legal requirements involved in conducting their business.

Lands' End runs a customs compliant business for all countries in which it does business. Business partners must be in compliance with customs regulations including:

- Country of origin and marking rules,
- Proper valuation of product,
- Clear product description allowing for proper classification,
- Proper quota and visa application,

- Record keeping requirements,
- Rules preventing transshipment intended to circumvent regulation,
- Unfair trade practices as defined by the customs laws, such as dumping.

**Contract relationship**
Sub-contracting without Lands' End prior written approval is not permitted to an unrelated or affiliated company or facility.

Our business partners are required to provide full access to their facilities and to relevant records relating to employment practices. We will conduct on-site inspections including unannounced visits of facilities to monitor these standards and assure the quality of our products. Lands' End will use discretion in evaluating compliance with these standards and may terminate business with any partner found violating the intent or spirit of our agreement.

## Example codes of conduct from household retailers

### *MUJI*

---

All our products are offered to the consumer under our own brand 'MUJI'. More than 80% of our MUJI apparel products are being produced outside Japan, of which 90% are produced in China, while our household products are mainly made in Japan.

Although we do not own nor directly operate factories manufacturing MUJI products, we realise that we need to know situations surrounding workforces in the factories producing MUJI products in developing countries and to establish the policy on maintaining relations with existing suppliers/manufacturers and selecting new ones from the ethical and fair trade's point of view.

We must admit that we do not have a specific policy nor code of conduct on this issue at this moment but we are currently discussing to prepare our policy and hope to materialise it in the near future.

### *Argos – extract from Policy Statement on Sound Manufacturing Conditions*

Argos opposes the exploitation of child labour and will not knowingly make purchases from manufacturers who do not comply with the labour, safety and other relevant laws of their respective countries, or from manufacturing sources where workers of any age are expected to work in unreasonable conditions, ie where the level of hygiene, safety or general environment are clearly unsatisfactory taking account of local conditions. Argos opposes the exploitation of workers generally and supports a fair reward and good working environment, again taking account of local working conditions.

## Example codes of conduct from jewellers

### *Signet – extract from Annual Report 2000/1: social, environmental and ethical (SEE) matters*

**Suppliers**

The Group recognises that stakeholders expect companies to take responsibility for and, where possible, to exert influence over suppliers to ensure that SEE standards are upheld throughout the supply chain. Most of the raw and processed materials for the merchandise sold by Signet are traded on commodity exchanges, through multiple brokers and traders making the source difficult to trace.

The Group is considering how to effectively influence its supply chain. One of the issues facing not only the Group but also the entire diamond sector is 'conflict diamonds', which are diamonds being sold by rebel movements to fund military campaigns. The Group has been involved in industry debates aimed at identifying a way forward. The Group is a non-voting member of World Diamond Council ('WDC') which has proposed legislation in the US in connection with the import of conflict diamonds. The WDC is also working with the United Nations and government bodies to introduce a workable system for the certification of the source of uncut diamonds. The Group worked with Jewelers of America which issued briefing material to all its members, including vendor guidance and an industry position statement. Based on the Jewelers of America policy, the Group has sent a letter to all its diamond suppliers requiring them to use their best endeavours not to supply the Group with conflict diamonds.

In respect of supplier payment, Group policy is that the operating businesses are responsible for agreeing the terms and conditions under which business transactions with their suppliers are conducted, rather than to follow any particular code or standard on payment practice. Suppliers are accordingly aware of the terms of payment and it is Group policy to ensure that payments to suppliers are made in accordance with these agreed terms.

## Example codes of conduct from sports retailers

### *Blacks Employment Standards*[17]

The Group is committed to health and safety as a common objective for all management and employees. The Group will ensure, as far as is reasonably practicable, that a safe and healthy workplace and working environment is provided for all its employees to a standard which is at least as high as that required by law.

The Group purchases goods for resale from suppliers based in the UK and direct from manufacturers around the world. The Group endeavours to ensure that the suppliers of our goods provide reasonable working standards for their employees and do not contravene the employment laws of their country.

The Group is committed to a policy of equal opportunities for staff at all levels.

### *YHA Adventure*

We do produce own brand products in China; however we do not have a written policy.

We are very careful to ensure that all our own products are made under satisfactory conditions. For this reason we use two reputable agents in Hong Kong who we have known for many years. They visit factories in China regularly and we ourselves have been there on several occasions. The standard of the factories is high, most of the equipment is as modern as in Europe, and conditions and working hours are good.

We have also looked at other factories in the past and rejected them, not because we actually saw bad practice, but because we could not be certain that it was not taking place behind the scenes. As we cannot visit regularly we prefer to use a trusted agent in Hong Kong.

The fact is, that because of the high standard of competence required to construct products for the outdoor industry, it is not really possible for the standard of products we need to be manufactured without modern equipment and working practices.

## *JJB Sports – Code of Practice on Socially Responsible Trading*

JJB are the UK's leading sports retailer and a prominent FTSE quoted company. Furthermore, given the nature of our supply chain, JJB is also part of an international business. This fact, along with the ongoing globalisation of the world economy, brings with it exciting opportunities for the future of JJB, but it also raises genuine concerns over the conditions in which the goods we sell through our stores are produced. These concerns are real and important to JJB because they are important to our customers. Furthermore, we also recognise our responsibility as a business for working closely with our suppliers to ensure that decent working conditions are upheld across the supply chain. We also share our suppliers' beliefs that better working conditions result in better productivity and better quality of output and therefore socially responsible trading is in the interests of employees, suppliers, retailers and consumers.

It must be stressed that JJB itself sources almost no product directly from the factories where its products are manufactured. Subsequently, the vast majority of products are purchased direct from UK companies who themselves source the product from the manufacturers and therefore JJB's Code of Practice has to be initially discussed with JJB's UK suppliers.

This Code of Practice on Socially Responsible Trading clearly sets out what we expect from our suppliers in terms of labour conditions. The Code of Practice will be distributed to all of our suppliers. JJB will also work closely with key suppliers to monitor and review their processes for ensuring ongoing compliance with their own Codes of Practice and internationally accepted best practice principles of labour standards (for example, the Ethical Trading Initiative (ETI) 'Base Code' and the 'Model Code of Conduct' devised by the World Federation of the Sporting Goods Industry). We believe that this process, along with our suppliers' own processes and controls, will help to ensure that labour standards continue to improve across the global sports and leisure industry supply chains.

**The principles of socially responsible trading**

The principles adopted by JJB are based on the internationally accepted principles of the ETI Base Code of Labour Standards and the Model Code of Conduct devised by the World Federation of the Sporting Goods Industry. We expect our suppliers to comply with the principles outlined below:

- Employment should be freely chosen
  There should be no forced, bonded or involuntary prison labour and employees should be free to leave their work, after giving reasonable notice.
- Freedom of association and the right to collective bargaining are respected
  Workers are free to join trade unions and other such organisations and worker representatives will not be discriminated against.
- Working conditions must be safe and hygienic
  Workers must receive health and safety training, have access to clean toilets and potable water. Accommodation, if provided, must be clean and safe.
- Child labour shall not be used
  There shall be no new recruitment of child labour and companies must provide for the transition of former child labourers out of the working environment.
- Living wages are paid
  Wages must meet minimum national standards or industry benchmarks, workers must be aware of the conditions of their

employment and illegal deductions will not be made from wages.

- Working hours are not excessive
  Working hours must comply with local national law or industry benchmarks. Workers shall not on a regular basis be required to work in excess of 48 hours per week and shall be provided with at least one day off for every 7 day period on average. Overtime shall be voluntary, shall not exceed 12 hours per week, shall not be demanded on a regular basis and shall always be compensated at a premium rate.
- No discrimination is practised
  There will be no discrimination in hiring, compensation, access to training, promotion, termination or retirement based on race, caste, national origin, religion, age, disability, gender, marital status, sexual orientation, union membership or political affiliation.
- Regular employment is provided
  To every extent possible, work performed must be on the basis of recognised employment relationships established through national law and practice.
- No harsh or inhumane treatment is allowed
  Physical abuse or discipline, the threat of physical abuse, sexual or other harassment and verbal abuse or other forms of intimidation shall be prohibited.
- Health and safety
  Suppliers and their partners shall endeavour to provide working environments that comply with all relevant health and safety legislation and best practice.
- Environment
  Suppliers and their partners shall minimise adverse effects on the environment and demonstrate commitment to ensuring continuous improvement in terms of their environmental performance.
- Legal compliance
  Suppliers and their partners shall operate in full compliance with national and local laws, rules and regulations relevant to their business operations.
- Community development
  Suppliers and their partners recognise the economic and social

impact of their work and are committed to improving conditions in the wider community.

Furthermore, we expect our suppliers to comply with the following:

- Monitoring and compliance
  Suppliers are able to demonstrate that Codes of Conduct on social responsibility and environmental matters are being adhered to across supply chains, via effective and ongoing internal and/or external monitoring procedures.
- Awareness raising
  Suppliers and their partners will make efforts, in addition to the distribution of a Code of Conduct across their businesses and supply chains, to promote awareness and understanding of the principles amongst all employees.
- Fair trading
  The manufacturers used by our suppliers are treated fairly and with respect and undue pressure is not placed on them through terms and conditions of supply.

## Example codes of conduct from toy retailers

### *Hamleys*

---

Hamleys does not have direct contact with toy manufacturers.

It is our policy to only conduct business with established, reputable suppliers who take responsibility for ensuring that the working environment and conditions of the manufacturers used by them, meet the standards agreed between them.

In the majority of cases these suppliers are members of the British Toy and Hobby Association who have confirmed their agreement to ensure that the conditions of the toy factories' code of practice are implemented by them. This code has the approval of the World Development Movement. These suppliers also appear on the approved suppliers list published by the British Association of Toy Retailers.

Any suppliers who are not members of the BTHA are likely to be small, specialist companies who do not manufacture in the Far East.

## *Early Learning Centre*

We trade with many countries around the world including China. Each of the factories we buy from is visited by a Senior Manager of Early Learning Centre at least once a year. They agree to abide by our standards and as part of this agreement we expect health and safety standards to be observed and ensure that the market wage is paid. We specifically demand that no children are employed or prison labour used.

We understand your concern and would like to assure you that we do not condone any practices which abuse human rights. However, we believe that it is through the benefits of trade that change can be brought about in the long term.

## *Walt Disney – Code of Conduct for Manufacturers*

At The Walt Disney Company, we are committed to:

- a standard of excellence in every aspect of our business and in every corner of the world;
- ethical and responsible conduct in all of our operations;
- respect for the rights of all individuals; and
- respect for the environment.

We expect these same commitments to be shared by all manufacturers of Disney merchandise. At a minimum, we require that all manufacturers of Disney merchandise meet the following standards.

**Child labour**

Manufacturers will not use child labour.

The term 'child' refers to a person younger than 15 (or 14 where local law allows) or, if higher, the local legal minimum age for employment or the age for completing compulsory education.

Manufacturers employing young persons who do not fall within the definition of 'children' will also comply with any laws and regulations applicable to such persons.

**Involuntary labour**
Manufacturers will not use any forced or involuntary labour, whether prison, bonded, indentured or otherwise.

**Coercion and harassment**
Manufacturers will treat each employee with dignity and respect, and will not use corporal punishment, threats of violence or other forms of physical, sexual, psychological or verbal harassment or abuse.

**Nondiscrimination**
Manufacturers will not discriminate in hiring and employment practices, including salary, benefits, advancement, discipline, termination or retirement, on the basis of race, religion, age, nationality, social or ethnic origin, sexual orientation, gender, political opinion or disability.

**Association**
Manufacturers will respect the rights of employees to associate, organise and bargain collectively in a lawful and peaceful manner, without penalty or interference.

**Health and safety**
Manufacturers will provide employees with a safe and healthy workplace in compliance with all applicable laws and regulations, ensuring at a minimum, reasonable access to potable water and sanitary facilities, fire safety, and adequate lighting and ventilation.

Manufacturers will also ensure that the same standards of health and safety are applied in any housing that they provide for employees.

**Compensation**
We expect manufacturers to recognise that wages are essential to meeting employees' basic needs. Manufacturers will, at a minimum, comply with all applicable wage and hour laws and regulations, including those relating to minimum wages, overtime, maximum hours, piece rates and other elements of compensation, and provide legally mandated benefits. Except in extraordinary business circumstances, manufacturers will not require employees to work more than the lesser of (a) 48 hours per week and 12 hours overtime or (b)

the limits on regular and overtime hours allowed by local law or, where local law does not limit the hours of work, the regular work week in such country plus 12 hours overtime. In addition, except in extraordinary business circumstances, employees will be entitled to at least one day off in every seven-day period.

Manufacturers will compensate employees for overtime hours at such premium rate as is legally required or, if there is no legally prescribed premium rate, at a rate at least equal to the regular hourly compensation rate.

Where local industry standards are higher than applicable legal requirements, we expect manufacturers to meet the higher standards.

### Protection of the environment

Manufacturers will comply with all applicable environmental laws and regulations.

### Other laws

Manufacturers will comply with all applicable laws and regulations, including those pertaining to the manufacture, pricing, sale and distribution of merchandise.

All references to 'applicable laws and regulations' in this Code of Conduct include local and national codes, rules and regulations as well as applicable treaties and voluntary industry standards.

### Subcontracting

Manufacturers will not use subcontractors for the manufacture of Disney merchandise or components thereof without Disney's express written consent, and only after the subcontractor has entered into a written commitment with Disney to comply with this Code of Conduct.

### Monitoring and compliance

Manufacturers will authorise Disney and its designated agents (including third parties) to engage in monitoring activities to confirm compliance with this Code of Conduct, including unannounced on site inspections of manufacturing facilities and employer-provided housing; reviews of books and records relating to employment matters; and private interviews with employees. Manufacturers will maintain on site all documentation that may be needed to demonstrate compliance with this Code of Conduct.

**Publication**

Manufacturers will take appropriate steps to ensure that the provisions of this Code of Conduct are communicated to employees, including the prominent posting of a copy of this Code of Conduct, in the local language and in a place readily accessible to employees, at all times.

# Notes

## Preface

[1] Whysall, P (2000) 'Addressing ethical issues in retailing: a stakeholder perspective', *International Review of Retail, Distribution and Consumer Research,* 10 (3), pp 305–18.
[2] Fairtrade Foundation (2000) 'Facts and figures', http://www.fairtrade.org.uk/Factsfig.htm, 10 November 2000, Fairtrade Foundation, London.
[3] ETI (2000) 'About ETI', http://www.ethicaltrade.org/_html/about/faq/framesets/f_shell.shtml, 10 November 2000, Ethical Trading Initiative, London.

## Chapter 1

[1] Brown, M M (2000) 'Commentary – meeting the challenge of poverty', *UNDP Choices Magazine,* http://www.undp.org/dpa/choices/2000/september/sept.htm, 14 March 2001, UNDP, New York.
[2] DWP (2001) *Households Below Average Income (HBAI) 1999/00,* Department of Work and Pensions, London.
[3] UNEP (2001) *Poverty Overview,* http://www.undp.org/poverty/overview/, 14 March 2001, United Nations Development Programme, New York.
[4] World Bank (2000) *World Development Indicators: 2000,* The World Bank, Washington, Table 6.9 (net official development assistance valued at the cost to the donor, less any repayments of loan principal during the same period. Data are shown at current prices and dollar exchange rates).
[5] UNDP (1999) *Human Development Report,* http://www.undp.org/hdro/report.html, 7 November 2000, United Nations Development Programme, Oxford University Press, Oxford.
[6] Christian Aid (1999) *Taking Stock – How the Supermarkets Stack Up on*

*Ethical Trading*, http://www.christian-aid.org.uk/f_reports.htm, 19 August 2000, Christian Aid, London.

7 Barrientos, S (2000) 'Globalisation and ethical trade: assessing the implications for development', *Journal of International Development*, 12, pp 559–70.

8 Waridal, L and Teitelbaum, S (1999) *Research Report – Fair Trade – Contributing to Equitable Commerce in Holland, Belgium, Switzerland and France*, http://www.equiterre.qc.ca/english/coffee/rapport.html, 21 August 2000, Équiterre, Montreal.

9 Barrientos (2000).

10 Waridal and Teitelbaum (1999).

11 Anderson, S and Cavanagh, J (2000) *Top 200 – The Rise of Corporate Global Power*, Institute for Policy Studies, Washington, p 9.

12 Brown, M B (1993) *Fair Trade – Reform and Realities in the International Trading System*, Zed Books, London.

13 WTO (2000) *What is the WTO?*, http://www.wto.org/english/thewto_e/whatis_e/whatis_e.htm, 7 November 2000, World Trade Organisation, Geneva.

14 Christian Aid (1999) *Fair Shares? Transnational Companies, the WTO and the World's Poorest Communities*, http://www.christian-aid.org.uk/f_reports.htm, 7 August 2000, Christian Aid, London.

15 NI (2000) 'Fair trade', *New Internationalist*, 322, April 2000.

16 Numbers from NI (2000), p 19.

17 Litterell, M A and Marsha, A D (1999) *Social Responsibility in the Global Market – Fair Trade of Cultural Products*, SAGE Publications, Thousand Oaks, California.

18 Hurst, R and Arnesen, M (2000) *Where Did That Come From? A Study of Ethical Issues in the Supply Chain*, The Institute of Business Ethics, London.

19 UNITE (2001) *Consumer Guide to Decent Clothes*, http://www.uniteunion.org/sweatshops/cando/cando.html, 15 March 2001, Union of Needletrades, Industrial and Textile Employees (UNITE), New York.

20 Save the Children (2001) *Child Labour*, http://www.savethechildren.org.uk/labour/index.html, 15 March 2001, Save the Children Fund UK, London.

21 UNITE (2001).

22 NLC (2001) *Wages Around the World – How Much Do Apparel Workers Make?*, http://www.nlcnet.org/resources/wages.htm, 15 March 2001, National Labor Committee, New York.

[23] ILO (2000) *The Magazine of the ILO: World of Work*, 36, Sept/Oct 2000, http://www.ilo.org/public/english/bureau/inf/magazine/index.htm, 13 November 2000, International Labour Organisation, Geneva.
[24] ILO (2000).
[25] Anti-Slavery (2000) *The Bonded Labour Campaign*, http://www.anti-slavery.org/selection.htm, 13 November 2000, Anti-Slavery International, London.
[26] ILO (2000).
[27] Oxfam (2000) *The Clothing Industry: A Case for Basic Rights*, http://www.oxfam.org.uk/campaign/clothes/cloindus.htm, 13 November 2000, Oxfam, Oxford.
[28] UN (1998) *Universal Declaration of Human Rights*, www.un.org/Overview/rights.html, 13 November 2000, United Nations, New York.
[29] ILO (2001) *Fundamental ILO Conventions*, http://www.ilo.org/public/english/standards/norm/whatare/fundam/index.htm, 3 August 2001, International Labour Organisation, Geneva.
[30] Hurst and Arnesen (2000).
[31] Hurst and Arnesen (2000).
[32] House of Commons (1999) *Trade and Industry Select Committee Sixth Report – Ethical Trading*, http://www.parliament.the-stationery-office.co.uk/, 14 August 2000, Stationery Office, London.

## Chapter 2

[1] Co-op (2000) 'Co-op and Fairtrade Fortnight – press release', www.co-op.co.uk, 2 August 2000, Co-operative Wholesale Society (CWS), Manchester.
[2] RUGMARK International (2000) *The Basics of RUGMARK*, http://www.rugmark.de/english/e_basic.htm, 2 October 2000, RUGMARK International, Cologne.
[3] http://www.iccr.org/issue_groups/accountability/feature_codes.htm
[4] http://www.iccr.org/issue_groups/accountability/feature_codes.htm
[5] http://www.iccr.org/issue_groups/accountability/feature_codes.htm
[6] ETI (2000) *Annual Report 1999/2000 – Getting to Work on Ethical Trading*, http://www.ethicaltrade.org/_html/publications/annrep_2000/framesets/f_page.shtml, 4 August 2000, Ethical Trading Initiative, London.

[7] Hurst, R and Arnesen, M (2000) *Where Did That Come From? A Study of Ethical Issues in the Supply Chain*, The Institute of Business Ethics, London.
[8] SAI (2000) *A General Introduction*, http://www.cepaa.org/introduction.htm, 9 November 2000, Social Accountability International, New York.
[9] UN (2001) *What It Is – The Global Compact: What It Is and Isn't*, http://unglobalcompact.org/gc/unweb.nsf/content/whatitis.htm#Top5, 3 August 2001, United Nations Global Compact Network, New York.
[10] UN (2001) *What It Is – The Nine Principles*, http://unglobalcompact.org/gc/unweb.nsf/content/thenine.htm, 3 August 2001, United Nations Global Compact Network, New York.
[11] Co-op (2000).
[12] SAI (2000).
[13] Co-op (2000).
[14] Co-op (2000).
[15] Fairtrade Foundation (2000) *Why Fairtrade Labelling? Developing Fairtrade Standards*, http://www.fairtrade.org.uk/Criteria.htm, 10 July 2000, Fairtrade Foundation, London.
[16] Oxford Policy Management (2000) *Fair Trade: Overview, Impact, Challenge – Study to Inform DFID's Support to Fair Trade*, Department for International Development, London.
[17] New, S, Green, K and Morton, B (2000) 'Buying the environment: the multiple meaning of green supply', in *The Business of Greening*, ed S Fineman, Routledge, London.
[18] Blowfield, M (2001) 'Sustainable values chains: experiences from Africa', International Sustainable Development Research Conference, University of Manchester, ERP Environment, Shipley.
[19] Blowfield (2001).
[20] Blowfield (2001).
[21] Blowfield (2001).
[22] House of Commons (1999) *Trade and Industry Select Committee Sixth Report – Ethical Trading*, http://www.parliament.the-stationery-office.co.uk/, 14 August 2000, Stationery Office, London.
[23] Barrientos, S (2000) 'Globalisation and ethical trade: assessing the implications for development', *Journal of International Development*, 12, pp 559–70.

## Chapter 3

[1] World Commission on Environment and Development (1987) *Our Common Future*, Oxford University Press, Oxford.

## Chapter 7

[1] RUGMARK (2001) *How You Can Help End Child Labour*, RUGMARK Foundation USA, http://www.rugmark.org/help.htm, Washington.
[2] RUGMARK (2001).
[3] http://www.rugmark.org/purchase.htm
[4] http://www.rugmark.org/cert.htm
[5] http://www.rugmark.org/facts.htm
[6] http://www.rugmark.org/social.htm
[7] http://www.rugmark.org/profiles.htm
[8] Mintel (2000) *Carpets and Floorcoverings*, Mintel International Group Limited, London.

## Chapter 8

[1] Mintel (1999) *Retail Review 1999*, Mintel, London.
[2] Retail Intelligence (2000) *The UK Retail Rankings – 2000 Edition*, Retail Intelligence – Corporate Intelligence Group, London.
[3] http://www.iccr.org/index.htm
[4] http://www.iccr.org/issue_groups/accountability/index.htm
[5] http://www.iccr.org/issue_groups/accountability/feature_sweatshop.htm
[6] http://www.cleanclothes.org/intro.htm
[7] http://www.fairlabor.org/
[8] http://www.umich.edu/~sole/usassy1/about/
[9] http://www.labourbehindthelabel.org/

## Chapter 9

[1] Mintel (2000) *Departmental and Variety Store Retailing*, Mintel International Group Ltd, London.

## Chapter 10

[1] B&Q (2000) B&Q's consultation document *How Can We Be Better Neighbours?*, p 15, B&Q's approach to sustainable development, http://www.diy.com/bq/templates/contentlookup.jhtml?content=%2Faboutbandq%2Fsustainability%2Fdocuments%2Fmain.jhtml, B&Q plc,

Eastleigh, UK.
[2] Mintel (2000) *The DIY Consumer 2000*, Mintel International Group Limited, London.

## Chapter 12

[1] EIRIS (2001) *Your Bank*, http://www.eiris.org/pages/PersonalFinance/Bank.htm, 3 July 2001, Ethical Investment Research Service (EIRIS), London.
[2] Mintel (2001) *Current Accounts and Personal Loans*, Mintel International Group Limited, London.
[3] Ethical Consumer (1999) 'Holding the banks to account – buyers' guide: banks and building societies', *Ethical Consumer Magazine*, 60, pp 6–12.
[4] UK Social Investment Forum (2001) *About UKSIF*, http://www.uksif.org/about_uksif/welcome/frameset.shtml, 12 July 2001, London.
[5] EIRIS (2001) *Your Investment Funds*, http://www.eiris.org/pages/PersonalFinance/InvFun.htm, Ethical Investment Research Service (EIRIS), London.
[6] EIRIS (2001).

## Chapter 13

[1] Retail Intelligence (2000) *The UK Retail Rankings – 2000 Edition*, Retail Intelligence – Corporate Intelligence Group, London.
[2] Mintel (2000) *Food Retailing*, Mintel International Group Limited, London.
[3] EC (2001) 'Buyers' guides – supermarkets', *Ethical Consumer Magazine*, 71, June/July, p 14.
[4] EC (2001).
[5] EC (2001).
[6] EC (2001).
[7] EC (2001).
[8] NRET (2001) Applying codes of practice in Third World countries – what can supermarkets do to help?, Natural Resources and Ethical Trade Programme, Natural Resources Institute, University of Greenwich, Chatham Maritime.

## Chapter 14

[1] Ethical Consumer (2000) 'Kicking off – buyers' guide: sports shoes', *Ethical Consumer Magazine*, 62, pp 12–14.
[2] Ethical Consumer (2000).
[3] Ethical Consumer (2000).
[4] Ethical Consumer (2000).
[5] CAFOD (2001) *Shoe Phase*, CAFOD Policy Papers, CAFOD, London.
[6] CAFOD (2001).
[7] CAFOD (2001).
[8] CAFOD (2001).
[9] Mintel (2001) *Footwear Retailing*, Mintel International Group, London.
[10] Adapted from Mintel (2001) *Footwear Retailing*, p 72, Mintel International Group, London.
[11] Adapted from Mintel (2001) *Footwear Retailing*, pp 50–51, Mintel International Group, London.

## Chapter 15

[1] Mintel (2000) *Furniture Retailing*, Mintel International Group Limited, London.

## Chapter 16

[1] Mintel (2000) *Toiletries and Cosmetics Retailing*, Mintel International Group Ltd, London.
[2] http://www.bodyshop.co.uk/usa/aboutus/ctrade.html

## Chapter 17

[1] Mintel (1999) *Retail Review 1999*, Figure 108, Mintel International Group Limited, London.
[2] Mintel (1999) *Retail Review 1999*, Figure 107, Mintel International Group Limited, London.

## Chapter 18

[1] Mintel (1999) *Housewares Retailing*, Mintel International Group Limited, London.

## Chapter 19

[1] Ethical Consumer (2001) 'All that glitters…', *Ethical Consumer Magazine*, 70, pp 28–31.

[2] Mintel (1999) *Retail Review 1999*, Mintel International Group Limited, London.
[3] Mintel (1999) *Retail Review 1999*, Figure 100, Mintel International Group Limited, London.
[4] Ethical Consumer (2001).
[5] Ethical Consumer (2001).
[6] Ethical Consumer (2001).
[7] Ethical Consumer (2001).
[8] Ethical Consumer (2001).
[9] Ethical Consumer (2001).
[10] Ethical Consumer (2001).

## Chapter 20

[1] Mintel (2001) *Sports Goods Retailing*, Mintel International Group Limited, London.

## Chapter 21

[1] Mintel (2001) *Toys and Games*, Mintel International Group Limited, London.
[2] Mintel (2001).
[3] http://www.btha.co.uk/codeofconduct.html
[4] http://www.btha.co.uk/codeofconduct.html

## Appendix

[1] C&A Services, www.socam.org/conduct_e.pdf, May 1998.
[2] www.arcadiagroup.co.uk/
[3] http://www2.marksandspencer.com/thecompany/ourcommitmenttosociety/ethical/global01.shtml
[4] http://www.gapinc.com/social_resp/sourcing/commit.htm
[5] Mintel (1999) *Retail Review 1999*, Mintel, London.
[6] B&Q's *Ethical Code of Conduct for Supply Chains – Draft for Consultation*, 4 February 2001.
[7] Homebase (unknown date) *Sainsbury's Homebase Position on Socially Responsible Trading*, p 2, J Sainsbury plc, London.
[8] http://www.co-operativebank.co.uk/
[9] http://www.triodos.co.uk/
[10] http://www.abbeynational.plc.uk/webcode/gateway_frame.asp?area=about
[11] http://www1.hsbc.com/

[12] Safeway, *The Green Grocer* publication.
[13] http://www.sainsburys.co.uk
[14] http://www.tesco.com/everyLittleHelps/
[15] http://www.ikea.co.uk/about_ikea/facts_figures/facts_organised.asp
[16] http://www.bodyshop.co.uk/usa/aboutus/charter.html
[17] Blacks (2000) *Blacks Leisure Group plc Annual Report and Financial Statements 2000*, Blacks Leisure Group plc, London.

# Index

# About the Authors

## William Young

Born in 1971, William Young writes, researches and teaches on environmental, ethical and sustainable development issues facing business and consumers. He currently lectures in the School of the Environment at the University of Leeds in the UK, where he runs an MA Environment and Business course.

He has experience in advising British and international organisations drafting environmental management standards as well as companies on environmental and ethical issues.

## Richard Welford

Born in 1960, Richard Welford has been an academic for over 15 years. He has written many books on all aspects of environmental management and ethics in business and is the founder and editor of a suite of academic journals concerning sustainable development.

As well as being an academic Richard has worked as a consultant to a number of large international corporations. His mixture of academic and practical experience makes him one of the leading experts worldwide on the new ethical and environmental issues impacting on business.